Edgehill

The Battle Reinterpreted

Edgehill
The Battle Reinterpreted

Christopher L Scott,

Alan Turton

&

Eric Gruber von Arni

with illustrations by
the authors, Richard Ellis and Lesley Prince

Pen & Sword
MILITARY

Edgehill: The Battle Reinterpreted
First published in Great Britain in 2004
Paperback edition 2005

Pen & Sword Military
an imprint of
Pen & Sword Books Ltd
47 Church Street
Barnsley
South Yorkshire
S70 2AS

ISBN 1-84415-254-5

A CIP catalogue record for this book is available from the British Library

Typeset in Ehrhardt 10/12 pt by
Palindrome

Printed and bound in England by CPI UK

For a complete list of Pen & Sword titles, please contact
Pen & Sword Books Limited
47 Church Street, Barnsley, South Yorkshire, S70 2AS, England
E-mail: enquiries@pen-and-sword.co.uk
Website: www.pen-and-sword.co.uk

Contents

List of Colour Plates and Maps

List of Tables

Acknowledgements

As with all endeavours we are grateful to those who helped us to achieve our goal. Be they those who encouraged, advised and corrected us when we required it, especially our wives, Pam, Nicola and Elizabeth, or those who gave their time or abilities to aid the project, notably battlefield photographer and great friend Richard Ellis who gave so freely of his time, effort and expertise and remained extraordinarily enthusiastic about everything. We could not have done it without you all.

We would like to thank the following people, whose names appear in no particular order but whose help along the way has been gratefully appreciated:

Lieutenant Colonel Darrell Ingle of the Ministry of Defence Depot, Kineton.
Mr Kevin Thom of the Ministry of Defence Security Force.
Mr Keith Clowes of the Military Police Service.
Dr Lesley Prince of Edgbaston and the Roundhead Association.
Mr David Blackmore of the Royal Armouries and the Roundhead Association.
Mr Thom Richardson of the Royal Armouries.
Dr David Chandler.
Prof Richard Holmes.
Mr David Ellis, the pilot.
Dr Paula Turner of Palindrome, the editor.
Mr Rupert Harding of Pen & Sword.
Mr Glenn Foard of the Battlefields Trust.
Mr Peter Ellis of the Battlefields Trust.
Mr Robert Leedham of Aston Cantlow and the Sealed Knot.
The staff of the Public Libraries in Kineton, Warwick and Swindon.
The staff of the Warwickshire Record Office, Warwick.
The staff of the Warwickshire Museum Archaeology Department, Warwick.
The staff of the Bodleian Library, Oxford.
The staff of the National Monument Record Office, Swindon.
The staff of the National Archives, Kew.

We would also like to mention the following institutions whose names, events or services have helped to open doors, in order for us to meet people or to gather information and opinions.

The Royal Historical Society	The Guild of Battlefield Guides.
The Battlefields Trust	The British Commission for Military History.

And finally, but by no means least, Mr Donald Featherstone and Mr Roger Snell who ignited and fanned the flame of battlefield walking so many years ago and kept it burning brightly ever since.

Preface

There is always great Difference in Relation of Battles, which do usually according to the Interest of the Relators. Bulstrode.

So what are our interests and why write another book on Edgehill? Surely all that has to be written has been written? If we believed that there would be no point, but we do not. Our interest is driven by the belief that the authors of the majority of 'battle' books discuss and describe their subjects through what we are coming to perceive as a narrow and limited approach. They tend to focus upon only one third of the subject by diverting their full attention to the historical perspective while ignoring, or paying scant regard to, the archaeological aspect and, very strangely, even less to the topography of the battlefield itself. In so doing we feel they fail to achieve a truly holistic approach.

This book tries to understand the events that took place on a field and hillside in Warwickshire on Sunday, 23 October 1642, from a more inclusive approach. Naturally we began this study by reading and noting broadly, but we have also approached two other primary sources for evidence: archaeological discoveries made in both artefacts and landscape history, and the shape and nature of the land itself. Both have significant stories to tell. Admittedly both also have their pitfalls, but being wary of them is somewhat akin to taking cognizance of written sources' partisanship and subconscious bias. Much of our study has been directed towards the military and social documents of the period, but in equal parts it has been spent in studying various types of maps and records of finds and partial surveys, and on just walking and walking the field, looking at what can be seen and experienced today. We hope that what we have produced is a synthesis of these three perspectives.[1] This more inclusive approach leads, we believe, to a more rounded appreciation of a battle. There are only a certain number of contemporary sources available to all researchers and although occasionally a new discovery may give more information it rarely changes knowledge dramatically, unless it is something as startling as the Rev. Percy Sumner's discovery in the Royal Library of de Gomme's diagram of the Royalist deployment. What we have endeavoured to do is to focus upon our interpretation of the current sources by referencing across a wide range of aspects and experiences, such as relating what was written about the involvement of a unit with its hospital casualty figures, using researched work on strengths and drill books to determine frontages, seeking to identify where un-documented battlefield finds were actually made and trudging across the field in autumn to appreciate the nature of the ground. By these and other techniques, including discussing theories with known battlefield enthusiasts and re-enactors, we have tried to extend our perception in order that, although reading the same sources as those who have previously undertaken work on this battle, we come to a different, and hopefully deeper, understanding of Edgehill.

Even with this approach, however, there are times when we must admit that we just do not know what went on during this one afternoon over 360 years ago. Despite all the efforts to unravel the detail and put the jigsaw together, to make calculations and deductions based upon evidence, we must at times admit that we can only offer speculation. Major Alfred Burne offered such speculation in his battlefield books of the mid-twentieth century and coined the phrase 'inherent military probability'; this is derided in certain circles as 'guesswork'. We are not so dismissive. Where Burne 'comes unstuck' is that his appreciation of a situation was often coloured by his own military experience in the twentieth century. Writing about 'laying down patterns of fire' or 'firing on fixed lines' was just not in the early modern mind-set.

The three authors have been steeped in English Civil War History for many years and all three have taken part in re-enactments, from musketeer to 'army commander-in-chief', and they believe that their experience can aid understanding. It is currently fashionable to disparage the thoughts of re-enactors but, while retaining an extreme wariness of the false nature of the re-enactment battlefield experience, this should not prevent us from appreciating certain aspects of it, such as the understanding of how quickly one can load and fire a musket with ball, the problems involved in manoeuvring 600 to 700 men according to a seventeenth-century drill manual, how long extreme physical pike-handling activity can be sustained, or what a hedgerow can do to an orderly advance – let alone sharing the very real fear of being ridden down by panicking horses! Re-enactment is not the wonder its protagonists would suggest, but it is yet another tool to help understanding and battlefield interpretation.

We have also discussed the battle with numerous military, social and philosophical period experts, with local residents and those who have walked the field before the Munitions Depot, which now covers a crucial portion of the battlefield, was developed. We have sought opinions and interpretations from whomever and wherever they were proffered. We have read the modern published accounts, including those that have earned the scorn of more enlightened readers. Again we do not share this scorn, for everyone who writes about battlefields hopefully does his best, presumably does so to help others appreciate the importance of that site, and, usually, has nothing but the greatest respect for those who fought there.

It is also fashionable to deride the work of Victorian historians, and indeed some of them can be quite entertaining in their flights of fancy, but here too we believe one must be careful not to reject everything simply because the style is romanticized and the academic method was generally poor. They normally obtained their ideas from some-where. We should not condemn writers for not drawing similar conclusions to those who have had further decades, or even centuries, of discoveries from which to work. Sometimes the context is more enlightening than the content. The Rev George Miller may be somewhat suspect in his history, but as an amateur archaeologist he certainly knew his countryside and although his annotation and records of locations for his finds are, by our standards, appalling, his references to the topography of his and the previous age's Edgehill are priceless. His Georgian ancestor, Sanderson Miller, upon whose work he also drew, was a keen historian: rich enough to indulge his historical passion and even worse at substantiating and providing evidence for his assertions, but his ideas too were sparked by something.

To us all work is useful, as even rejection of it is all part of this inclusive approach to endeavouring to understand and write down what took place. We too have done our best. Where we have to resort to speculation we make it clear that is what we are doing. However, we trust our speculations, being based on our researching, reading, observing, listening, discussing, walking and mock-fighting experiences, are reasonable.

The intention of this book is to try to understand Edgehill. In publishing it we hope to serve the interests of those who share with us the enjoyment of history and battlefield walking. Despite often knowing the historical significance of a conflict, the enjoyment of visiting a battlefield can be impaired by a lack of understanding of the nature and the operation of the action, a lack of appreciation of the landscape in which it happened, and, perhaps more importantly, how the two impacted upon each other. Often left to flounder in a bewildering array of classroom recollections, pictures based on Victorian engravings, tree plantations, modern roads, field drainage and clearances, the National Savings costume time-line poster, and with only a crossed-swords symbol on a map as a guide, battlefield visitors need information and routes to the understanding of both these elements, if they are to benefit fully from their visit. During our visits we noticed how the work of many previous writers was inherently biased towards the King's cause. We would like to apologize if our bias in favour of Parliament's cause is too evident but we have endeavoured to limit its influence on our judgement.

Finally we would like to acknowledge that much of our work is interpretative, hence the title, and that, regardless of anyone's experience or powers of battlefield analysis, a series of conclusions can only be as good as the source material available. It is possible that some of our opinions will not be accepted by the more traditional reader. We have tried to be as wide-ranging as possible in sources and opinions, but future discoveries may disprove much of what we currently hold to be probable. Some sources, such as the original copy of de Gomme's deployment map, we have been unable to see. Further work, such as Oliver and Pollard's archaeological report, remain in preparation at the time of writing. Perhaps yet more lies hidden waiting to be unearthed. Should anyone ever find Essex's Battle Plan we would be among the first to join the queue to see how it upsets what we have written. As with many of England's battle sites, a full archaeological survey has never been done but, fortunately, battlefield archaeology is at last gaining a higher profile thanks in no small part to the work of Glenn Foard and the Battlefield Archaeology Annual Conference. Within days of going to the publisher we heard that part of the Battlefield Trust's plans to construct an 'Edgehill to Edgecote Battlefield Trail' involves an attempt to secure community activity funding which could lead to such a survey being undertaken. As two of us are Trustees of the body we look forward to any results this may bring, whether they confound our current beliefs or confirm them. Our efforts are based upon what was available from Summer 2003 to February 2004.

We hope you will enjoy our efforts but we would draw attention to the rest of our opening quotation from Sir Richard Bulstrode's memoirs:

> it is certain, that, in a battle, the next Man can hardly make a true Relation of
> the Actions of him that is next [to] him; for in such a Hurry and Smoke as in
> a set Field, a Man takes Notice of nothing but what relates to his own Safety:
> So that no Man give a clear Account of particular Passages.[2]

Abbreviations

Abbreviations used in the Notes and References

BL	British Library
BodL	Bodleian Library.
CSPD	Calendar of State Papers, Domestic
CSPD Add.	Calendar of State Papers, Domestic, Additional
CSP Venetian	Calendar of State Papers, Venetian
E	Exchequer Papers
Harl. MSS.	Harleian Manuscripts
HMC	Royal Commission on Historic Manuscripts
HMon.C	Royal Commission on Historic Monuments
NA	National Archives, Kew
SP	State Papers
TT	Thomason Tracts
WO	War Office

Official Parliamentary Account: BL *TT* E 124 (26): Anon., *An Exact and True Relation of the late Battell neere Kineton* (London, 1642).

Official Royalist Account: BL, *TT* E 126 (24): Anon., *A Relation of the Battel fought between Kineton and Edgehill, by His Majesty's Army and that of the Rebels* (Oxford, 1642).

Note on dates and spelling

Throughout this work, the year is assumed to begin on 1 January and transcribed dates have been amended accordingly. Days of the month have not been altered and remain as originally expressed according to the Julian calendar.

Idiosyncratic seventeenth-century spelling frequently resulted in the same word being written in different ways in the same passage. In this book the spelling of words transcribed from original documents has been standardized according to modern practice, except where the original spelling assists in conveying the contemporary sense or idiom of the text.

Chapter One
Preceding Events

Their troops were discovered upon Edgehill in Warwickshire. Ludlow.

During the mid-seventeenth century England and Wales were plunged into a series of civil wars that gradually engulfed Scotland, then Ireland, and had repercussions on Continental Europe. There have been many attempts to explain why this happened, ranging from the simplistic to the highly complex, but by far the most convincing view is an holistic one. It was the result of a desire for change which embraced the inter-related social, economic, religious, political and philosophical aspects of society at all levels: international, national, local and personal. This was fuelled by a growing individualism, the confidence in self, and a sense of opportunism, seen so frequently and strongly expressed in Milton. All was contained within a major change in the fundamental operating system of society; one which had its roots in the thinking behind the Reformation.

This shift can be seen in isolated instances such as James I's selling of knighthoods or in subtler, more permissive examples such as the building of Littlecote House in Wiltshire. Encouragements and inducements had enabled both William Daryll in the fifteenth century and John Popham in the sixteenth to make lavish changes to the old fortified manor of the de Calstones. Daryll was a loyal supporter of Edward IV, and he was rewarded with the office of Keeper of the Royal Wardrobe, which meant he controlled private interviews with the King. His rise came from the feudal concept of 'shield-service', whereas Popham had risen by industrious investment of profits and from favours derived from his legal business. In the eyes of the old nobility he was 'trade' and he reached the dizzy heights of Lord Chief Justice by his own multifarious efforts. New men with new money were the new power.

During the first half of the seventeenth century the new force of reason-led capitalism demanded change, and faith-based feudalism resisted. The all-round pressure for change was enormous and permeated all walks of life including that of the monarch, the magnitude of it being described by those who lived through it as 'the world turned upside down'. Such dramatically changing times called for great statesmen at the helm.

England did not have them. Its king, Charles I, blinkered by his father's doctrine of Divine Right, stubbornly resisted all evolutionary moves apart from those in which he was personally interested. Never born to be king, Charles was elevated to Prince of Wales on the death of his elder brother and crowned in 1625. Although compared with those of his his predecessors such actions were far from exceptional, within five years he had called and dismissed three parliaments and reverted to the practice of personal rule. Over a period of eleven years he devised several money-making schemes desperately attempting to stave off national bankruptcy. These included selling commercial monopolies, instigating benevolences or forced loans, the selling of crown property above the market value, re-instituting the purchase of titles, the marketing of wardships and the imposition of Ship Money nationwide. None of these measures raised sufficient monies to meet the demands on the Treasury. As a ruler beset with fiscal problems he should have focused on the economy; instead he turned to religion and endeavoured to impose the Anglican English prayer book upon Presbyterian Scotland. This had dramatic results in widespread civil unrest, and led to the military and financial debacle known as the First Bishops' War. Having failed miserably to bring the Scots to heel, Charles's belief in Divine Right induced him to make another attempt, and the Second Bishops' War was even more humiliating with the Scots invading England. Almost destitute, the King was obliged to summon his fourth parliament, which met in 1640.

This Parliament epitomized the forces of 'new money' and the desire for change from that class, but now it was fanned by resentment that had built up during the period of personal rule. Instead of being subservient to instruction, members began making speeches eulogizing change and moves designed to bring it about. Royal prerogative was attacked and the House split into Court and Country parties, dividing roughly along political and religious lines, but with a dangerous undercurrent of being for or against the King's will. The wrangling grew bitter as they reacted to a rebellion in Ireland that ignited passions and fuelled prejudices. Parliament then set before Charles a list of their grievances. Angered, the King responded by abusing parliamentary privilege. He led an armed body into the House and tried unsuccessfully to arrest five of the most politically active members. Thwarted and frustrated, the King left London and, after an embarrassing attempt to demonstrate his power in the North, returned to the Midlands where he made Nottingham the base for his operations on 21 July 1642. Six days later the first blood of the looming civil war was spilled in Manchester during a skirmish between local forces. This was soon followed by further military action at Marshall's Elm on 4 August, the King's failure to take Coventry on 20 August, and Colonel George Goring, at Portsmouth, declaring for Charles only to come under siege on 26 August by Sir William Waller with newly raised troops from London.

On 22 August 1642 the King raised his standard against the representatives of his own people. The hoisting of the standard at Nottingham was a very sorry affair, taking place on what is still known as Standard Hill outside the walls of the derelict castle. Charles had issued a proclamation on 12 August, requiring every man capable of bearing arms living within a twenty-mile radius of Nottingham to repair there for the ceremony. In the event, the King was only able to recruit 300 men after repeating the unfurling on three successive days. However, it did cause consternation in Parliament. The members were divided, and those who did not go to the King in answer to his Commission of Array, passed the Militia Ordnance to be read across England to raise troops to defend themselves and the rights of Parliament. The need for change was driving events. When change by constructive means is denied them, men will affect it by destructive means – or as Clausewitz was to say 'war is… a continuation of political activity by other means'.[1]

In the opening stages of any war there is always a race for territory and men, and in 1642 both sides made strenuous efforts to secure garrisons and gather soldiers. After

Raising the Royal Standard – although of the nineteenth century, this illustration captures the atmosphere of the rain-soaked occasion and the lack of enthusiasm that greeted the King's call to arms.

almost five generations of relative internal peace, and the union of the crowns of England and Scotland, most of Britain's great medieval castles had been allowed to fall into decay, many serving purely as county gaols and militia magazines. The exceptions were the forts and castles on the south coast of England, many of which still maintained small regular garrisons. One of these was Southsea Castle, which was described in 1635 as 'the most exquisite piece of fortification in the Kingdom'. Most of Britain's major trading cities declared for Parliament. By the mid-seventeenth century London was one of the most populous and wealthy cities of western Europe. It contained the Tower of London, reckoned to be the largest magazine in England, and the city boasted many manufacturers of arms and equipment. The Royalist Lord Mayor was quickly ousted for a pro-Parliament man and the city's merchants and citizens were leaned upon for loans and subsidies. Parliament always held on to London with a firm grip despite the city containing a sizeable Royalist minority. However, like many areas of England, the country's second city, Bristol, tried to remain neutral until overtaken by events not of its choosing. Its near neighbour, Gloucester, however, was predominantly Parlia-mentarian from the start under the leadership of its MP, the Mayor and its Council who, setting up a Committee of Defence, quickly put the city on a war footing. On the other side, Newark, 'The Key to the North', and Worcester were to be staunchly loyal to King Charles, a frequent and popular visitor to both places before the war. The trading and fishing ports of England also tried to carry on life as normal until one side or the other occupied them, but the naval establishments on the Thames and Medway rivers and virtually all the Royal Navy's ships came quickly under Parliament's control. Only the great naval port of Portsmouth, under its unpopular Royalist governor, George Goring, initially was held for the King.

The dominance of Parliament over London and the populous counties of the south-east gave it a considerable manpower advantage, and the London Trained Bands and the apprentices served as sources of men. The King's army was obliged to recruit in the more scattered areas of the north and west. Parliament could equip its forces from material drawn from the capital and what it could not obtain there it could easily purchase from overseas; its merchant vessels were protected by ships of the Royal Navy. The King on the other hand lacked both money and equipment and what arms he could afford to procure in Europe had to run the gauntlet of the Navy.

The King had hoped to assist Goring in Portsmouth with reinforcements sent from the West Country but they, in their turn, became besieged at Sherborne Castle by troops under the Earl of Bedford. On 7 September, Goring and his desertion-depleted garrison surrendered to Waller and Meldrum, who then rejoined Essex's army massing at Northampton, where the Earl himself arrived three days later.

This build-up of rebel strength so alarmed the King and his council that Nottingham was abandoned and he marched with his little army, via Derby, to Shrewsbury, which they reached on 20 September. Charles had been informed that the Severn-side town was well affected to his cause, and he was not to be disappointed, for on the day of his arrival, his force was joined by the regiments of Rivers, Fitton and Aston, mostly raised in the Marches and north-west Midlands.

On 19 September, to shadow the King's movements, Essex marched from Northampton towards Worcester. On the same day, Worcester was occupied by Sir John Byron who had just arrived there, accompanying a convoy of plate intended for the King's treasure chest. The King's German nephew, Prince Rupert, was immediately dispatched with a considerable force of cavalry and dragoons to support Byron, but upon arrival he judged Worcester to be indefensible and decided upon evacuation once he had rested his men and horses. It was during this rest-break in the fields alongside Powick Bridge that the advance party of Essex's cavalry, under Colonels Sandys and Brown, appeared on the opposite side of the river Teme. The ensuing skirmish was a Royalist victory, the repercussions of which were out of all proportion to the actual event. The Parliamentary force was driven from the field and, in their panicked flight, they surprised the cuirassiers of Essex's Lifeguard, who were coming up the road some distance behind them, and they, in turn, fled. This loss of face and confidence infected the whole of Essex's Horse and was no doubt one of the reasons for their poor showing at Edgehill.

The next day, after addressing his assembled army, Essex entered Worcester, immediately setting his Lieutenant General of Ordnance, Du-Bois to fortify the city. A detachment under Lord Stamford was sent out to take Hereford and forward posts were set up at Bewdley and Kidderminster. Satisfied with these dispositions, Essex awaited the expected Royalist advance.

The King was not ready to make his next move but, since his arrival at Shrewsbury, he had seen a great improvement in his fortunes. More regiments were arriving and his excellent Lieutenant General of Ordnance, Sir John Heydon, had managed to assemble from various sources a small but effective train of artillery. By 4 October it comprised the ordnance shown in table 1.1:

Table 1.1 Royalist Ordnance available within the Train of Artillery.

2 demi-cannon	2 3-pounders
1 culverin	6 falcons
3 iron demi-culverin	5 falconets
1 iron saker	3 robinets
1 iron minion	

Source: I Roy (ed.), *The Royalist Ordnance Papers, 1642–1646* (Oxford, Oxfordshire Record Society, vol. I, 1963), pp 1–16.

Charles himself temporarily left Shrewsbury to take part in a successful recruiting drive in the Welsh Marches and Chester before returning and busying himself in the modelling of his new army. Sir Jacob Astley was made Sergeant Major General of Foot with three brigades (tercios) of infantry under his command led respectively by Sir Nicholas Byron, Colonel Henry Wentworth and Colonel Richard Fielding. The newly arrived Patrick Ruthven was created Field Marshall and attached to Rupert's staff in the cavalry, another professional soldier, Colonel General Sir Arthur Aston, was given command of all the King's dragoons.

With these preparations made, the King and his council debated their next move and came to the conclusion that a rapid advance on London could end the war quickly, and if Essex interposed his army, then so be it, they would give him battle. As a cover to gain time on the march, Rupert's cavalry demonstrated towards Worcester, causing a Parliamentary garrison at Kidderminster to fall back on the main army, convinced that Charles's main force was following them. Charles in fact led his army out via his outpost at Bridgenorth on 12 October, and then by stages to Wolverhampton, reaching Birmingham five days later. Clarendon claims the Royalist army travelled light 'there being not one Tent, and very few Wagons belonging to the whole Train'.[2] The problems that they probably experienced can be appreciated when it is realized that Charles's Ordnance Office estimated that a minimum of eight carts were required for artillery projectiles, twelve for powder, twenty-two for shot and five for match – that is, forty-seven vehicles, before taking any other train stores or equipment into account. If this was considered to be 'travelling light', one can but wonder how much greater were Essex's logistical problems when Clarendon went on to state that Essex's 'train was so very great, that he could move but in slow marches'.[3]

On 18 October the King's army regrouped at Meriden Heath then marched on to the area around Kenilworth. The next day, Essex at long last began his pursuit, leaving the regiments of St John, Stamford and Merrick to cover Worcester. His army marched on a broad front that funnelled them across the Avon at the two bridges of Evesham and Stratford, a dangerous thing to do when he had no idea where his enemy actually was. Equally, the King, lacking any intelligence of the route of Essex's march, surprisingly decided to divert from his plan of a quick descent on London and to pause and take Banbury. As the King's forces gave a wide berth to Lord Brooke's powerful castle at Warwick, some of his baggage fell into the hands of a patrol from its garrison, and his plans for Banbury were discovered and carried to Essex.

On 21 October Charles ordered a muster at Southam, a small town that had witnessed a sharp local skirmish earlier in the campaign when both armies were marching west. Here his footsore soldiers were given a brief rest. The next night they were billeted in villages around the Wormington Hills and the King and his officers

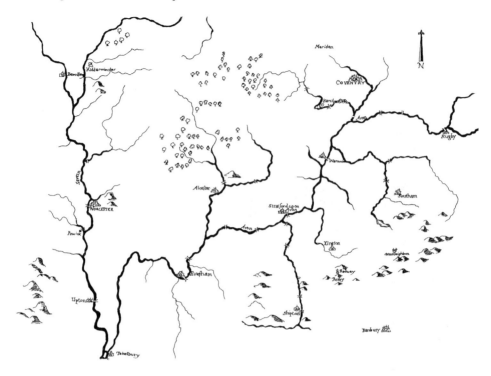

The campaign area, based on Speed's map of Warwickshire. This is the style of map and type of information that was available to both armies.

made detailed plans for the assault on Banbury the next day, with Sir Nicholas Byron's Brigade assigned to the task, the rest of the army taking a rest day. A scouting party of 400 horsemen had searched in vain that day to find any sign of Essex's forces. So it was that when both Charles and the Earl of Essex retired to their respective quarters for the night of Saturday, 22 October, neither of them had any idea that the next day they would fight a major pitched battle.

Essex had chosen the market town of Kineton as a rendezvous point for the re-grouping of his army that was still marching gradually eastward in a number of disparate parties along several different roads. A section of Essex's train of artillery was so far behind that Hampden's and Grantham's Regiments of Foot were forced to march with them as guards. Once the junction of his forces had been made, Essex had intended to march the thirteen more miles to Banbury to prevent the King's designs on that town. Kineton itself was quite a small town, the parish church of which stood sentinel over the junction of four minor roads near its centre. On the south side of the town, in a deep gully, ran the little river Dene. Essex's infantry would have been allotted unit billets in the town and immediately outside in the surrounding fields. A main court of guard was probably set up somewhere near the church. It is also likely that the baggage train, and that part of the artillery that was with the main body of the army, was parked somewhere near the river to enable the watering of the hundreds of draught animals; the carters sleeping in or under their wagons.

There would have been no room for the majority of the cavalry to quarter within the

'An Army Marches Through a Town'.
Armies had to carry everything they
needed with them, and their passage often
occasioned the requisition of carts,
animals and supplies.

town, so, as was normal practice, they were billeted in neighbouring villages for miles around. The overnight stops were sought out by troop and regimental quartermasters, who rode out well in advance of the army, and allocated who should be accommodated where. It was one of these quartermasters' parties entering Wormleighton that fell foul of a group of Prince Rupert's who were also out looking for billets, and were all taken. This was the first indication on either side of how close the armies were. Rupert immediately sent out a scouting party of twenty-four men to confirm Essex's presence at Kineton. In the meantime, other Royalist units had spied the campfires around the little town and had stood-to at their billets. Rupert's first inclination was to order a beating up of Essex's quarters with as many cavalry as he could muster in the darkness, but his Staff Officers persuaded him to consult the King first. The King received Rupert's intelligence at Sir William Chancies's house in Edgecote that:

> the Body of the Rebel's Army, was within seven or eight miles, and that the head quarter was at a village call'd Keinton on the edge of Warwickshire; and that it would be in his majesty's power, if he thought fit, to fight a Battle next day; which his Majesty liked well.[4]

At four o'clock in the morning Charles returned this answer to Rupert,

> Nephew, I have given order as you have desired, so that I doubt not but all the foot and cannon will be at Edgehill betimes this morning, where you will also find, your loving uncle and faithful friend, Charles R.[5]

Dragoon scouts – the eyes and ears of the army were its Horse and dragoons whose job was often to seek out the enemy.

Upon receipt of these orders, the Royalist troops began to leave their quarters and pick their way through the dark country lanes up to the army rendezvous. They mustered upon the narrow plateau between the steep northern escarpment of Edgehill and the little village of Ratley. Rupert arrived at daybreak but it would be gone midday before the rear of the army came up with the train of artillery.

Meanwhile down in the valley, the Parliamentary army was beginning to stir, the troops looking forward to a quiet Sabbath day of rest. Cavalry pickets would have been sent out at daybreak to expand the tight overnight security perimeter of the camp and to take in any high vantage points. It was probably such a picket sent to take in Edgehill that first became aware of the Royalist presence upon it and reported back to the officer of the watch. The Reverend Adoniram Bifield claimed to have made the first visual confirmation sighting of the Royalists from the valley 'by help of a prospective Glass'.[6]

The news of the Royalists' appearance reached Essex at about 8 a.m. as he and his senior officers were making their way to church for Sunday service. The alarm would have sounded through the town, and Essex ordered in his cavalry from their scattered overnight stations and, no doubt, sent urgent messages to Hampden's distant detachment to hurry to the rendezvous.

Essex now had to make the decision whether to stand and fight where he stood, fall back to join Hampden, or advance and attack. The pressure on Essex at this point was enormous, the whole weight of Parliament's 'Good Old Cause' rested upon his shoulders. If he failed in the coming fight, that cause would be utterly lost. Critics of Essex have frequently attacked him for being lethargic and indecisive, but he displayed neither of those traits that morning. He would take the fight to the King, but not on the ground the monarch had chosen.

Chapter Two
Weapons

Before the 8,016 muskets can be again supplied with rests and bandoleers, six months time will be necessarily employed. A Copy of the Remonstrance to be Exhibited to the Parliament, 12 February 1641.

Having reached Essex's decision to fight, we now have to examine the weapons employed by the soldiers in both armies. Understanding the operational ability of each arm and the technology involved helps us to appreciate more fully what happened during the battle. Even knowing something as simple as the ranges of the guns helps us deduce where they could have been deployed and how they could have been used. Compared with twentieth-century battlefield weapons those of the seventeenth century forced combat to be a much more personal thing; although here too, change was beginning. Drill manuals and treatises on the *Art Militaire* were forging a science of mutual bloodletting. Gunpowder had revolutionized warfare by the fact that even an untrained, half-starved conscript could point a musket and pull a trigger. No longer did the missile arm require powerfully built archers bred to their weapons from boyhood, while the more 'noble and puissant pike' which required more practice and physical robustness to handle, was hardly a weapon requiring great skill. Both the pike and the musket were the arms of the unified mass – what they lacked in quality they made up for in quantity.

Muskets
The smoothbore, muzzle-loading, matchlock musket was the main weapon of the Civil Wars. Most existing examples are about four feet long and weigh about twelve pounds. Calibres, or barrel widths, vary from half to three-quarters of an inch and the weight of the musket balls they fired varied from 10 to 16 to the pound, giving rise to the expression 'bore' meaning the diameter of a barrel capable of firing the relevant size and weight of ball. Earlier muskets fired balls of about two ounces (8 bore) but, on average, those of the mid-seventeenth century were between one-and-a-quarter to one-and-a-half ounces (12 to 14 bore). The muskets manufactured under the influence of the Dutch military system tended to be 12 to 14 bore, while those of the Swedish pattern were made, on Gustavus Adolphus' advice, with a heavier projectile, 11 to 12 bore. Their weight also varied and could be from 14 to 20 pounds.

At Edgehill there would have been a mixture of old and new muskets, the older, heavier weapons necessitating the use of the rest. Possibly there were more rests used at Edgehill than in any subsequent battle of the wars. This was a hand-held barrel support, a simple metal 'U' shape (looking like a rowlock) mounted on a shaft about four to five feet high and resembling a walker's thumb-stick. Manipulating the musket and the rest was a complicated business especially as musketeers firing in deep formations had to handle their rests every time it came to their turn to fire. When wishing to fire the musketeer would ram his rest upright into the ground (they were often fitted with spikes to make this easier) and place the musket barrel in its U–piece. Balancing the musket in the rest he secured it against his right shoulder and also supported it with his left hand. He then fired it by squeezing the trigger with his right hand. Rests came to be frowned upon by young men or those equipped with the more modern, lighter pieces. As Parliament had access to the London gunsmiths they were able to order and supply cheaper styles to their soldiers. These mass-produced versions did not have as much wood in the stocks and were consequently lighter, thinner and easier to handle. Being cheaper they also broke more easily but even without a serpentine to grip the match they could still be used effectively by manual touch-firing *if* they could be pointed in the direction of the foe without recourse to a rest.

Old or new, expensive or cheap, they were all single-shot muzzle-loaders fired for the most part by soldiers using a burning 'match', a saltpetre-soaked cord, which, when the trigger was pulled, was pushed into the priming pan by means of a cheap pivoting mechanism, the serpentine, that had probably developed in German lands. The barrel was loaded with charges of poor-quality, black gunpowder, which before use were contained in lead-capped wooden bottles suspended from a leather belt worn across the shoulder. Some musketeers also used paper cartridges, pieces of parallelogram-shaped, possibly greased, paper, wrapped around a stick and twisted or glued into a tube. A measured charge was poured into either the bottle or the cartridge. Each man carried one collar of about twelve bottles, plus perhaps some cartridges in either his bullet bag, an additional dedicated cartridge pouch or even his snapsack; some Continental accounts state that English musketeers were also noted for the practice of carrying cartridges in their breeches' pockets![1]

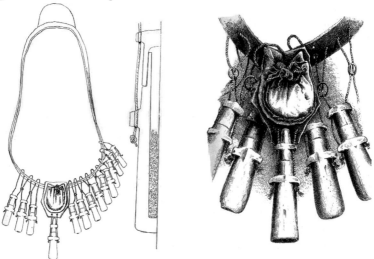

A bandolier with its bottles and accoutrements (left) plus a cutaway of a bottle (centre) and a bullet pouch, priming flask and the arrangement of bottle cords (right), from S D Scott, The British Army, Its Origin, Progress and Equipment *(London, Cassell, 1868).*

When ordered to load, the musketeer checked that he held his burning match in his left hand well away from the loading process. Bringing his musket across his body he would 'open and clean the pan' by moving the pan-cover out of the way and exposing the firing pan itself. Cleaning it meant making sure there were no embers left from the previous shot to cause a pre-ignition and was effected by a combination of blowing across it and/or wiping it round with the little finger or thumb of the right hand. He then 'primed' by going to the flask of finer powder (if available) he also wore suspended from a thin shoulder strap, or, he extracted one cartridge from wherever he kept it, conveyed it to his mouth and used his teeth to tear open the paper tube, often getting the acrid, salty powder into his mouth. With either flask or opened cartridge, he then used a pinch of the powder to fill his pan and flipped the pan cover over it to keep this primer in place.

Reversing his weapon he 'charged his musket' by uncapping one wooden bottle on the collar or bandolier or using the previously opened cartridge. Having twelve charges suspended about the body, or cartridges in the pocket, could be a dangerous practice and, although not frequent, accidents could cause them to ignite, seriously burning the musketeer. Sometimes there was a flap of leather stitched to the belt which covered the bottles and kept them protected from stray sparks or glowing match coals but usually the simple lead cap which clipped over the open mouth of the drilled out wooden container was deemed sufficient. Most caps were pierced and threaded with thin cords to keep them attached to the bottle once opened. However, these cords sometimes snapped in the heat of battle and, when discovered in numbers by archaeologists, the caps can give us a good idea of where bodies of shot stood to fire.

The opened bottle or the torn cartridge was then conveyed to the muzzle where the musketeer poured the charge down the barrel. It fell to the bottom, into the chamber and piled up against the end plug. It was important that the measure was sufficient to form a pile high enough to reach and cover the touch-hole on the inside. There is no surviving evidence to prove that wadding was in fact used, but to gain maximum effect the musketeer would possibly insert something to keep this powder charge in place and help seal and compress it. Modern re-enactment practice is to use pieces of paper, often thrust into pockets or kept in the cuff of the coat, but in the seventeenth century paper was not as cheap a commodity as it is today. Grass might have made a reasonable wad. Paper was used, however, for cartridges and it would be likely that musketeers crumpled the cartridge paper in behind the powder. Those without cartridges or bottles were probably pouring handfuls of loose powder extracted from a bag down their muzzles.[2] If taking care and loading without haste the musketeer would then withdraw his 'scouring stick' from its groove in the underside of his musket, and putting it into the barrel, 'ram home his charge'. He rammed by holding the stick between finger and thumb, and giving two or three sharp taps when he was sure it was at the bottom to compress the charge in the chamber. At any stage during this process he would also have reached into his bullet bag and transferred a ball to his mouth. Covered with saliva as a lubricant he then spat that bullet from his mouth into his hand and then dropped it on top of the wadded charge. Taking out his scouring stick once again he then rammed the ball against the compacted charge. This all took time and short-cuts were common. The musketeer then returned his stick to its proper place in the stock. We believe experienced soldiers tapped their ramrods with the flat of their hands after they

'Ram home your charge', and 'Give fire!', copied from drawings of soldiers on the Artillery Ground, London.

had put them back so as to hear a reassuring 'clack' which told them they had not left it down the barrel. If they had done so it would make a fine body-piercing projectile – much like an arrow – but it made all future reloading operations very difficult. It would be silly to suggest that tap-loading (slamming the butt on the ground while holding the musket upright) was unknown, especially in the heat of battle, but compression would always be minimal and thus reduce range dramatically.

After returning his scouring stick the musketeer then took one end of the burning match from his left hand and put it into the serpentine of the lock, all the time keeping the other burning end between the fingers of the left hand, and away from the loaded bottles which garlanded his chest. The musket was thus loaded and only needed the pan cover to be swung clear before it could be fired. On command, the weapon was brought up to the 'present' position, pointed at the enemy with the left hand under the barrel and with the butt resting in the right shoulder. This may seem obvious, but the butt, as most people think of them today, was still a fairly new development and some old-fashioned drill manuals still advocated the sixteenth-century practice of holding the 'handle' into the centre of the chest. The pan cover was then pulled clear.

Squeezing the trigger caused the serpentine, with the burning match between its jaws, to pivot towards the gunpowder-primed pan. This action brought the burning coal of the match into the pan, and the resulting ignition of coal and priming powder caused a minor explosion that flashed through the touch-hole into the chamber of the weapon. There it ignited the main charge. The resulting explosion caused vast amounts of gas to be created – about 1,000% by volume – and these expanded gases, initially imprisoned by the plug and the chamber, sought, found and then rushed along the line of least resistance along the barrel. They forced the ball before them and out of the muzzle at about 500 miles per hour, the recoil delivered a hearty thump to the shoulder. After repeated firing in action, men had bruised and tender shoulders for days.

Smoothbore muskets had not developed very far in the technology race from the

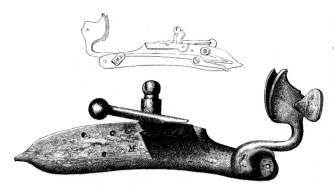

A lock, the firing system of the matchlock musket, from S D Scott, The British Army, Its Origin, Progress and Equipment *(London: Cassell, 1868).*

firearms of the previous 200 years; they were still a metal tube secured to a piece of wood using gunpowder to explode and propel a lead ball. They remained limited to an extreme range of about 300 yards and the same accuracy factors. The ignition systems of the wheellock and flintlock, including the snaphaunce and the dog lock, carried by artillery guards, cavalrymen and wealthier musketeers, were significant refinements, but the musket of the Civil War era was a 'barn-door' weapon that relied upon massed fire rather than individual accuracy.

Accuracy came from the reduction of 'windage', meaning the ball had a snug fit in the barrel. However, the last thing a soldier wants in action is a jammed ball, which would render the weapon useless, so they were cast slightly smaller than the calibre of the barrel. This had the effect of rattling the ball up the tube, and as it left the muzzle it would fly out at the angle of the last deflection of its bouncing journey. Accuracy, even for aimed shots, was erratic. At 100 to 150 yards muskets tended to fire one foot higher than the point of aim. At 200 yards aim and hit points were roughly the same but, at 250 yards, the ball would strike three to six feet lower than where it was aimed. So, firing at over 200 yards meant aiming over the enemy's head. Veterans could attempt a shot at 200 yards for the first round which was aimed at a man's chest, and then another at one 150 yards aimed at the groin. Most soldiers however did not open fire until at 100 yards when the knees became the best target. At less than 100 but above 50 yards, the aim should have been at the feet. At less than 50 yards the trajectory was fairly straight, but practice still encouraged soldiers to aim low to allow for the kick. Edgehill was an early battle and many of the men did not have this experience. It is conjecture but perhaps the experienced officers and sergeants of muskets only fired their blocks at distances below 100 yards and preached the universal doctrine of aiming low.

However, there were other associated drawbacks besides having to aim low, firing the scouring stick and having to keep the lighted match away from the charges. If the measure of compacted powder did not cover the touch-hole inside the chamber, any wad would prevent the flash igniting the charge and the piece would not fire. In the heat of battle the soldier might 'double-shot', that is load another charge on top of the one already in the chamber. If, by chance, it then fired, the force would have given the firer a severe blow to the shoulder, or if the barrel had not been well made, it could have been powerful enough to blow the plug or split the chamber. If it did not fire, and several charges and bullets were jammed on top of each other, the weapon would be useless and dangerous until carefully 'wormed out' with a special corkscrew-like device fitted

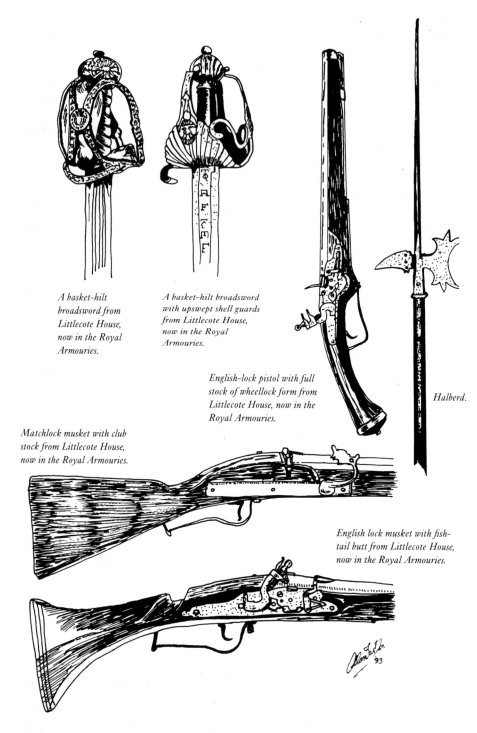

A basket-hilt broadsword from Littlecote House, now in the Royal Armouries.

A basket-hilt broadsword with upswept shell guards from Littlecote House, now in the Royal Armouries.

English-lock pistol with full stock of wheellock form from Littlecote House, now in the Royal Armouries.

Halberd.

Matchlock musket with club stock from Littlecote House, now in the Royal Armouries.

English lock musket with fish-tail butt from Littlecote House, now in the Royal Armouries.

Muskets, a pistol and swords – styles of weapons used at Edgehill.

to the scouring stick. Wind also caused problems by blowing the powder out of the priming pan and extinguishing the match or causing it to rapidly burn down. These may have been contributing factors to the emphasis placed by various contemporary writers upon gaining the wind from the enemy.[3]

Musketeers would also have probably encountered clogging of the touch-hole caused by the high sulphur content of powder of the period. This was cleared by inserting a thin needle-like pricker into the hole and prodding the blockage through into the chamber. Heavy use could also cause a build up of detritus inside the barrel necessitating musketeers to wash their barrels through, preferably with hot water, which was a frequent post-action task. We have nothing to prove that Civil War soldiers discovered the Napoleonic veterans' practice of clearing clogged barrels in action by urinating down them (the chemical action caused the fouling matter to dissolve more easily). The poor powder also produced vast quantities of smoke – literally the fog of war! After several volleys, musketeers' lines would be wreathed in thick, acrid, grey smoke which seriously limited their ability to see their target. Although also being hidden from view themselves, an opposite musket block which had not fired could always fire into the smoke. On a still day, especially when the atmosphere was heavy, this smoke would hang in the air and soon engulf large portions of the field. At Edgehill we learn from comments in several accounts that at the end of the fight the Parliamentarians gained an advantage of the wind, apparently a light south-westerly, which hampered the Royalists' ability to return fire and hit their enemy.[4]

Hitting the human target was one thing, but injuring him was another. Many of the Horse and pikemen wore armour, much of it supposedly shot-proof (for the Horse) and bearing 'the testing dent' as a supposed guarantee. It was not always bullet-proof. Various claims in period drill manuals extol the matchlock musket's ability to penetrate armour at 'ten score paces' (200 yards). Target-shooting tests undertaken by one author of this work suggest these figures are a little optimistic and possibly based on manufacturers' best estimates – in other words 'advertising hype'.[5]

The matchlock musket may not be as mighty a weapon as the longbow in legend but it had advantages in the hands of common men.

Rifles
Spiral grooves inside the barrels of firearms had been introduced during the sixteenth century but these weapons, although more accurate, were bespoke, only produced in small numbers for the hunting market, and consequently expensive. A few hunting rifles might have been on Edgehill in the hands of privileged individuals, but the lack of references make it currently of little interest to the story of the battle.

Pistols
Although officers of Foot might have carried pistols, they were essentially a cavalry weapon that belonged to the age when formations of Horse were considered chiefly as mobile fire platforms and massed pistols were used to deliver close-range fire on targets in order to soften them up before the action deteriorated into a melee. The matchlock was too complicated an arrangement to use mounted and so the wheellock mechanism was developed in order to make firing on horseback more practical. The wheellock did away with match by means of winding up a clockwork serrated steel disc or wheel. They

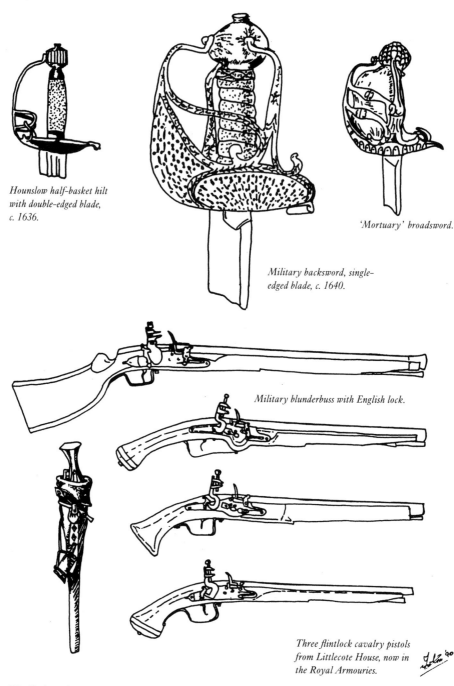

Hounslow half-basket hilt with double-edged blade, c. 1636.

'Mortuary' broadsword.

Military backsword, single-edged blade, c. 1640.

Military blunderbuss with English lock.

Three flintlock cavalry pistols from Littlecote House, now in the Royal Armouries.

Wheellock pistol complete with holster, spanner, bullet bag and powder flask from Cruso's Militarie Instructions for the Cavalerie.

Sword hilts and firearms – styles of weapons used at Edgehill.

were reliable weapons but had to be carefully made, especially the short piece of chain which connected the wheel's spindle to a powerful mainspring. When the spindle was wound, or spanned, by use of a crank key, or spanner, this chain wrapped around the spindle under tension from the mainspring which was locked by a standard trigger mechanism. Just before firing another moving part, the dogshead, which held the flint or pyrites in a set of screw-up jaws, was clicked down on to the wheel so that on squeezing the trigger the spring was unlocked and it pulled the chain back, rapidly unwrapping it and causing the spindle to revolve. The rapidly rotating serrated wheel grated against the iron pyrites to produce sparks which ignited the priming charge in the pistol's pan. Wheellocks were quite robust but if they malfunctioned it required a specialist with purpose-designed tools to repair them whereas any competent blacksmith could mend a matchlock. Firing by use of flint was problematical because flint was too hard and damaged the wheel, but the more common use of pyrites, a soft mineral that quickly broke, chipped or wore away, necessitated frequent replacement. Added to this, small fragments often worked their way into the mechanism. However, it worked well and could usually be relied upon to fire first time but, with its operation dependent upon a detached spanner, reloading in action was probably difficult.

Pistols varied in length according to the beliefs and styles of the gunsmiths. Contemporary examples are between 16 and 25 inches and thus required a substantial holster. Most pistols were issued in pairs and slotted into holsters strapped over the pommel of the saddle. Pistol bores varied too with examples ranging up to 36 balls per pound weight (36 bore), although the 32 bore appears common.

At Edgehill evidence suggests that the Parliamentarian Horse was still reliant upon its firepower from carbines and pistols. Parliament's control of weapon manufacture meant most of their Horse carried pistols. We have no evidence of similar issues to Royalist troopers and Roberts and Tincey state they would 'pass muster if armed only with a sword'.[6] Cavalrymen, however, considered themselves socially superior to the Foot and the pistol was not deemed a gentleman's weapon of choice although Rupert, who was known to be interested in them, owned a pair of rifled pistols whose accuracy he supposedly demonstrated to his royal uncle by twice hitting a church weathervane.[7] Tests made in 1620 with standard wheellocks recorded an 85 per cent success rate for hitting a man-sized target at 30 yards plus reasonable rates of penetration of ³⁄₁₆" (2 mm) steel plate.[8] However, those performed by the author with a reproduction wheellock showed accurate shooting was possible at 10 yards, up to 20 yards it was reasonable, about 80 per cent, but beyond that rather haphazard. A flintlock pistol fared somewhat better but was more prone to misfires. Perhaps the 1620s man was a better marksman, or perhaps it was for this reason that at Edgehill the experienced prince ordered that his mounted command should, 'receive the Enemy's Shot, without firing either Carbin or Pistol, til we broke in amongst the Enemy, and then to make use of our Fire-arms as need should require'.[9] In other words, do not fire until you can see the whites of their eyes!

Carbines

The 'hook-gun' and harquebus of the previous century had virtually vanished along with the practice of holding these shorter firearms against the chest. A need for a long-range firearm for the Horse had caused the evolution of this weapon into something supposedly nicknamed the 'dragon' which has become one of the traditional derivations for the term dragoon – meaning a man who rode into battle but fought not with his sword and mounted, but dismounted with an infantry-style weapon. One line of thinking argues that as the musket was the weapon of the musketeers, so the dragon was the weapon of the dragoneers, as Lord Bernard Stuart calls them.

The use of carbines by the Horse at Edgehill was severely limited, for their numbers would have been very small. It was not until later in the war that this weapon went fully into production and then it was either using the expensive wheellock mechanism or the new snaphaunce or flintlock. Most of the snapping locks of this period imitated the then common household practice of striking flint against steel to produce sparks. The lock was a mechanism to bring the flint, held in the jaws of the cock, at speed into contact with the steel frizzen. It worked by the shank of the cock going through the lock plate with a lug that, when rotated, compressed the mainspring allowing the end of a horizontally moving sear to also slip through the lock plate and hold the mainspring in its depressed position. The action of the trigger withdrew the sear, released the mainspring, driving the lug forward, rotating the cock and throwing the flint against the steel. A refinement incorporated a built-in plunger that automatically opened the pan cover. At Edgehill the firelock artillery guards and perhaps some of Parliament's dragoons carried these more modern weapons.

Holland had become Europe's major weapons manufacturer and the Dutch snaphaunce would probably have been the most common version. It is easily recognized by its large S-shaped cock and a round disc set on the outside of the pan which itself was usually a half-cylinder with a sliding cover. Although uncomplicated, the inner mechanisms varied between national gunsmiths, such as the English doglock and the French and Spanish miquelets, but the detailed description of these patterns is beyond the scope of this book and, so early in the war, few would have been at Edgehill.

The dragoons at Edgehill were more likely to have carried matchlock muskets, especially those on the Royalist side, for we find a reference in the papers of the royal trayne to them carrying the dragoons' match.[10] References to Wardlaw's and Brown's Parliamentary dragoons state that they were issued with 'short' or 'bastard muskets' and since there is no reference to match being issued to them, it would suggest they were firelocks.[11]

As to range and accuracy, these shorter-barrelled firearms, 20 to 26 inches long rather than 40 to 48 inches, were smaller, 24 bore to the musket's usual 12 or 16 bore, and were thus likely to have fired a smaller charge, to have been more susceptible to 'last bounce syndrome' and without the range or accuracy of the musket. Carbine tests performed by the author have been limited but were roughly the same as recorded for pistols except that reasonable accuracy could be expected up to 40 yards, but over 50 yards the accuracy rate dropped dramatically. Neither was the author on horseback, although he experimented with firing preloaded, 16 bore, reproduction muskets while mounted, with the result that his horse, although declared by its owner to be of a docile nature and accustomed to gunfire, bolted everytime.[12] Perhaps many of those horses ridden by Ramsey's troopers at Edgehill were similarly disposed to their riders shooting carbines while on their backs and consequently behaved in an identical manner?

Pikes

The pike was regarded as the more noble weapon of the Foot. It took time to master and the associated postures and drill movements were considered a display-art worthy of

'Advance your pike' and *'Charge your pike'*, *copied from Hexham,* The Principles of the Art Militarie (1642).

public demonstration on London's Artillery Ground. It also took physical prowess to handle a pike properly and fighting with it required discipline and trust in one's neighbours. In its crudest form it was a long, straight pointed stick with a fire-hardened, shaped point for thrusting at the enemy any way the men could manage. At its best it was a 16-foot long, rounded, ash pole, which was tapered at both ends and fitted with a socketed, razor-sharp, steel head with protective steel bands, or langets, and a steel butt ring. The taper of the fighting end was thinner but more gradual than at the butt so as to compensate for the weight of the steel point. The weapon had a precise point of balance about six feet from the butt. Handling the pike depended upon the user becoming familiar with this balance until control could be established by almost delicate shifting of handgrips or even movement of the fingers. Pike drill was complicated and exponents were required to learn a series of postures which were executed in unison. It was this cohesion which made pike fighting so effective. When a body of pikes was charged, the enemy saw a mass of sharp, steel, stabbing spikes pointed directly at them. If this entity was moving with the impetus of a steady advance then the sight was both awe-inspiring and daunting.

The optimum shape of the point of the pike was much debated in military manuals of the period. Types range from square-section spikes to flat-section lozenges. There was no universal pattern of pike point at Edgehill but, at this time on pikes of English manufacture, various leaf shapes including an inverted kite were current. Most were fashioned by blacksmiths from hollow round tubes, which were flattened and beaten into shape on the anvil. This process case-hardened the metal. The other end of the tube was left rounded to take the tapered end of the shaft and was probably mounted while hot to shrink into its fit. Nails then secured the pre-pierced tubular section of the point to the shaft. Two strips of steel, each about two feet long, were then similarly fastened on either side of the head of the shaft just below the point. These 'langets' were in place to stop the heads being lopped off in battle. On the more expensive pikes the langet was a forged part of the whole head and a counter-weight butt ring or short spike was also added, but economies could see both of them vanish altogether.

On long marches pikes could be transported by wagon but were more usually carried by the men 'at shoulder', which is with the shaft pivoting on the shoulder and held in point of balance by the weight of a hand resting on the lower section; this can even be done by simply hooking a finger over it. In all likelihood the men in 'Kineton Fight' had carried theirs for days. Marching with the pike on the shoulder is easy as long as the soldier keeps his eye on the butt and avoids the ankles of the man in front. However, manoeuvering is more complicated and demands that the pike is held upright to allow turning. The pike is 'advanced' so that the butt rests in the palm or underside of the fingers of the right hand. The left hand can come across the chest to secure the long shaft in windy weather, but a skilled pikeman can balance his weapon easily and finds it fits into collar depression of the ball and socket shoulder joint or into the niche created between the coat and the breastplate's shoulder strap. With pike held upright the man may turn and march in whichever direction ordered without clashing pikes with anyone else or creating havoc in the synchronized body.

The pike was to evolve into an essentially anti-cavalry weapon, but Edgehill was the first battle of the war and the notion that it was the primary infantry melee weapon persisted. Writers of contemporary drill books looked back to the age of Classical Greece and found descriptions of operational pike practice in the writings of ancient historians. The Dutch system favoured the eight-by-eight block, based upon the work of the scholar Lipsius who studied the writings of Asclepiodotus on the Macedonian phalanx (with files doubled for extending their fighting line), while the Swedish system went back even as far as Polybius' writings for his Roman master, about the six-by-six arrangement of the Spartan *enomotia*. Lipsius also worked on the writings of Aelian, Leo and Vegetius, as did several other military historians of his age.[13] Although fascinating, the origin of drill sources are beyond the scope of this book, but suffice it to say that in all these models, men were arrayed in files. Each file was under fighting command of its front man, or 'file leader' (*lochagos*) and a further complex arrangement of 'dignities' that revolved around responsibilities in any change of order or formation. This included 'bringers up' or 'file closers' (*ouragoi*) and half-file leaders (*hemilochites*), whose job was to move up next to his 'file leader' with his half-file behind him if the formation was to double its front. The better trained seventeenth-century units could perform the advised methods of countermarching or even the modern evolution of wheeling, albeit slowly. These classical models were followed, however, to the point of adopting the practice of regimental commanding officers 'trailing their pike' in the front rank, as did the *syntagmatarchs* of Hellas.

Two basic fighting methods were in use: one for fighting Foot the other for defending against Horse. Both involved coming to 'closest order', with the men packed together, shoulder-to-shoulder, to give density to the fighting mass, fusing disparate individuals into a solid, unified block. On coming close to enemy Foot the order to 'charge your pike' was given; experienced soldiers could do this on the move but it was not unusual to halt first, perform the posture and then move off again. It involved planting a stance with the right foot drawn back and turned at 90 degrees to the left so that the body-weight was in balance – much like a fencer's *en garde* position. The left hand came across and secured the shaft chest high, and the pike was then allowed to fall forward from the upright advance position with its weight being taken by the left hand as the body weight was adjusted to the front foot. The right arm was allowed to rise outstretched and, with the fingers of the right hand checking the impetus, the heel of the hand, now on the top of the flat-held weapon, pushed downwards to bring the whole pike into balance with the left hand acting as the fulcrum. This was then locked into place by the right arm rolling over the top of the shaft which also added more weight to the rear portion and gave better control of the point. Simply by leaning forward the steel tip could stab forward several inches but with a leaning-forward accompanied by a step and a push forward of both hands, the thrust could reach another three to four feet, with almost the whole body-weight of the man concentrated behind its point. Some drill books advised against thrusting, preferring to rely upon the impetus of the unified mass.

> When Battells commeth to push of pike, good commanders say that your pikemen must not push by advancing and retiring their arm as commonly is done; but onely go jointly on together in a rout without moving their arms.[14]

No matter which fighting style was preferred the force, focused on a sharp steel tip, was easily great enough to pierce cloth and flesh. If the target was advancing the collision effect would nearly double its piercing effect. If the target was a mounted trooper and the horse going at a trot then it could penetrate a reasonable-quality buff coat. The old-fashioned and complicated 'charge for horse' posture was probably not used at Edgehill having been found to be a fairly pointless refinement, and the standard Foot 'bright hedge of steel' was sufficient to deter most cavalry attacks, especially if the muskets had emptied a few saddles as they rode in.

The use of the pike in action at Edgehill would depend upon the type and level of training received and the manual or treatise read and understood by the officers. One modern authority on pike fighting methods is David Blackmore of the Royal Armouries upon whose work these few paragraphs heavily rely. His work extends well beyond the range of those sources which would have been available to the officers in 1642 but, in order to appreciate what went on in the battle line, we can look at those of the preceding age for an understanding of how the Edgehill men may have been taught to fight.[15]

Our best indication comes from the Earl of Essex on the occasion of his reviewing the army at Worcester on 24 September 1642, the day after Powick Bridge. He took pains to explain to his men the cause of the war as he conceived it to have been and then advised his officers:

> to be careful in the exercising of your men, and bring them to use their arms readily and expertly, and not to busy them in practising the cere-monious forms of military discipline; only let them be well instructed in the necessary rudiments of war, that they may know to fall on with discretion, and retreat with care.[16]

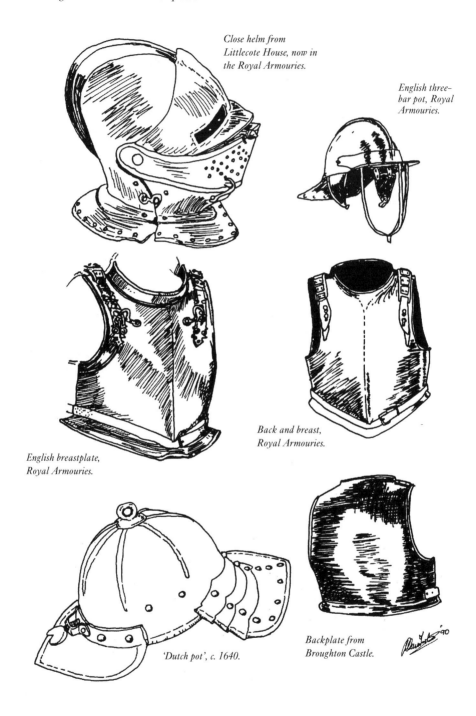

Close helm from
Littlecote House, now in
the Royal Armouries.

English three-
bar pot, Royal
Armouries.

English breastplate,
Royal Armouries.

Back and breast,
Royal Armouries.

'Dutch pot', c. 1640.

Backplate from
Broughton Castle.

English Civil War armour. Types of personal body protection used at Edgehill.

Lord Brooke's buffcoat, helmet and armour, probably worn at Edgehill, from S D Scott, The British Army, Its Origin, Progress and Equipment *(London, Cassell, 1868).*

He then announced nine articles of war, which formed the basic military code for the ensuing campaign.[17]

We know that not all six or eight ranks of pikes were lowered towards the enemy. One much-read writer, Ward, states 'the front Half of Pikes are onely to charge their Pikes, the Rere half-files to port them in time of fight'.[18] Under these instructions the Royalist pike blocks had three ranks of points stabbing forward, while Parliament had four, a 25 per cent advantage. Ward was published in 1638 but his views on this are echoed by both the authors of two more popular drill manuals published in 1643 and 1649.[19] This would suggest the practice was common throughout the war. We know also that they probably dressed their order and drew together to gain control and cohesion. Sir John Smythe advises that prior to engaging the ranks and files be closed: 'armed men in the field, being ready to encounter with… their enemies, ought to straighten and close themselves by front and flanks'.[20] Smythe also recommends that, as far as possible, all these points strike into the enemy at the same time. He further stipulates that all pikes should be relatively the same length so that: 'with their pikes bent against their enemies, [they] may altogether give a great blow and thrust to the repulse of either horsemen and footmen than if they were of divers lengths'.[21]

The intention was to come to 'push of pike'. The front ranks were responsible for thrusting and striking, searching for advantages, or openings in the opposition's guard through which they could drive their long steel spikes. The front ranks were also supposedly well protected. Smythe tells us armour was hard to pierce. If supplied, each man wore a wide-brimmed, steel pikeman's pot to shield the skull and cause the enemy's pike points to glance away. They kept their faces down and, protected by the leather gauntlets on their left hands, if they had them, they aimed their pike by peering along the shafts of their weapons through slits between their headgear brims and their hands. Their throats were covered by steel gorgets and added padding came from knotting their collars. Breastplates were sought after by the front ranks and, early in the war, backplates too were issued. Both were of a good thickness. Finally they wore articulated and flared tassets to protect the groin and upper thighs.[22] Arms were unprotected but difficult to stab, and faces were accessible, but the favourite target was the armpit, for it afforded an unarmoured access to the body and a well-positioned thrust could drive through the side of the ribs and into the lungs at an angle that could, potentially, sever a major blood-vessel. For all this accurate positioning, fencing, pushing and warding with pikes, 'quickness of foote and hand ys much advisable'.[23]

There was also a minor on-going debate as to the speed of the advance to contact. A few officers might have preferred the running charge advocated by Blaise de Monluc: 'as the Swiss do, run headlong to force and penetrate into the midst of them, and you shall see how confounded they shall be'.[24] However, despite the advantages of running into combat or advancing slowly and striking as a unified body, there must also have been a lot of falling over as they clashed. Monluc continues 'as well on their side as ours all the first ranks either with push of pike or the shock at the encounter, were overturned'.[25] The same author also records that at Cerisoles in 1544 he was in a pike block and beaten to his knees 'above three times' without hurt, while later, at Stratton in May 1643, Sir Bevil Grenville himself was bowled over in a disordered scrimmage instigated by a charge of pikes led by his old adversary, Major General Chudleigh.[26]

Being knocked over, or tripped by stumbling over those already down, caused the front ranks of any pike clash soon to become a tangled mess of desperately fighting men. Ranks would become mixed as those initially standing behind men who fell would close up into the gaps and charge their pikes into the chaos. Pikes would become unmanageable in the tightness of the press; some would bend and snap while others would be dropped. Although he was writing before 1590, Smythe records how, in these situations, soldiers would resort to their other weapons when, with 'the use and execution of the pikes of the foremost ranks being past, they must presently betake themselves to the use of their swords and daggers... the nearness and press being so great'.[27]

Despite the ferocity of the fighting and the terrible wounds which must have been inflicted, it would seem that the number of men killed outright was surprisingly few. This is borne out by the casualty figures for Edgehill. For those who had it, their armour prevented many deaths. Wounds to legs, arms and even faces may be dreadful but they are seldom mortal, at least on the field. It would appear that actually killing as many enemy as possible was not the purpose of the push of pike. Sir James Melville's memoirs may give us a lead as to the intention of the pike conflict when he states that at the Battle of Langside the men 'forced them incontinent to give place and turn back, after long fighting and pushing others to and fro with their spears (pikes). There were not so many horsemen to pursue after them'.[28] Of Edgehill itself, we can read in James II's account 'the Foot being thus engaged in such warm and close service, it were reasonable to suppose that one side should run and be disordered'.[29]

Apparently their job was to break the enemy and cause such disorder and exhaustion that they would be forced to flee the field or at least give ground. The killing was the job of the cavalry pursuit. At Edgehill we see Meldrum's and Ballard's Brigades practising the typical infantry role of breaking the enemy's formation and holding ground.

Artillery

Artillery was also dependent upon established, if not outdated, technology. Henry VIII had overseen and financed developments in design and manufacture which were still in use during the early seventeenth century. Metal barrels were cast from various alloys of bronze, iron or brass according to the specifications of the person placing the order. Bronze resists corrosion better than iron and it can also withstand greater pressures without cracking. It was, however, a softer component and reportedly gave problems in the casting. Although this had been a period of stagnation in artillery technology, improvements had come in the development of the poundage system and the beginning of a movement towards agreement on calibres and weight of shot in respect to charge.[30] Artillery had begun to separate its weaponry into two distinct types: guns needed to fire upon troops in the field and those required to batter down walls or lob bombs into defensive works, but they had not yet developed the exploding shell.

Accuracy was dependent not just upon the skill of the man who aimed the piece but also on precision-casting of the barrel, quality of powder and calibre of shot (which effected windage). A gunner who 'knew' his guns was a most valuable asset. Powder was usually of poor manufacture early in the war and the powder granule or 'corn' variety used by the muskets was deemed too powerful for the age of some of the guns. The following details are taken from Ward's *Animadversions of Warre* but we have deliberately edited the information to try and give a simple picture of what was available to the gunners at Edgehill:

Table 2.1 Comparative statistics of various artillery pieces.

Name	Diameter inches	Shot Wt pounds	Charge pounds*	Pt Blk yards	Utmost	Weight pounds	Horses
Demi-cannon	6	27	18	340	1,700	4,000	16/20
Culverin	5	15	12	400	2,500	3,400	10/12
Demi-Culverin	4½	11¾	9	380	1,800	3,000	7/8
Saker	3¾	5½	5½	300	1,500	1,900	5/6
Minion	3¼	3	5	280	1,400	1,100	4
Fawcon	2¼	2½	2½	260	1,200	750	3
Robinet	1½	¾	¾	150	700	300	2

*in lb of serpentine (not corned) powder.

Source: National Archives, SP 12/242, ff 64 and 65; R Ward, *Animadversions of Warre* (London, 1639); W Eldred, *The Gunners' Glasse* (London, 1646); A R Hall, *Ballistics of the Seventeenth Century* (Cambridge University Press, 1952).

Different ranges were still achieved by varying the angle of elevation by driving a wedge, called a quoin, between the back of the chamber and the carriage, which forced the barrel to pivot on its trunnions and so change angle. These ranges were approximately:

Table 2.2   Comparative ranges according to elevation.

	1°	2°	3°	5°	10°
3-pounder	700	950	1,150	1,400	2,390
6-pounder	750	1,050	1,310	1,800	2,800
12-pounder	800	1,150	1,450	1,900	3,200

Source: National Archives, SP 12/242, ff 64 and 65; R Ward, *Animadversions of Warre* (London, 1639); W Eldred, *The Gunners' Glasse* (London, 1646); A R Hall, *Ballistics of the Seventeenth Century* (Cambridge University Press, 1952).

The make-up of the artillery trains at Edgehill is very pertinent. The Royalist Ordnance Papers tell us that the King's Army had twenty guns: two demi-cannons, two culverins, two demi-culverins (which must have formed the six-gun battery on Bullet Hill) plus six falcons, six falconets and two robinets that were deployed in the Swedish method as battalion guns, i.e., spread out along the line.[31] Belasyse's secretary Joshua Moore states that two cannon were placed 'before every body of foot' but exactly where we do not know.[32] The most likely scenario is that they were drawn up in pairs, directly forward of the brigades but in the intervals between the constituent regiments allowing sufficient space for the Foot to manoeuvre around them. There is no evidence to support an advance of these guns with the Foot when the latter attacked but, after an initial bombardment, they would have been in a position to act as a defensive base upon which the Foot could fall back.

There was no standard arrangement for manning a gun. From various accounts we can arrive at an approximation that a big gun, such as a demi-culverin (a 10- to 12-pound field gun) needed quite a team of men and horses to get it into action. Usually there were about eight men serving the piece: five working the gun directly, including one gunner and one or two assistants, called matrosses, with three men serving ammunition. The period authority, William Eldred, states, 'one may well make 10 shots an hour if the peeces be well fortified and strong, but if they be ordinary peeces then 8 is enough, always provided that after 40 shots you refresh and cool the peece and let her reste an houre'.[33]

The casualty effect of round shot was nowhere near as devastating as the bursting shells of later periods. A flying ball could only hit those in its direct path, but it did have what Leedham calls an 'earthquake effect' on those in the proximity of its strike. The violent disruption of the air caused by the flying or bouncing ball would be sufficient to set up a stun wave, especially in its initial flight.[34] Accounts from soldiers in action during later periods suggest that the passing of a ball was sufficient to knock the wind out of a man and leave him on his knees gasping for breath. The ball from a big gun such as a demi-culverin passing through an advancing formation might, in optimum bounce circumstances, kill or maim a complete file of eight men but the shock wave could also knock over the file on either side. These men would later get up and not even be counted as wounded but they would have been effectively removed from the fight for some time.

Of course, to achieve this effect they had to reach their target. We have already discussed accuracy and range but getting a ball on to a target was also a matter of striking the right type of ground at the correct angle. Effective long-range bombardment involved striking hard ground at about a 45 degree angle causing the shot to ricochet. Bouncing balls were the bane of deep formations and could plough through first and

A heavy gun on a travelling carriage, based upon an engraving by S della Bello.

second lines, while even a shot rolling along the ground having spent most of its kinetic energy could still be dangerous. At Edgehill the King placed his long-range guns on Bullet Hill which gave them the advantage of height to reach further but worked against their trajectory. It is supposed that the reason they did so little damage was that the balls dropped at too steep an angle for an effective bounce which was compounded by firing at troops stood on recently turned fields fronted by wet headwater heath. The shot ploughed in and did not bounce; much of it thus fell short. Although also at utmost range, Parliament's guns could fire so that their shot struck the drier, harder ground of the lower slopes of the escarpment at a more reflex angle and so bounced several times increasing their propensity to do hurt.

Nevertheless, the overall ability to inflict casualties was small compared to the effect guns had on morale. The noise and the smoke produced must have terrified men and horses. When this is added to their ability to hit from such a long distance the fear induced must have been substantial let alone the psychological demands placed on men having nobody to fight but ordered to 'just stand firm and take it'.

The train of artillery was responsible for the provision of ammunition to the whole army. Transporting sufficient stocks as well as their guns about the countryside was a mammoth task requiring exceptional organizational and administration skills, more than basic understanding of engineering, animal husbandry and considerable diplomacy. In addition, vast quantities of material, seemingly limitless numbers of horses, carriages, wagons, drivers, carters, pioneers, craftsmen and labourers were essential. It was a very expensive instrument which Clarendon calls 'a spunge that could never be…satisfied'.[34] At Edgehill the task of moving the big guns down the escarpment took all morning and, while forming six-gun batteries was not usual practice, the establishment of a platform on Bullet Hill must have provided the gunners with considerable relief at the prospect of not having to move them further.

Armes Blanches
The sword was the symbol of the soldier and every fighting man wanted one. Parliament was able in part to meet this need by commissioning vast numbers of cheap (they cost 4*s* 6*d*), unbalanced, hacking broad or short swords with a rudimentary guard. The Horse too carried something similar: but the tuck, or mortuary sword, had the advantage of being slightly longer, useful for both cutting and thrusting, and its guard gave better protection to the user's hand. Longer still and much more efficiently balanced was the more expensive *Pappenheimer*, a German-designed rapier carried by many of the those who had seen foreign-service. Cheap swords were notoriously weighty, blade-heavy, clumsy and difficult to use. The idea of a trooper placing the point just to the side of a cuirass and thrusting in under the armpit as opposing lines met was most likely an

elusive dream. More usual was the crash of horseflesh followed by a protracted maul as the men engaged in chopping and hacking coupled with punching with their large hand guards. Their target was more often than not their enemy's mount which, if felled, took its rider out of the fray as well. The swords used by the Horse could cut, but their design was nowhere near as good as that of the extremely effective light cavalry sabre of later eras. Consequently they were not good for slicing down fleeing infantry.

The poleaxe, or pollaxe, was a favourite cavalry weapon early in the war and its effective use features in several accounts of Edgehill. Although it was a development from the medieval battleaxe with a longer handle, the pattern was eastern European and was brought in by returning veterans from the Continental wars. As well as a cutting edge it usually had a hammer head for crushing and a spike for thrusting which made it a very useful all-round weapon. For a skilled smith, it was not difficult to produce; it just took time and was consequently more expensive. Any used at Edgehill were not issue items but were personal possessions brought from a private arsenal, or were specially commissioned by the owner for 'going to the wars'.

Lances

Despite their appearing in von Walhausen's manual there is no record of lancers, or indeed mounted pikemen, in English service at this time. There were none at Edgehill although they were in use in Scots armies and were employed effectively on Marston Moor during 1644.

Effect

The weapons employed during the Civil War were designed to produce crude, extensive injuries upon anyone unfortunate enough to be the target of their owners' aggression. Cannonballs and grape shot could smash the human frame into a quivering bloody mess or remove heads and limbs in an instant. Shot weapons, albeit of relatively low velocity in comparison with later firearms, could, nevertheless, inflict fatal or severe life-threatening injuries. The effects of shot on flesh has been the subject of research but as yet the calculations remain unconfirmed. Tests performed in the 1970s involving firing at suspended sheep carcasses suggested fairly easy penetration at 50 yards getting progressively weaker up to 200 yards, when they hit! At 300 yards shot, more often than not, bounced off – and this was using modern, more refined gunpowder. At this range they could still deliver a significant punch and cause severe bruising but death was a rarity. The entry wound caused by a soft lead ball at effective range is about two inches across and quite neat in appearance. It does however, seriously damage the skin and the tissue it penetrates. Unlike modern high-velocity projectiles the musket ball's relatively slow speed and non-streamlined shape cause it to tear and batter its way into the body rather than piercing and slicing, and jagged flesh marks its destructive path to the point where it runs out of impetus and comes to rest. Sometimes at close range it will channel through muscle, almost tunnelling, but it remains a crude projectile. The musket ball, being of soft lead, will absorb shock and partially flatten on impact with something as resistant as human bone. The effect would be determined by the shape and type of bone struck. A chest shot hitting a rib snaps the individual bone, but the spring of the rib-cage absorbs much of the impetus and deflects the now partially flattened projectile, causing it to sheer and spin away from its initial pathway. The effect can be likened to a rough-edged, heavy coin spinning at random through the lungs. However, the ball is at its most deadly when it impacts upon a soft target such as the abdomen. Quickly ripping through the body wall, it tears through the internal organs before either lodging in or leaving the body through the back creating a three- to four-inch exit wound. Torn muscle tissue is relatively simple to treat compared with the massive damage inflicted upon the internal organs and even modern surgeons find this kind of wound challenging. It is not known whether the medical care of the day operated a triage system, but one suspects that they would have made those suffering from abdominal wounds as comfortable as possible without spending more time upon them than was necessary.

Assistance could, however, be rendered to a man whose limb had been struck by a ball. Unlike the thin ribs, which tend to simply snap, the femur, radius and ulna are prone to shattering. Not only would the surgeon have to deal with the torn tissues and muscle of the entry wound but also with bone splinters driven into the surrounding tissue in all directions. Unlike a simple break, inflicted by a sword that was frequently incapable of cutting though a buff-leather sleeve, these wounds meant that the limb could rarely be salvaged by contemporary surgical practice and amputation was the simplest, most effective and humane treatment. Recent work by Professor Carole Rawcliffe, of the University of East Anglia, has shown the painstaking care demonstrated in removing an arrow from Prince Henry's cheek after the battle of Shrewsbury in 1403.[36] Had his wound been inflicted by a musket ball it would probably have torn his eye from its socket, shattered the side of his skull and destroyed his upper jaw.

The standard musket ball, an ounce of lead, may well have torn through muscle and tendons inflicting potentially massive tissue damage, bone fractures and loss of blood, but should the victim survive the initial wounding, gross infection would probably ensue, owing to the clothing, soil and other materials that would, inevitably, have been forced by the missile into the soldier's head, chest, abdomen or deep muscle layers of the limbs. Swords and long arms, such as poleaxes and halberds, each with the capacity to slash and stab, were no less damaging in their action. Slicing through muscle, tendon or bone their effect could be likened to that of a butcher's cleaver with the added potential to produce penetrating wounds that could sever vital internal organs and blood vessels.

The threat posed by these weapons was a major factor in establishing the mind-set of the troops before the first shot was fired. Later, in chapter 4 below, it will be shown how the bulk of the troops engaged were drawn from raw, poorly trained volunteers or levies, each of whom would have had only an extremely vague impression of the nature of armed combat. The mental imagery and psychological effects induced by anticipating personal injury by these crude tools of war cannot be overestimated. An accurate appreciation of the state of mind for the majority of the soldiers present during and after the battle of Edgehill cannot, therefore, be achieved without considering the impact that recent preceding events exerted upon the minds and attitudes of the combatants. Inevitably, the ill-trained, raggle-taggle troops of the opposing armies were already suffering from the problems that follow in the footsteps of poor discipline, lack of experience and minimal training. In situations familiar to all armies at the beginning of every subsequent campaign, there were several recorded instances of accidental or negligent injuries, such as the twelve Parliamentary soldiers 'wounded by the firing of some powder; [including one who] shot himself through the foot with his Pistoll and another through the back'.[37]

Although the first skirmish of the war at Powick Bridge on 23 September 1642 only lasted for about fifteen minutes, the exaggerated, florid horror stories that circulated after the incident were rapidly disseminated through both armies and found fertile soil in the soldiers' impressionable minds. For example, one Parliamentarian author stated:

> That many of their soldiers and Cavaliers, being fled into Worcester before the end of the skirmish, were seen in the streets most woefully cut and mangled, some having their ears cut off, some the flesh of their heads sliced off, some with their very skulls hanging down, and they ready to fall down dead, their pistols and carbines being hewed and hacked away in slices, which it seems they held up for guard of their heads.[38]

In a similar vein, the letters of Nehemiah Wharton, a London volunteer sergeant in Colonel Denzil Holles's Regiment of Parliamentarian Foot, provide a colourful summary of his experiences during the first few months of the war and reflect the contemporary prevalence of exaggeration, rumour and speculation:

> Our wounded men they brought into the city, and stripped, robbed, and slashed their dead bodies in a most barbarous manner, and imbued their hands in their blood. This relation I had from an gentleman that was in the front of the battle, and was wounded with the sword and bullets in seven several places, was stripped naked, and yet liveth. He afterwards thought that there were ten for one, yet there were more slain and wounded of them than of us and I spoke with one that heard the Prince, at his return, say, that our men fought more like lions then men… Since their departure we hear that the Prince [Rupert] is wounded, but it is certain Duke [Prince] Maurice is mortally wounded. They report unto the king that they have slain eight hundred of our men, when there were but twenty-eight slain in all, and some of them were Cavaliers.[39]

In reality, casualties at Powick Bridge were very light. For the Royalists, Prince Maurice received two cuts on the head, Lord Wilmot was cut on the arm, Sir Lewes Dives was wounded and the son of Sir John Strangeways taken prisoner. Total losses on the Parliamentary side were no more than fifty including Colonel Sandys who was mortally wounded.[40] Quartermaster Douglas was killed, and about ten junior officers were taken prisoner including Captain Wingate, who was quickly exchanged for the young Strangeways. Nevertheless, the widespread, over-blown and sensationalized images that circulated freely exerted a considerable and lasting influence upon the troops' morale, attitudes and subsequent folk-lore.

Chapter Three
Command

He shall have power to assign ... also to command all forts, castles and ships, and to give instructions for the punishment of all mutinies. The Earl of Essex's Commission.

Seventeenth-century armies had, in theory, a simple structure with a commander-in-chief, a second and a third in command, and a field marshal (not to be confused with the modern rank). Each arm had a general with a lieutenant general to assist him. The Foot also had the services of a sergeant major general and the Horse a commissary general. These vacancies were usually filled by professional soldiers whose advice was sought by their frequently less experienced superiors. These men formed the army Council of War with their numbers being supplemented by various colonels, military appointments (such as the Adjutant General or Scout Master General) and indeed civilian officials (the King had several Ministers of State).

As Edgehill was the first major battle of the Civil Wars, commands and posts in both armies were awarded to those deemed suitable for the job by either the King or Parliament. The criteria for the suitability of an individual for their nominated role appear to have been founded upon a mixture of social rank and status, political and personal influence, and military experience and professional expertise. The result was an interesting cross-section of factions present in both camps, and the friction was exacerbated by the military use of the council. Designed to advise the commander, councils often became lobby-based debating chambers. It was believed that with shared understanding of plans, execution of them would be easier and more effective. However, clarity of thought and maintenance of objective were frequently sacrificed to personal interest; the Royalist council suffered from this more than Parliament's and had a reputation for bickering and full-blown quarrels.

Senior officers included everyone ranked as a general, be they from the Foot, Horse or ordnance, but frequently experienced men with the official rank of colonel were placed in charge of larger formations than just the single regiment that their rank would appear to imply. Most of Essex's Brigades of four regiments (sometimes called tercios or brigados) were commanded by colonels. Foot regiments were often commanded by lieutenant colonels ('lieu-tenant' meaning literally 'place-holding' in French) who were supported by a (sergeant) major, several captains, a captain lieutenant and a range of lieutenants and ensigns, plus a quartermaster and provost master. To this number of commissioned officers were added a significant number of non-commissioned officers (NCOs). In the Horse the colonel was supported by a lieutenant colonel, a sergeant major, quartermaster and several captains each commanding a troop and aided by a cornet and non-commissioned officers.

Both sides nominally subscribed to the ranking structures and areas of control specified in contemporary drill books. Appointments to ranks were made, but the defining boundaries of senior command appear to have become blurred in the field due to various circumstances.[1] The following table lists the initial appointments for both sides, but already there is deviation from the theory:

Table 3.1   Comparative Headquarters Staff Appointments

Parliamentarian	Royalist
The Authority of Parliament	**Charles Stuart, King of England**

Lord General

Commander in Chief with overall and universal authority, recommended by drill manuals to be stationed behind the second line where he could see, interpret and react to the action. He was frequently accompanied by a small staff, bodyguard and advisors.

Robert Devereux, Earl of Essex	**Robert Bertie, Earl of Lindsey**[2]

Lord General of the Horse or Lord Lieutenant General

The second-in-command of the army, usually an experienced general officer, who advised his political and social superior in matters military and, at times, shared command decisions. He was the senior cavalry officer commanding all the cavalry, usually leading the right wing of Horse.

> *must be a soldier of extraordinary experience and valour; having in charge the nerve of the principle forces, and on whom the good success of many designs and actions dependeth. The General of Horse was want to supply the place of Lieutenant General of the Army, and in the absence of the Ld.Gen. to command the whole army.*[3]

William Russell, Earl of Bedford	**Patrick Ruthven, Earl of Forth**

Sergeant Major General

Had overall command of the infantry, was usually positioned in front of the first line of Foot, but often rode along the line with nominal local control and powers of decision-making.

Philip Skippon (absent)	**Sir Jacob Astley**
Thomas Ballard (acting)	

Lieutenant General of Horse

The second-in-command of the Horse. He commanded the body on the opposite wing to that chosen by his superior – usually the left.

> *The charge of the Lieutenant General of the Horse hath ever been held of very great importance; and therefore must be supplied by a person of great experience and valour: one that must be very carefull and diligent, because he usually marcheth and logeth together with the cavallrie.*[4]

Sir William Balfour	**Prince Rupert of the Rhine**

Commissary General

Despite the name this was a cavalry rank which indicated a senior officer usually in command of the second line of Horse but who deputized for any senior cavalry commander whose fighting duties took him out of control range.

> *He must be vigilant and carefull to appease dissensions which grow among the soldiers, as he which dealeth with them. He is to send and distribute the orders and keep record of the lists of ye guards, convoys and other services.*[5]

Table 3.1   continued

Parliamentarian	*Royalist*
Sir James Ramsey	Henry Wilmot

Horse Brigade Commanders
Officers commanding and coordinating the fighting of a group of Horse regiments, usually in the second line and often including their own.

Not applicable	Sir John Byron
	George, Lord Digby

Sergeant Major General of Dragoons
In charge of all the army's dragoons, he could be deployed anywhere. Commanded from where he thought best, often leaving local decisions to regimental or troop commanders.

Unknown	Sir Arthur Aston

General of the Ordnance
The holder of this appointment was in command of the train of artillery, this was often a political or social appointment guided by professional advisors, although he was often a skilled administrator who left fighting the guns to others.

Henry Mordaunt, Earl of Peterborough	Mountjoy Blount, Earl of Newport

Lieutenant General of the Ordnance
The fighting field commander of the artillery who placed and supervised the guns.

Philibert Emmanuel Du-Bois	Sir John Heydon

Foot Brigade Commanders
Officers commanding and coordinating the operations and fighting of a group of Foot regiments allocated to a specific section of the line of battle.

Sir John Meldrum	Charles Gerard
Charles Essex	Richard Fielding
Thomas Ballard	Sir Nicholas Byron
	Henry Wentworth
	John Belasyse

Field Marshall
An officer entrusted with the overall deployment array.

John, Lord Robartes	Not known (Probably Prince Rupert)

Quartermaster of Horse
An officer entrusted with the care, equipping and provision of the Horse.

Captain John Dalbier	Not known

Provost Marshall
In charge of 'policing'; the maintenance of discipline and order.

Captain James Seigneur	Captain William Smith

Carriage Master General
In command of wheeled transport, problem solving and being responsible for keeping the Army moving.

Captain Thomas Richardson	Not known

Although in command, many of these men in fact relinquished control by placing themselves in the forefront of the fighting, several indeed joined their own regiments and took post in the front rank, including Essex and Lindsey. Wharton says of Essex's conduct during the battle that he

> began to show himself to be more than an ordinary man and indeed more than I have heard tell of any man, for he charged up at several times, once with his own troop of horse [Draper's in the Reserve], as I remember, but I am sure with his own Regiment of Foot … and fell upon the King's own Regiment.[6]

Leading by personal example may have been a Continental practice of the Thirty Years War, but it cost Gustavus Adolphus his life and brought about the collapse of the Swedish war effort. It may have been an extremely brave and soldierly thing to do, but it was very restricting in terms of maintaining control and readiness to react to changing tactical situations.

The Royalist army suffered from confusion in command. If not exactly whimsical, Charles I displayed an unfortunate knack of favouring the opinion of the last influential man who spoke with him. He also had a peculiar style of management in that he was often ambiguous and also adept, through royal prerogative, at sidestepping responsibility for these decisions. One of his more irksome traits was to grant personal deviations from the accepted practice in the chain of command. One of these was afforded to Rupert whose commission made it clear that, although a subordinate officer, and thus normally subject to the orders of both the Lord General and the Lieutenant General of the Army, he need not actually obey orders of anyone save those of the King! Rupert exploited this loophole unmercifully and engaged in a number of quarrels with his uncle's nominated Lord General, Lindsey, who, although senior in rank, years and experience, seems to have been a target for the ambitious young foreigner. Rupert also seems to have manipulated the army's Lieutenant General, Patrick Ruthven, Earl of Forth.

Where to place bodies of pike and muskets for the best effect was the subject of great contemporary military debate and the Thirty Years War had seen three distinct deployments emerge. As they were favoured by different national forces they acquired the national name of each army that employed them and were known as the Dutch, the Swedish and the German systems or styles. Each had its strengths and each its weaknesses, and each had its supporters and detractors. Roberts and Tincey suggest Forth's extensive experience would have alerted him to problems inherent in arraying the inexperienced army in the Swedish method of deployment.[7] He may well have kept his own counsel during the dramatic final quarrel between the upstart Prince and the established officer cadre, but Bulstrode seems to have heard a tale that Forth, having been a Lieutenant General under Gustavus Adolphus, was requested by the King to take over the deployment. Nevertheless, it appears that Ruthven, Aston and Astley had already drawn up an order for a 'Swedish' deployment. Either they had fallen in with Rupert's scheme or else Rupert was acting as the public face for a more insidious high-command coup.

Robert Bertie, Earl of Lindsey was Lord General, effectively in overall command and empowered to carry out the strategic instructions of the King; a position that should have been impregnable. He should have had the same authority as that enjoyed by Essex but, being subject to the King, he was also subject to his royal master's whims! Lindsey had actually had a regiment in Dutch service and learnt his trade under Prince Maurice of the Netherlands. He spent time training his men to fight in what was known as the Dutch system and had both formed and exercised his army in the three large brigades– the usual English practice of having a Van, a Battle and Rear Ward. Virtually at the last moment, Rupert, who had studied the military practice of Gustavus Adolphus, suggested to the King that the Royalist army be deployed in the Swedish system of checker-boarding five brigades. Charles, who 'was so indulgent to him... concurred entirely with Prince Rupert's advice, and rejected the opinion of the General'.[8] In one ill-conceived decision, the King had managed to undo all the army training his hard-working senior officers had managed to effect in the short period he had given them to create a fighting force out of enthusiastic but militarily ignorant men. At best it could be described as folly to allow the figure of battle to be altered the night before a major engagement, but it is bordering on supreme ignorance to expect hundreds of officers to relearn everything they had picked up so far from the *ad hoc* training on the march which Lindsey had tried so desperately to have delivered.

We know that two Councils were called: one at midnight on Saturday, 22 October, where the decision to turn and fight Essex was agreed; and a second at about noon on the 23rd on Edgehill. We also know that the Lord General's Regiment was the rearguard of the march and, if Lindsey had marched with his regiment, as Rupert marched with his, perhaps he arrived to find much of the deployment discussion had already taken place. It could be that the decision to fight in the Swedish formation had been previously proposed by Rupert, debated and agreed, and the battle plan revealed, so that the old Lord General was presented with a *fait accompli*. Even so, this did not prevent a public quarrel. For all that Rupert was influenced by the great victories of Gustavus Adolphus, and saw the coming battle as a chance to win the war in one decisive stroke, this quarrel was not just about a young man challenging the authority of his seniors. Rupert was young, but he was not averse to using his royal birth, proximity to the King and social position to insist upon public acknowledgement of his superior military expertise. This was distasteful enough, but his vaunted superiority had serious implications for the fate of the battle and for the army.

Perhaps we can excuse Charles his part in the matter by acknowledging that the two deployment systems may appear similar on paper. However, the underlying fact remains that the drill necessary to effect them efficiently and the fighting styles they delivered and demanded were widely different. Lindsey, completely undermined by his sovereign, kept his dignity, if not his command, and retired, expressing his intention of serving the next day as a field colonel in the front rank of his own regiment of Foot. This gesture cost him his life and Rupert's petulant ploy of using his uncle to override his superior officer cost the Royalist cause any future service from this highly experienced man. It also cost the army any flexibility and proficiency they might have had, and very likely the battle. These deductions may well offend many readers, especially devotees of the 'Stranger Prince', but in the annals of command and control one is hard pressed to find a greater example of donkeys leading heroes.

Overall command of the Parliamentarian army was vested in the Earl of Essex as Lord General and to some extent he was fortunate in having a reasonably clear chain of command under him. Although there were some who would have liked to question his authority, he held his commission from Parliament and the terms expressed therein made it very clear who was in control. Essex was granted sole command with powers to carry out the strategic instructions of the Parliament:

> The Earl shall have power to raise forces … and to lead them against … all unlawful violence, oppression and force, howsoever countenanced by any pretended commission of authority from his Majesty or otherwise. He shall have power to assign…also to command all forts, castles and ships, and to give instructions for the punishment of all mutinies … . The Earl … shall be … defended by the power and authority of both Houses of Parliament.[9]

Essex had also commanded a regiment in Dutch service and was a military contemporary of Lindsey.[10] Unlike the latter, however, he had no formal opposition to the adoption of the Dutch system and so arrayed his force in the classic Dutch formation of three large brigades. This coincided with established English practice of three fighting divisions flanked by Horse on each wing. He must have had a carefully considered and drawn-out battle plan, most probably drawn up at Worcester, and from most accounts we read the titles of the Van and Rear being ascribed to Meldrum's and Ballard's Brigades. Without having to justify his decision to his inferior officers, Essex adopted and trained his army in the established and passably familiar methods of deployment and engagement. He might have forfeited command and control for long periods while he stood or rode with his units, but at those times he did at least have the luxury of knowing that his officers understood what they were supposed to be doing. On the royal side the lack of command and control went unnoticed; one is tempted to pronounce: Forth did not speak, Lindsey did not see, Rupert did not care and Charles did not understand.

Nevertheless, lack of command and control was not restricted to the Royalists. The Royalist army is said to have adopted an inspiring 'The King and the Cause!' which was shouted enthusiastically. Bernard Stuart wrote of the fleeing Parliamentarians that 'a great many of them saved their lives by getting our word For God and King Charles' – albeit two passwords must have been confusing![11] However, according to Vicars, Essex issued no field word for the army.[12] This may have been due to the fact that the usual Sergeant Major General, Philip Skippon, whose duty it was

Bernard, Lord Stuart

to decided and promulgate the field word was absent, and the temporary Sergeant Major General, Sir John Merrick, was with the force holding Worcester. Ballard was acting in the role but appears to have had little previous experience of it or its duties. No matter the blame, this was an oversight as it deprived them of the ability to determine friend from foe and hindered any attempt at uniting behind a common watchword or chant. Both armies at Edgehill were essentially volunteers and both had men break and run away. Perhaps failings in command and control could provide a clue as to why this happened. The experience of war is terrifying and it has long been believed that discipline was the key to keeping a man in the line. Edgehill was fought long before Prussian drill was inculcated into the army, nevertheless emphasis would still have been placed upon the soldiers' confidence in knowing what they and their officers were doing.

A General Officer.

The presence of the officers was essential in maintaining the fighting line.

There is evidence to indicate that many of the officers of Parliament's army were not very capable. By mid–August 1642, complaints were being made that Essex's soldiers had committed various disorders that had outraged local civilian populations, and one of the most frequently cited reasons for such occurrences was the lack of officers to control the men. Lack of experience in managing other people was probably a root cause, and lack of military experience another. Men who had seen previous service were so prized that, against normal social patterns, promotion was available and a regular sergeant of good family with influence could achieve a lieutenancy and, as a result, be removed from the men that he previously controlled so effectively. In addition, many officers were temporarily sojourning away from the army for a variety of valid and not-so-valid reasons. Absenteeism was common across all ranks, even among the high command. As previously mentioned, Skippon was absent on the day of battle. As well as mistakes and disorders, absenteeism also induced an air of nonchalance about drill, cynical fatalism and irregularities in duties and pay, factors which undermine the efficient operation of an army in the field and in battle.

Coupled with absenteeism was pluralism, whereby commanding officers held other posts that took them away from their duties. Several of the colonels of Essex's Foot Regiments were also appointed to command regiments or troops of Horse, while others were to abandon unit command altogether in favour of controlling brigades, arms, wings or even armies; Essex himself was titular commander of the army, his Regiment of Foot his Regiment of Horse, and his Troop of Lifeguards. While this was common practice in both armies and remained so for hundreds of years, it did mean that junior officers or nominated replacements held command and that experienced officers were not controlling the ranks.

We have already seen how appointments made according to social status interfered with the smooth running of the army, and in this respect Essex was fortunate to have such an affable peer in the Earl of Bedford who seems to have demurred to Balfour and Fielding without the slightest hesitation or resentment. Added to this impediment to efficiency caused by social rank was the scourge of nepotism, where inexperienced or even totally unsuitable family members and protégés gained junior, although sometimes independent, commands in regiments. To be commanded by a foolish teenager because he is the colonel's wife's cousin's son could have a deleterious effect upon unit morale. Added to this we should also consider the practice of selecting friends, colleagues or neighbours to be officers. Their word seldom carries authority and their lack of military experience is often widely known, while in a status-conscious age, their equal social position opens their orders up to debate or disagreement.

The officer ranks of those early civil war armies, from senior command to more humble field and non-commissioned ranks, were, in general, largely full of enthusiastic volunteers. Many had military experience, but most did not. Some were promoted to a rank beyond their capabilities or comprehension and the efforts of some were impeded by the common contemporary practices. Without traducing their reputations or feats, it is probably fair to say that command and control were not at their best, but Edgehill was, for many, their first taste of war and their enemies were their fellow Englishmen.

Chapter Four
Combatants

the Army of Cavaliers and of those Evil Persons who, upon Sunday the 23rd of this Instant, engaged his Majesty in a dangerous and bloody Fight against his faithful Subjects in the Army raised by Authority of Parliament, for the Preservation of his Crown and Kingdom. Official Parliamentarian Account

Thus reads the opening of the account of the battle compiled by six Parliamentarian senior officers. From it we can gain an insight into the complicated attitude taken to the person of the King whose belief in Divine Right had brought about this armed conflict. Being the first battle of a civil war there was hesitancy and confusion on both sides. It was not a new experience for England, the history of the power struggles to rule this country is littered with battles for the crown and political power, but it was the first in the emerging 'Age of Reason'. Many Englishmen had been in action before Edgehill. Some senior officers and men had taken part in campaigns including the two rather humiliating Bishops' Wars, and others had fought in various battles abroad, so there was a cadre of men who knew what they were doing and what to expect, but many did not. To them this was to be their baptism in warfare. To understand more fully what happened at Edgehill and why certain decisions were taken we have to examine the relative military experience of the various commanding officers. Some had military experience but that could mean political rather than fighting appointments or long periods without being in action. This brief resumé seeks to give the background of these men at the time of the battle in 1642 with minimal reference to their subsequent reputations and developed skills.

The Royalists

Charles Stuart, King of England   At this first major engagement he was inexperienced and, despite having some appreciation of the problems of administration gained during his distant command of the Bishops' Wars, he had little idea of the application of his military studies. Although he sought advice from the best and most able quarters, he was frequently prone to listening to favourites. He was, however, keen to prove his personal bravery and accept the mantle of the warrior king.

King Charles I

Robert Bertie, Earl of Lindsey   Essentially a courtier but vastly experienced in warfare having seen action both on land and at sea. Having first been to war in 1597/8 he had a long period of in-activity before being recalled. He served with the armies of

The Earl of Lindsey

Patrick Ruthven, Earl of Forth

Prince Rupert

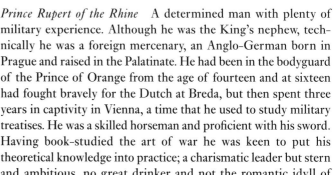

Sir Jacob Astley

Henry, Lord Wilmot

John, Lord Byron

George, Lord Digby

England, Denmark and Holland, become an Admiral, and had held Berwick during the First Bishops' War.

Patrick Ruthven, Earl of Forth   A man of vast military knowledge who had seen action with the Swedish army under Gustavus Adolphus. He had held Berwick in the Second Bishops' War, was a trusted supporter of the king and, although seventy years of age, was still an able soldier, if no longer at the height of his powers. Holmes styles him 'a somewhat bibulous veteran'.[1]

Prince Rupert of the Rhine   A determined man with plenty of military experience. Although he was the King's nephew, technically he was a foreign mercenary, an Anglo-German born in Prague and raised in the Palatinate. He had been in the bodyguard of the Prince of Orange from the age of fourteen and at sixteen had fought bravely for the Dutch at Breda, but then spent three years in captivity in Vienna, a time that he used to study military treatises. He was a skilled horseman and proficient with his sword. Having book-studied the art of war he was keen to put his theoretical knowledge into practice; a charismatic leader but stern and ambitious, no great drinker and not the romantic idyll of fiction.

Sir Jacob Astley   An experienced soldier and one-time teacher of matters military to Rupert. Described by Holmes as 'a small taciturn man', he had served with commendable spirit and ability in the Dutch, Danish, German and English armies and was respected as an authority on training infantry. He had been Governor of Plymouth and held a colonelcy during the Bishops' Wars.[2]

Henry, Lord Wilmot   Having fought bravely and well as a captain of Horse for the Dutch at Breda he was appointed Commissary General during the Second Bishops' War. He showed understanding of horse tactics and was deemed reliable, hard but fair; although he was also regarded as a politician.

Sir John Byron   He had seen action in Dutch service and held command in both the Bishop's Wars. He had been a Governor of the Tower of London and was thought, and showed himself to be, a gallant and able soldier, but inexperienced in tactical command.

George, Lord Digby   Having seen his first action at Powick Bridge where he had fought bravely, he had precious little common sense about command or warfare in general. Clarendon was particularly scathing of him and his performance.

Sir Arthur Aston A Catholic who had been in service with both the Swedish and the Polish armies. He had served alongside Gustavus Adolphus and had fought in Russia, Poland and Germany where he had gained experience and an understanding of warfare which he showed during both Bishops' Wars. He was, however, regarded as an argumentative, easily irritated, arrogant martinet.

Mountjoy Blount, Earl of Newport His was a court appointment but he was an able administrator and someone who could plan well ahead.

Sir John Heydon A scholar of mathematics who had held the post of Lieutenant General of the Ordnance during both Bishops' Wars and proved to be both efficient in organization and field practice. He was deemed a tried and tested officer, skilled in practice and keen in the execution of his duties.

Charles Gerard A man of some military experience and skill learnt as a captain with the Dutch. He had been in the English army for a few years. A friend of Rupert's, he was eminently brave but said to have been arrogant and cruel.

Richard Fielding After serving in various countries he had accepted a colonelcy in the English army in 1640. He was a professional soldier who knew his business and had a reputation for competence.

Colonel Charles Gerard

Sir Nicholas Byron He had been in Dutch service along with his nephew and returned to England to take up a colonelcy in the Bishops' Wars where he proved able and won many well-placed friends.

Henry Wentworth Another Scots' Wars colonel whose appointment owed much to family connections, yet he proved competent.

John, Lord Belasyse A man promoted to command due to social status, (Fauconberg's son) despite having no military experience.

John, Lord Belasyse

The Parliamentarians

Robert Devereux, Earl of Essex Possibly the most experienced officer in the army having seen action and held command on land and sea. Essex began his military career in 1620 with the Earl of Oxford in the Low Countries where his performance as a colonel of Foot for the Dutch was competent. Created Lieutenant General of the Army for the 1639 war against Scotland he was greatly frustrated in his plans and execution of his duties by Court politics, although he was one of the few English generals to come through the affair with credit. In 1642 he readily accepted Parliament's offer of command. He also had a reputation for being quarrelsome and difficult although he was well liked by the army, 'the most popular man of the kingdom, the darling of the swordsmen'.[3]

The Earl of Essex

The Earl of Bedford

Sir William Balfour

Bazil, Lord Fielding

The Earl of Peterborough

Sir John Meldrum

Phillip, Lord Wharton

William Russell, Earl of Bedford   Said to have been likeable and easy to get along with, he had no military experience and was chosen for his social standing rather than his ability. Although brave he was not a fully convinced Parliament man.

Sir William Balfour   A Scot who had taken English nationality in May 1642. He had seen Dutch service and had served as Governor of the Tower of London, but had been replaced for 'conduct unbecoming his post'. Holmes says he was 'an experienced and thoroughly able officer'.[4]

Sir James Ramsey   A highly respected Scottish professional soldier.

Bazil, Lord Fielding   An English professional soldier and member of the Committee of Safety.

Henry Mordaunt, Earl of Peterborough   Another with no military experience who held the titular post of General of the Ordnance due to his social status. However, he appears to have been an able administrator and well disposed to leaving the field business to professionals.

Philibert Emmanuel Du-Bois   Described as being the only man who had confidence in his ability. Young states simply he was 'useless'.[5]

Sir John Meldrum   A professional Scottish soldier with great experience and a good record.

Charles Essex   A competent English professional.

Thomas Ballard   Another English professional soldier.

There was experience among the Parliamentarian colonels and captains, such as Lord Wharton who had been chosen as an Irish Expedition officer and, although several were novices to military command at Edgehill, many, such as Brooke, Holles and Robartes, fought well and showed considerable bravery. Others, like Waller and Ludlow, later acquired formidable reputations or died in their making, like Hampden. Among the Royalist colonels and captains were also men of skill and experience like William Legge, others who were always ready with their sword like the Earl of Carnarvon, who had served in the Scots Wars and was to die at Newbury, and his lieutenant colonel, Sir Charles Lucas, who had fought in the Low Countries and whose loyalty to the Royalist cause burned so ardently he broke his parole, levied another civil war and was shot for it at Colchester.

As well as those who made the command decisions we must also consider those who did the actual fighting and examine those who were in the ranks; where did they come from and why were they there? The two armies that blindly circled around the midland counties of England in the autumn of 1642 were, by and large, made up of volunteers between the ages of sixteen and sixty. One regiment 'of blewe coate soldiers, in number about 450, from Tame or Aylesbury, but originally from Lundon', possibly Lord Saye's, was described as 'most of the Company very younge and but meanely apparelled and very unexpert in their armes'.[6] They probably believed, like most soldiers on their first campaign that it would all be over soon, and that they would 'be home in time for Christmas'. We have no surviving letters from any of the rank and file of either army to inform us of their motives for being there, whether it was for conscience's sake, loot, adventure or a mixture of some or all. However, militant puritan, Nehemiah Wharton, a sergeant of Holles's Regiment of Foot, writing from Northampton in September 1642, gives us some indication. He describes with indignation the attitude of part of his unit, drawn up for exercise, 'many of them discovered their base end in undertaking this design, and demanded five shillings a man, which they say was promised them monthly by the Committee or they would surrender their arms'.[7] Such scenes were probably common, but we do know from surviving records that some of the ordinary private sentinels were committed for the duration to their cause and to their regiments. Men like Thomas Hart, who enlisted in Merrick's Regiment as it passed through his home town of Wootton Basset in Wiltshire, William Stokes of Shepton Mallet of Lunsford's, who had already seen action at Babylon Hill, and would go on to make sergeant, and William Allen, a felt-maker by trade, of Holles's Regiment who would later, as a prisoner of the Royalists, escape hanging and rejoin his regiment.[8]

The prospect of pay and plunder, a word introduced to the English language by veterans of the Thirty Years War, from the prosperous land of England attracted considerable numbers of foreign mercenaries to both sides from a war-exhausted Europe, particularly French and Dutch. Some came from further afield, such as the Croatian Carlo Fantom, who commented 'I care not for your Cause: I come to fight for your half crown, and your handsome women'.[9] In later years, Fantom was to have the reputation among the superstitious as a 'hard man', only killable with a silver bullet! However, serving as a Lieutenant in Arthur Goodwin's Horse at Edgehill, he was to be badly wounded.

Professional Scots officers were much in demand by the

Robert, Lord Brooke

Colonel Denzil Holles

John Lord Robartes

Colonel Edmund Ludlow

Colonel William Legge

Robert, Earl of Carnarvon

Sir Charles Lucas

Colonel Arthur Goodwin

Parliamentary Army; the King taking most of the English professionals, 'for want of others, many Scotch men are entertained to assist the Commander of the Parliament forces'.[10] Essex's two regiments of Dragoons seemed to have been almost entirely officered by 'North Britains'.

The literate English middle and upper classes have left us more detailed information regarding their feelings on what Sir William Waller was to call 'this war without an enemy'. Sir Edmund Verney, hereditary standard bearer to the King, reluctantly took up his duties, 'I do not like the quarrel, and do heartily wish that the King would yield and consent to what they desire; so that my conscience is only concerned in honour and in gratitude to follow my mastr'.[11] He went on to say that he would 'not do so base a thing as to forsake him, and choose rather to lose my life'. From the other side, brewer and political celebrity John Lilburne, serving as a captain in Lord Brooke's Regiment wrote 'I scorned to be so base as to sit down in a whole skin... while the liberties and freedoms of the kingdom was in danger'.[12] Lilburne sold his business and went off to the wars with his wife 'as ready and willing to adventure my life as any man I marched along with'.[13]

Understanding why men enlisted is a difficult task, but we do have some indication of where they came from. The main known geographic areas for recruitment were as shown in the following table:

Table 4.1   Regimental recruitment areas

Parliamentarian[14]		Royalist	
Colonel Brooke	London	Colonel Lunsford	Somerset
Colonel Holles	London	Colonel Belasyse	Yorks/Notts
Colonel Cholmley	London	Colonel Gerrard	N. Wales/Cheshire
Colonel Merrick	London	Colonel Bolles	Staffordshire
Colonel Wharton	London & Middx	General Lord Lindsey	Lincs
Colonel Ballard	Bucks		
Colonel Hampden	Bucks & Suffolk		
Lord General Essex	Essex		

An estimated 10,000 volunteers from London and Southwark paraded in Moorfields on 26 July 1642 and two days later enlisted at the 'new ground of the Artillery Company'.[15]

The recruiting areas for individual troops of Horse are far more difficult to pinpoint. For instance, many gentlemen officers brought with them entourages of servants from their home estates, as well as enlisting friends and relatives. In London, cavalry volunteers were instructed to leave their names and address with officials at the Guildhall, and once a full sixty had enlisted, officers were put in charge of them by a committee of five noblemen including the Earls of Essex and Warwick. That the cavalry arm of both armies considered themselves socially superior to the infantry is very apparent, and caused a great deal of friction between the two branches. To quote Wharton again, 'there is also great dissension between our troopers and foot companies, for the footmen are much abused and sometimes pillaged and wounded'.[16]

Knowing what the soldiers of both sides wore is a lot easier but we must discount those fanciful images of cavaliers in lace and velvet and roundheads in hooped sleeves. Similarly we must shed the idea of regular uniforms beloved by film-makers. In the early weeks of the campaign, the infantry on both sides went to war in their civilian clothing and there is no indication that the Royalist Foot received any uniform coats until after Edgehill. On the Parliamentary side, an ordinance was passed on 6 August 'that all soldiers shall have delivered unto them at their first marching coats, shoes, shirts and caps, in all to the value of seventeen shillings for every man'.[17] The caps were never issued but the men were issued with a supply of snapsacks. On 22 August, for instance, the agents of the three London regiments of Merrick, Holles and Cholmley received coats and snapsacks mostly taken out of the stores intended for troops in Ireland that had then to be subsequently transported to the respective units at Portsmouth and Coventry.

Colonel John Hampden

Sir William Fairfax

The ordinary soldier's coat of the period was straight-fitting and skimpily cut from heavily felted woollen cloth with prominent shoulder rolls. In most cases it was lined with a contrasting coloured cloth.

Table 4.2   Parliamentary regimental coat colours

Lord General's Guard	Grey with silver buttons
Lord General's Regiment	Orange
Lord Brooke's	Purple
Lord Wharton's	Grey?
Lord Rochford's	Blue lined white
Lord Mandeville's	Blue?
Lord Robarte's	Red lined yellow
Lord Stamford's	Blue
Lord Saye and Seles's	Blue
Sir John Merrick's	Grey
Sir Henry Cholmley's	Blue
Sir William Constable's	Blue
Sir William Fairfax's	Grey?
Colonel Ballard's	Grey lined white
Colonel Hampden's	Green lined yellow
Colonel Grantham's	Tawny lined white
Colonel Essex's	Tawny lined yellow
Colonel Holles's	Red

Beneath the coat the soldier would have worn a woollen or linen waistcoat, if he possessed one, over the issued shirt of linen or hemp. No breeches were issued to the Foot at this stage in the war. The stockings, if received, were either knitted or cut on the cross from linen or flannel. Infantry shoes were usually of the low-fitting latchet variety, straight-lasted and made of leather. The durability of this kind of footwear in the foul weather conditions of autumn 1642 must have been very poor.

Initially, with no recorded issue of headwear to either side on this campaign, the

Top: a musketeer of the London Trained Bands, one of the few common soldiers to wear a sleeveless buff coat; right: unarmoured pikeman; below: a dragoon, an unarmoured cavalryman who usually fought on foot.

recruits would have been wearing whatever they brought from home. This could have been one of the various types of knitted Monmouth caps that were popular among ordinary working people of the time or, depending upon status, the more fashionable broad-brimmed felt or beaver hat. Foreign mercenaries would have brought a number of exotic varieties of headwear with them and one style, introduced earlier in the century and known as a Montero cap, was to become a particular favourite with the military.

Armour in the form of helmets, back and breast plates was supplied to pikemen on both sides, when available, although on the King's side there was a definite shortage. This deficiency in the Royalist army may account for the poor showing of some of the Foot regiments in the later phases of the battle. Musketeers wore little or no armour.

The clothing and equipment of the cavalry was an altogether different matter to that of the Foot. There was no wholesale central supply of clothes to the Horse by either side and it was left very much to the individual troop captains to organize and finance supplies for their sub-units. On 20 May the first unit raised was the King's Lifeguard of Horse and, being made up of volunteers drawn from the nobility and rich gentry, the recruits' social status was very much reflected in their dress. They became known as 'The Troop of Show'; a name with derisory connotations that, in their efforts to live it down, led to serious repercussions at Edgehill. The Earl of Bedford, writing early in 1642, had recommended that cavalry troopers 'be handsomely furnished [in] comely apparel with coat of buff with long skirts [and a] coat of cloth to keep both himself and furniture from the violence of the weather'.[18] The buff coat was the most sought after item of cavalry and officer wear, but was more expensive than the back and breast plates that were supposed to be worn over it. Nevertheless, so common did the coat become that the nickname for a cavalryman became 'buff coat'.

The average cost of a trooper's buff coat was between twenty-five and thirty shillings, with a good-quality officer's coat costing considerably more. The material of the coat was usually bull hide and ranged in colour from white to bright yellow ochre. In contemporary usage, yellow ochre was used as an early form of disinfectant on the walls of stables and cow sheds. Its use on buff coats may therefore have been, similarly, to suppress lice! The better-quality coats usually had double sleeves, the inner full length pair being made of chamois to allow easy movement of the arms. A number of contemporary portraits of officers reveal their sitters in buff coats with fabric sleeves, usually decorated with bands of gold or silver lace. Very few of this particular style of coat survive and on most the fabric sleeves have disintegrated, giving the impression that they were always sleeveless. The only infantry rank and file known to have worn buff coats were the richer members of the London Trained Bands, whose only appearance in the post-Edgehill campaign was at Turnham Green.

Full armour was still worn by some, particularly life-guard units and officers. The King himself probably wore full armour on the day of the battle over which it is recorded he wore a black velvet coat lined with ermine, and a steel cap covered with velvet. This last item was almost certainly a form of Montero cap similar to the head-piece owned by the Earl of Denbigh, and described as 'after the Montero fashion with one skirt of quilt'.[19] The young Prince of Wales probably also wore a full set of armour, one which had been made for his father earlier and is still in the Royal Collection. There is no surviving account of what any of the senior Parliamentary officers wore at Edgehill, although almost certainly they would have resembled their Royalist counterparts.

Top: A cornet of Horse carrying the troop captain's flag; below:a harquebusier, an ordinary heavy Horse trooper.

That the officers and cavalry of both sides looked exactly alike is obvious, and the difficulties resulting from this are only too apparent – 'ye great inconvenience we find it upon service we cannot know one another from the enemy'.[20] It was therefore necessary to issue each trooper with a scarf of his general's colour. The King adopted the traditional English colour of red and Parliamentary tawny orange, a colour associated with Protestant forces fighting on the continent. Parliamentary scarves were made of taffeta and cost ten shillings each, more than the cost of a foot soldier's coat. There is no definite information on what the dragoons wore on either side, but it was probably a cheap version of cavalry attire without the buff coats and scarves.

The colours and standards carried by both sides followed the normal English style of the seventeenth century. In the Parliamentary army, eighty pounds was allowed for the purchase of colours, partizans, halberds, and drums for each regiment. The infantry colours were about 6 foot 6 inches by 6 foot, made of silk and mounted on a short pike. Each infantry company had a colour, carried by the ensign, the most junior officer. Each colour differed slightly in a systematic way from those of the other companies in the regiment. All, apart from the colonel's plain colour, had the Saint George's cross stitched in the top canton next to the staff. There are no known descriptions for Essex's infantry colours during the Edgehill campaign, but a number of captured Royalist colours were drawn in a contemporary trophy book and follow this pattern exactly. Regiments were sometimes known by the tincture of their flags, for example the 'Blue Regiment', or the 'Red Regiment'. The flags or cornets carried by the cavalry differed greatly from those of the foot. The cornet of each troop was about 1 foot 6 inches square, made of silk and usually edged with a heavy parti-coloured fringe. The colour of the fringe matched those of the rest of the cornets of the regiment and each captain would have his own skilfully painted with his personal 'impresse' or armorial achievement. The cornet was attached to a medieval style lance by silk cord and tassels. Dragoon colours, or guidons, were similar in size to the cavalry cornets but were more elongated, generally with two swallow tails, and with their devices resembling those of the infantry.

Chapter Five
Deployment

... and there drew into Battalia, where we saw there Forces coming down the Hill, and drew likewise into Battel in the Bottom, a great broad Company. Official Parliamentary Account.

Two of the many problems that beset writers about battles concern deployment: which unit fought where, and who was next to whom. Students of more recent conflicts have written orders of battle or even deployment battle maps available for study but to historians of the middle of the seventeenth century and before such things are luxuries. Commanding officers of armies usually drew up battle plans as part of general military planning at the commencement of each campaign. They were normally done in consultation with a Council of War and ratified by any controlling influence such as a monarch. Plans were probably constructed by moving rectangles of card to the required deployment on a large sheet of paper. Each rectangle would be a scaled down representation of individual battalia based upon the known regimental establishments and the depth of files required by the drill manual 'figure of battle', which, in turn, depended on the military system favoured by the general. Copies were made of the plan and distributed by the sergeant major general to the senior officers to ensure that there was a unified understanding of what was to be done when the army deployed for battle.

Most battle plans of the period would have had the main body of the infantry positioned in the centre of the army's line with guns dispersed along its length and protecting wings of cavalry on either flank. The Foot was then sub-divided into three large brigades, the van (or right), the battle (or centre), and the rear (or left). These brigades were made up of individual regiments, roughly equal in numbers or strengths. Each brigade was placed under the command of a senior officer, usually a colonel of one of the brigaded regiments, command of which would then devolve upon its lieutenant colonel. The Dutch system called for the line of battle to be formed in battalia, with each one being approximately 550 men strong. Large regiments deployed on the field in two Grand Divisions forming two battalia, while under strength regiments were usually amalgamated to form one. The separate companies of each individual battalia were then arranged 'in line of divisions', each division comprised of six files of six, or eight files of eight, all armed with the same weapon. While the pike divisions were grouped together, the musketeer divisions were placed in equal numbers either side of them so that each battalia had a centre of pikes and two wings of shot.

The Horse was allocated its position in a similar way except that the basic unit was the sixty-man troop. Six or more troops under their individual captains were grouped together to form a regiment under the command of the senior man who became its colonel.[1] These regiments were then allocated to either the left or right wing or the reserve with the senior officer of each formation also being elevated to general rank for command purposes.

At the start of a battle each brigade or wing would be placed according to its position in the line of march. Ideally the right wing (which also supplied the scouting patrols) would be the first to deploy into its fighting position. The van, headquarters and reserve, battle, train of artillery, rear and left wing (including the flank and rearguard patrols) would follow in sequence.[2] An army would usually deploy in the same manner according to a pre-arranged plan. Scouting patrols located and secured the field and then, under the direction of the field marshal, the right wing formed first to face the enemy. The van would then deploy on its left with the headquarters and reserve taking position behind it, while the battle deployed on the left of the van. The train of artillery would move behind the battle and begin to site its guns along the line starting from the right and working to the left. The rear would come up and deploy on the left of the battle and, finally, the left wing would arrange itself left of the rear. Sometimes, and this seems to have been the case at Edgehill, the left wing came up earlier and deployed where Ramsey or the field marshal thought it ought to be.

As each Foot brigade came on to its ground the brigade commander would array the constituent battalia in the pattern required by the chosen figure of battle. Under the Anglified Dutch system this would mean in a checkerboard pattern with several battalia forming a front line with others placed in a second line to provide mutual support, alternating one up and one back. This gave both a degree of manoeuvre flexibility and 'refused protection' against Horse. It also broke up the massed artillery target, as well as allowing room for units to be advanced into the fighting line, or withdrawn from it, without disorganising their neighbours. Under the Swedish system the infantry 'chequers' were arranged in a lozenge with companies from the constituent regiments sometimes becoming intermingled.

Cavalry regiments were also deployed in battalia. Much smaller than the 550 of the Foot, these consisted of 120 troopers in two troops; one in the front line and the other in the second. A six-troop regiment would thus form three two-troop battalia. Each troop was arrayed in three squadrons, line abreast, with each squadron numbering approximately three files of six under the Dutch system or six files of three under the Swedish. The reason for the Dutch system's depth of deployment was because of the manner in which the Horse was actually fought at this period, as mobile platforms for fire power. The intention was that they would weaken their enemy with carbine and pistols and then disperse the shot-shattered formation with the sword. The Horse operated very much as did the rotating files of the Foot's musketeers before closing to melee. To increase the defensive fire power of the cavalry wings while stationary, the troops of Horse could be interspersed ('interlarded') with bodies of musketeers deployed in the intervals between the units of the first line, which is exactly what Essex and Ramsey did at Edgehill. Gustavus Adolphus's system relied upon the use of the sword rather than firepower and so thinned the depth in order to cover more ground and overlap flanks, making better use of troopers who would otherwise have been wasted ineffectively at the rear. Swedish deployment called for the regiments to be arrayed in a line of troops with a second line being formed by a different brigade.

Further support for both Horse and Foot was provided by the field guns of the artillery. Normally these were sited in the intervals between divisions of the front line and consisted of guns up to the calibre of culverin (12 lb). In theory these guns could be moved during the battle but, in practice, they seldom were because of their weight. This meant that the bigger guns, demi-cannon and above, were generally used purely for siege work. However, at Edgehill the King was so short of field pieces that in his battle plan he was forced to use his big guns in a fixed battery in the rear. It has been suggested that the formation of this large battery was an accident of the road system and time, both of which may have been influential factors in associated decision-making.

Once the battle plan had been decided upon the sergeant major general would translate it into an order of march and discuss it with the brigade commanders who would, in their turn, pass both it and its implications to their regimental colonels. Marching, moving and fighting in formation were not arduous tasks, but they took time and training to perform correctly and to prevent formations from falling into disorder. At the beginning of the war, both armies would have been trained in the Dutch manner with files eight deep, a practice with which most English professional officers who had served on the Continent would have been familiar, although other variations would have been available from the large number of foreign military text books hurriedly translated into English at the first signs of the coming war. Regimental commanders on both sides would have instructed their officers to train their units and, once an opportunity arose on campaign for the majority of the army to be rendezvoused in the same place, the general would attempt to drill his entire army and exercise his troops in their battle formations. They would practise forming up, advancing and firing while maintaining their essential formations in accordance with the battle plan. Essex would have had a greater opportunity to do this than the King, the majority of his army being assembled for a longer period of time.

For Edgehill we have the luxury of a deployment diagram produced by the Dutch-man Bernard de Gomme, Rupert's engineer. This document survives in the Royal Library at Windsor Castle and was reproduced by Peter Young in his study of the battle.[3] It was drawn after the battle as a record of the day and was not, presumably, the prepared battle plan that may have reflected a deployment in the Dutch style that was familiar to Lord General Lindsey. This plan gives us both the brigade structure, manner of deployment and the relative field positions of the King's forces. Its key tells us which regiments stood where and the alignment indicates the intended manoeuvrability expected of the constituent elements in action. Unfortunately it does not dictate the projected positions for the guns but the inclusion of Colonel Legge's Firelocks, raised to guard the artillery, provides a good indication of where the main battery was sited. Working off this plan and cross-referencing it to the various accounts, especially that of Richard Bulstrode who states 'our whole Army was drawn up in a body, the Horse Three deep in each Wing, and the Foot in the Centre Six deep', we can confirm the preference for the Swedish system and form a picture of the Royalist order of battle.[4]

Reading the memoirs of old soldiers is a fascinating thing, but care must always be taken to remember that, even though the writer was an eyewitness, this does not mean that his recollections are infallible. Much of the surviving early material was written many years after the battle and there are dangers in assuming that all is the result of memory recall and not interpretation developed over the years or modified according to the accounts of others.[5] However, as with piecing together a jigsaw puzzle, one extracts elements of the fragmented picture, examines them, and by carefully comparing and considering the evidence from various sources, cross-references them to those already in place, and, if it all fits, puts the new piece of information in place, and moves one step nearer to a complete picture. To continue the analogy, with de Gomme we are also able to look at the picture on the box lid! We know that the actual placing of the regiments was left to Ruthven, Aston and Astley but, without full written evidence, it is impossible to state that ours is a correct picture, but it is the best possible interpretation that we can make based upon current research and understanding of period practice.[6]

Royalist Order of Battle

Right Wing   Prince Rupert of the Rhine. 27 troops of Horse + 3 troops of dragoons

Avant Garde Colonel James Usher's Regiment of Dragoons, Lieutenant Colonel Henry
Washington   3 troops
    1 Colonel James Usher's
    2 Lieutenant Colonel Henry Washington's
    3 Major Hutchinson's

First Line (from right to left)   20 troops:

His Majesty's Lifeguard Regiment of Horse: 150 in 1 troop
    1 Lord Bernard Stuart's

His Highness the Prince of Wales's Regiment of Horse   500 in 8 troops
    1 Colonel Sir Thomas Byron's
    2 Duke of York's Troop, Lord d'Aubigny's
    3 Earl of Newcastle's Troop, Colonel Charles Cavendish's   120
    4 Earl of Lindsey's, Colonel ?
    5 Earl of Northampton's, Colonel ?   100
    6 Earl of Westmorland's, Colonel ?
    7 Captain Davidson's (servants of the regt.)
    8 Earl of Crawford's, Colonel ?

His Highness Prince Rupert's Regiment of Horse   465 in 7 troops
    1 Prince Rupert's Lifeguard, Sir Richard Crane's   100
    2 Lieutenant Colonel Daniel O'Neale's   70
    3 Major William Legge's   15
    4 Sir Lewis Dyve's   140 }
    5 Sir Thomas Dallison's
    6.Lord Dillon's   140 }
    7 Sir William Pennyman's

His Highness Prince Maurice's Regiment of Horse   180 in 4 troops
    1 Prince Maurice's Lifeguard
    2 Lieutenant Colonel Guy Molesworth's
    3 Captain Thomas Sheldon's
    4 Sir Ralph Dutton's

Second Line Sir John Byron   7 troops

His Majesty's Lifeguard Regiment of Horse *   150 in 1 troop
    2 Sir William Killigrew's (servants of the regiment)

Sir John Byron's Regiment of Horse   250 in 6 troops
    1 Colonel Sir John Byron's
    2 Lieutenant Colonel Frank Butler's
    3 Major Gilbert Byron's
    5 Captain Sir Richard Byron's

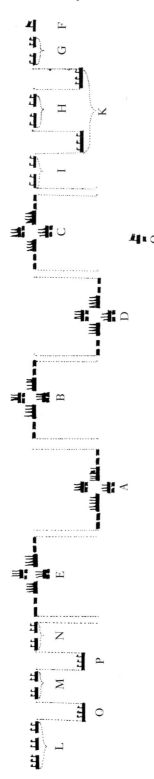

De Gomme's deployment map of the Royalist army at Edgehill (redrawn).

A Lifeguard of Foot, Lord General, Beaumont   B Lunsford, Bolles, Fitton, Stradling

C C. Gerard, Dives, Dutton   D Blagge, Belasyse, Pennyman

E Gerard, Salusbury, Molineux   F Lifeguard of Horse

G The Prince of Wales' regiment   H Prince Rupert's Regiment

I Prince Maurice's Regiment   K Lord Byron's Regiment

L Lord Wilmot's Regiment   M Lord Grandison's Regiment

N Lord Carnarvon's Regiment   O Lord Digby's Regiment

P Sir Thomas Aston's Regiment   Q The Lifeguard (Pensioners) and Legge's Firelocks

6 Captain Allen Apsley's
7 Captain Edward St John's
* *De Gomme shows Killigrew's Troop and Legge's Firelocks with the King on Bullet Hill. This may have been where they started.*

Centre   Sergeant Major General Sir Jacob Astley. 17 regiments of Foot

Front Line 11 regiments	
On the Right: Charles Gerard's Brigade	1,985 in 3 regiments
1 Charles Gerard's Regiment of Foot	740
2 Sir Lewis Dyve's Regiment of Foot	575
3 Sir Ralph Dutton's Regiment of Foot	670
In the Centre: Richard Fielding's Brigade	2,545 in 5 regiments
1 Colonel Richard Fielding's Regiment of Foot	460
2 Sir Thomas Lunsford's Regiment of Foot	350
3 Colonel Richard Bolle's Regiment of Foot	560
4 Sir Edward Fitton's Regiment of Foot	460
5 Sir Edward Stradling's Regiment of Foot	715
On the Left: Henry Wentworth's Brigade	1,790 in 3 regiments
1 Sir Gilbert Gerard's Regiment of Foot	560
2 Sir Thomas Salusbury's Regiment of Foot	910
3 Lord Molineux's Regiment of Foot	320
Second Line 6 regiments	
On the Right: John Belasyse's Brigade	1,880 in 3 regiments
1 Colonel Thomas Blagge's Regiment of Foot	690
2 Colonel John Belasye's Regiment of Foot	505
3 Sir William Pennyman's regiment of Foot	685
On the Left: Sir Nicholas Byron's Brigade	1,830 in 3 regiments
1 His Majesty's Lifeguard Regiment of Foot	670
2 The Lord General's Regiment of Foot	84
3 Sir John Beaumont's Regiment of Foot	320

Left wing   Lord Wilmot 16 or 18 troops of Horse + 6 troops of dragoons

Avant Garde Sir Arthur Aston	6 troops
Colonel Edward Grey's Regiment of dragoons	3 troops
1 Colonel Edward Grey's	
2 Lieutenant Colonel ?	
3 Major Ralph Hebburne's	
Colonel Sir Edward Duncombe's Regiment of Lifeguard dragoons	3 troops
1 Colonel Sir Edward Duncombe's	
2 Lieutenant Colonel ?	
3 Major ?	
First Line 14 or 15 troops	
Lord Wilmot's Regiment of Horse	355 in 6 troops
1 Colonel Lord Wilmot's, Captain Lieutenant Robert Walsh's	90
2 Lieutenant Colonel Edward Fielding's	85 ⎱
3 Major Paul Smith's	
4 Captain John Harvey's	70
5 Captain Price's	40
6 Captain John Frenchville's, Lieutenant Jammot's	
Lord Grandison's Regiment of Horse	200 in 4 troops
1 Lord Grandison's, Captain Lieutenant Edward Gerard's	

2 Major Sir Richard Willys's	
3 Lord John Stuart's	
4 Captain Francis' Bertie's	
Earl of Carnavon's Regiment of Horse	200 in 4 or 5 troops
1 Earl of Carnarvon's	
2 Lieutenant Colonel Sir Charles Lucas's	
3 Major Richard Neville's	
4 Captain Alexander Standish's	
5 ?	

Second Line Lord Digby 6 or 7 troops

Lord Digby's Regiment of Horse	150 in 3 or 4 troops
1 Lord Digby's, Captain Lieutenant Henry Harris	
2 Thomas Weston's	
3 Richard Herbert's ?	
4 John Lane's	
Sir Thomas Aston's Regiment of Horse	150 in 3 troops
1 Colonel Sir Thomas Aston's	
2 Lieutenant Colonel Sir James Bridgeman's	
3 Captain Flemming's	

In the Rear with the King

His Majesties Gentlemen Pensioners	50 in 1 troop
Lieutenant Sir William Howard KB	

In the Rear
Colonel Legge's Regiment of Firelocks

The largest pieces of artillery	2 demi-cannon
	2 culverins
	2 demi-culverins

Along the Line

The lighter pieces of artillery	6 falcons
	6 falconets
	2 robinets

Deploying the armies took time. Apparently the Earl of Essex eschewed the comforts of the village and had his tent erected, for Kightley tells us that 'my Lord Generall did quarter in a small Village where this Battel was fought, in a field called Great King's Field, taking the name from a Battel fought there by King John as they say'.[7] However, he was an early riser, and was either in Kineton Church or on his way there for prayers, when, at about eight o'clock, he received news of the appearance of a significant number of Royalist Horse on Knoll End. This news came as a surprise as he and his officers 'intended to rest the Sabbath-day, and the rather, that our Artillery and the Forces left with it might come up to us'.[8] The Royalist general rendezvous was on Edgehill, and Rupert, presumably eager and possibly the nearest, arrived first. A larger number of the King's Horse arrived between ten and eleven o'clock in the morning and the van came up within an hour, but the rear (which happened at that time to be the Lord Lieutenant General's Regiment) with the artillery, did not arrive until a further two hours had elapsed, certainly not before one o'clock. As it came up the Royalist army fell into battle formation. This must have taken even more time because it was

The Royalist cavalry deployment area on the top of Edgehill.

unfamiliar to the officers and men alike. As the realization dawned that Essex had no intention of attacking up such a steep slope as the Edgehill escarpment, an advance guard of dragoons and some Horse were sent down on to the bottom slopes to secure the Radway hedges, the roadside briars, and to cover any approaches which might threaten the army's descent. Meanwhile the Royalist battle array was completed on the plateau above Ratley.

As a result, Essex had time to assemble his army and march it out of Kineton on to the field. He also had time to ride forward and reconnoitre the ground and make *ad hoc* plans for the deployment of his force. The Parliamentary high command had 'all morning to draw up their army, in a great plain Field, which they did to their best Advantage' while 'the Earl with great dexterity performed whatsoever could be expected from a wise general'.[9] Although his decision impressed his peers, Essex's deployment in 'the Vale of the Red Horse' was severely limited in the application of his preconceived battle plan because of the dispersed nature of his army. One of Essex's failings that military historians have criticized him for was his division and delegation of executive command. He had been campaigning in the region and had left various regiments to garrison what he believed to be strategic bases so, by the time he came to fight at Edgehill, the following regiments were missing from his army:

In Worcester	Sir John Merrick's and Lord St John's
In Banbury	Earl of Peterborough's[10]
In Hereford	Earl of Stamford's
In Coventry	Lord Rochford's
With the Train	Colonel Hampden's, Colonel Grantham's and Colonel Willoughby's Horse

Colonel Bamfield's Regiment, which Young positions in Northampton, was never part of Essex's field army and was at this time only a cadre of officers supposedly recruiting in the Bath and Bristol area.[11]

In addition to this, the cavalry were spread widely across the country in order to obtain billets, take some pressure off the immediate inhabitants of Kineton, and to act as eyes and ears of the army. Some were over five miles away and, as a result, arrived at various stages during the action and either had to find their own way into the line or attach themselves to various temporary commands such as the one assembled by Fiennes, that included Kightley's, Cromwell's and the remains of Douglas's troops. Essex obviously sent out riders to call in his outlying forces and garrisons who, to their credit, made excellent speed to come up as best they could. Hampden's and Grantham's Foot and Willoughby's Horse arrived with the main body of artillery in the early evening, while Rochford's appeared on the Monday.

However, although no battle plan for the Parliamentary army has yet been discovered, there can be little doubt that one existed, and several copies would have been made and handed out to the brigade commanders, probably at Worcester. When the fight was forced upon him, Essex would have tried to maintain what he could of his original plan with what he had been able to assemble as it would have been folly to undo all of the training previously undertaken by introducing a completely different formation and deployment. Without a contemporary diagram to guide us we must look closely at the written sources and see what information we can glean.

To begin we need to establish how many units Essex had at his disposal. We can draw up a simple chart to plot numbers according to various writers:

Table 5.1   Constituent units of the Earl of Essex's army at Edgehill

	Foot Regiments	*Troops Horse.*	*Dragoons*
Official Account	11	42	700
Fiennes	12	42	
Bifield	12	50	1,000
TC	13	38	1,000

Source: BL, *TT*, E 85 (41); E 86 (23); E 124 (18) and (21); E 126 (13) and (38); E 128 (20); E 200 (67); 669. f 6 (85) and (88).

Fiennes listed an additional regiment of Foot but, as he failed to mention the dismounted dragoons, we feel it safe to equate the two. The inflation of the dragoon numbers by Bifield and TC is probably the result of counting a portion of the commanded musketeers as dragoons. Wharton and Kightley both agree along the same lines as the Official Parliamentary Account although Wharton underestimates the cavalry.[12]

We now need to examine how these units were deployed. Firstly, we are told that they were all drawn up in 'battalia', that is in the fighting formation blocks described above. There is evidence to suggest that the Prince of Nassau's practice of dividing Foot regiments into two grand divisions may have been utilized in certain cases at Edgehill.[13] Although Holles's Regiment was over 1,000 strong, his numbers had been reduced by the detachment of 400 to act as commanded musketeers but the Lord General's and Cholmley's were also both large regiments and may have been set out in two grand divisions. We have no certain way of clarifying their status but, despite the lack of detailed deployment evidence, we know that Essex used the Dutch style of setting out his army and his battalia. It is, therefore, reasonable to suggest that, at Edgehill, the foot battalia were formed as a central body of pike with musket on both flanks, leaving small intervals between each body and slightly larger gaps between each battalia. Essex's army was drawn up in two major lines with the second line created by deploying each brigade in checkerboard fashion. The intervals between battalia were one battalia wide, over 120 metres, and were covered by a battalia in the second line. The width of the interval would thereby permit the covering unit to come up into the line when required without disrupting the formation or order of the fighting line. There is an argument that disputes this practice by advocating the use of a continuous line, but we believe that such a formation was only formed once the distance between armies had closed and the threat of Horse had been negated. For this reason it is probable that each of Essex's Brigades were drawn up in two lines, some battalia of each brigade in the front line and some in the second. We can find no evidence to suggest Essex would deviate from the normal pattern and allocate a specific brigade to form the second line. To the best of our researches we believe that neither army at Edgehill had a reserve of Foot. This later evolution could only be achieved as later armies grew in size and, by examining contemporary battle maps for Marston Moor and Naseby, it is possible to observe just such a gradual evolution of deployment practice. Nevertheless, it is appropriate to suggest that, at this early stage of the war, Essex would be swayed by his earlier personal experience in the Dutch service coupled with that fact that his rather dogmatic personality would not allow him to be tempted into experimentation with new ideas.

Although prepared to accept correction, we know of no Dutch-based, pre-1642 battle formation that placed a separate brigade as the second line. Added to which, to array the army so that the battalia of one brigade formed the second line of another would lead to confusion and would create a fighting line of mixed command and control. This is just one of the problems that we associate with the notion of Ballard's Brigade being spread along the rear as a second line. Once called forward the component battalia would alternate and interlard with those of Meldrum and Charles Essex thereby destroying any cohesive command structure.

We suggest that Parliament's Horse was drawn up in their basic Dutch fighting formation of the troop, six ranks deep and up to ten files wide although, with the campaign being several months old, the Edgehill numbers suggest that each troop was arrayed in three squadrons, each being three files wide. Further, we believe that Ramsey and Balfour formed their battalia in the normal, checkered manner. We can find no reference to suggest that either of these commanders adopted the Swedish three-deep formation or indeed placed one troop directly behind another. Like their Lord General, both of these officers had seen Dutch service as had several of their colonels. There appears to be no reason to assume that either of them would opt for a Swedish deployment and we firmly adhere to the view that both the left and the right wings of Parliament's army would have been set out with the troops in checkerboard fashion. Ramsey interlarded with musketeers and, despite some references stating that this pattern was used by Gustavus Adolphus at Lutzen, it also featured in various contemporary Dutch deployments. Balfour's command, however, had a closed flank with bushes and a small stream that made his front somewhat constricted. It was Essex's decision to place guns in support because some of the troops, and indeed regiments were absent and, incidentally, he may also have influenced the placement of Fielding's

Regiment well behind the front two lines in order that those precious guns would be 'guarded by two regiments of Foot, and some Horse'.[14]

Use of the Dutch system would require the Horse to fire and retire by files to reload. This was done in two ways. Firstly, by virtually countermarching and moving down the gaps between each file and, secondly, by each rank turning their horses to the right and peeling off to ride down the flank in single file until they could turn right again and rejoin their own file at the back. The latter choice was the was the most probable option although we do not know if this was done by nine men across the troop or by three across the squadron which would have been quicker but called for greater gaps between squadrons. In either case, setting troop or regimental intervals wide enough to create a clear passage for the first line troop to wheel by rank, in order to retire to the rear, was unnecessary – five yards would suffice. Ramsey's troop intervals would have been wider than Balfour's so as to bring in the bodies of commanded musketeers, however, we think his deployment may have changed during the late morning. Studying the deployment of his opposite number Ramsey would have noticed the build up in numbers and the most likely extension of the line, especially when the Lifeguard was apparently added into it at a late stage. This caused Ramsey to respond: 'we were inforced to draw out our Left Wing to a great breadth'.[15] Ramsey could only draw out his formation by three methods. Firstly, by increasing the width of all intervals, which would put gaps in the line and weaken its concentration of firepower. Secondly, by reducing the depth of files from six to three thereby decreasing the frequency of firepower. Thirdly, the most likely option, he would commit the second line of his troops thereby sustaining their concentration and firing frequency while sacrificing the support element. We believe Ramsey took a decision to forgo having a second line in an attempt to match Rupert's width. He had personal battlefield experience and knew that several of his troops had previously been defeated in melee by the opponents facing them. His enemy was to be made to come to him, standing as he did on a good defensive position. It is likely that he believed his troops could shoot their enemies down with massed firepower before they could approach near enough for close action. Post-civil war cavalry tactics would not embrace such thinking, but to the seventeenth-century military mind, fixed upon the tried and tested practice of Horse as mounted firepower, it was a sound decision.

Dragoons usually fought on foot, with their horses used primarily for rapid battlefield movement, although there is little to show they ever fought a fluid action. With Horse considered a mobile firepower arm, dragoons were employed as skirmish troops used to breaking up or covering attacks, frequently doing so from the protection of hedges, ditches, brushwood or trees. They seldom, if ever, fought mounted but would swarm forward in loose order, indeed even open order; normally on the flanks, and do whatever damage they could before falling back to their horses. At Edgehill Essex found a position that had its flanks on wetlands and small streams and loaded his dragoons towards his right where they could hold their ground by operating among the briars, furze and scrubland trees, protected by a watercourse that crossed their front and flank and also by ditches and a reasonable slope. On his left the ground provided a few hedges that angled to permit enfilading fire and therefore he also deployed commanded musketeers to hold that flank using the natural obstacles in like manner as on the right.

The guns were still an emergent weapon of war, especially where field battles were concerned. Their effectiveness is discussed elsewhere but, when considering deployment, their lack of mobility needs to be understood. In chapter 2 we have already noted the numbers of horses required to move each type of gun. In addition it is necessary to understand that many of the transport drivers and their teams were contracted or pressed civilians who, having deposited their load on the field of battle, retired to some place of safety as soon as they could. In essence, once deployed the guns did not tend to move. The smaller, lighter pieces could be manhandled, and perhaps they were. Gustavus Adolphus had used his famous leather guns to support his attacks, but the age of dedicated battalion guns was yet to come. It required enormous effort to drag even a 3-pounder and all of its paraphernalia around a field, especially across the soft headwater land of Edgehill, nor do we have any evidence to confirm that they were used in this way. Equally, we have no source from which to determine the exact positioning of guns although Essex appears to have spread his artillery along his line according to the accepted practice of the day. We know he put his best pieces on his right flank, Ramsey had three on his wing but, other than that, we have to assume that he deployed the remaining guns either in the intervals between, or forward of, each battalia in the front line. If attacked the gunners would normally retire to the protection of the Foot while their abandoned guns would act as obstacles to break up the formation and order of any assaulting unit.

Although we are dealing with conjecture we can gain a fair picture of where the rest of the army fought by returning yet again to original sources:

The Official Parliamentary Account:

> We presently marched forth into a great broad Field, under that Hill, called The Vale of the Red Horse, and made a stand some half a Mile from the Foot of the Hill, and there drew into Battalia, where we saw their Forces come down the Hill...
> ... the Wind was very much for their Advantage, and they endeavoured to get more of it; which, to prevent, we were inforced to draw out our Left Wing to a great breadth ... In our Right Wing were Three Regiments of Horse, the Lord General's ... Sir William Balfour's and the Lord Fielding's; Sir John Meldrum's Brigade had the Van, Col. Essex was in the middle, and Col. Ballard's with the Lord General's Regiment, his own, the Lord Brooks and Col. Hollis in the Rear. In the Left Wing were twenty-four Troops of Horse commanded by Sir James Ramsey.
> ... and so stood when our Rear came up; and then Charging altogether, especially that part of our Rear which was placed upon the Right hand, and so next to them which was the Lord General's Regiment and the Lord Brooks, led on by Col. Ballard who commanded that Brigade...
> The other two regiments of our Rear, Col. Hollis and Col. Ballard Charged those which were before them ...
> Now for our Rear...before it, toward the outside of it, stood our Left Wing of Horse, advanced a little to the Top of a Hill where they stood in a Battalia, lined with commanded Musketeers...they wheeled about ... and came running down ... just upon Col. Hollis's Regiment ...Col Hollis's Regiment ...together with the other Regiments of the Brigade, marched up the Hill, and so made all the haste they could to come to fight, and got the Wind of the enemy, and came on...and Charged the enemy who were in the fight with our Van, and the Right Wing of our Horse.[16]

Nathaniel Fiennes' *Most True Relation:*

> For our Army, it was drawn up upon a little rising ground, and being
> amongst the horse, I could not well discern how the foot were drawn up;
> only I know they were most of them a good space behinde the horse, there
> were three Regiments on the Right wing of our Army, vis, The Lord
> Generalls; Sir William Belfore's; and the Lord Fielding's Regiment, which
> stood behinde the other two, in the way of a reserve.
> On the right* [left] Wing of our Army, was Sir James Ramsey with some
> 24 Troops, for many of our Troops were not in the Field that day.[17]

* a slip of the pen.

Edmund Ludlow's *Memoirs:*

> The best of our field pieces were planted on our right wing, guarded by
> two regiments of foot and some horse.
> ... a party of the enemy being sent to line some hedges on our right
> wing,...were repulsed by our dragoons.[18]

Rev. Adoniram Bifield's Letter:

> our enemy had the wind more with them, but we had more of the Hill.[19]

The Official Royalist Account:

> We saw the Rebels Army drawing out, and setting themselves in Battalia.
> The Rebels had placed some musketeers under a Hedge that crost the Field,
> where the Encounter was to be made, that flanked upon their left wing.[20]

Sir Richard Bulstrode's *Memoirs:*

> The Enemy had all the morning to draw up their Army, in a great plain
> Field, which they did to their best Advantage, by putting several; Bodies of
> Foot with Retrenchments and Cannon before them, and all their Foot were
> lined with Horse behind them, with Intervals betwixt each Body, for their
> Horse to enter, if need required and upon their right Wing were some
> Briars covered with Dragoons, and a little behind, on their left Wing, was
> the town of Keinton, which supplied them with Provisions, and where their
> Baggage and Carriages were.
> ... and when we came within Cannon Shot of the Enemy, they discharged
> at us three Pieces of Cannon from their left Wing ... on the other side of
> Keinton towards Warwick ... we met with two Foot Regiments ... and a
> Regiment of Horse.[21]

James II's Account:

> He saw the van of the Rebell's Army down in the bottom by Keynton,
> which soon after began to draw up in battell in the plain before that village,
> but advanced no further.
> As for their order of battell, they had not made their wing so equal as his
> Majesty's, for knowing Prince Rupert was to command the King's right
> wing, they put the greatest part of their best cavalry into their left... Besides
> this, to strengthen that wing, they had small platoons of musquetiers
> betwixt every squadron, and on their left hand some dragoons; As for their

right wing of horse, which were not all come up, they drew that part of them which was present behind their foot, seeing they were not strong enough to encounter with the King's left wing, and lin'd the bushes with some dragoons to make a shew.[22]

Lord Bernard Stuart's Letter:

They stood still all the while upon the hill … we were fain to charge them uphill and leap over some five or six hedges and ditches … Upon our approach they gave fire with their cannon lined amongst their horse, dragoneers, carabines and pistols.[23]

John Belasyse's *Memoirs*:

The enemy's army…were drawn up in several bodies and reserves, much in the same manner of ours, but plainer order.[24]

From these brief statements we shall now attempt to more accurately define the Parliamentary army's artillery deployment.

Essex was drawn up on the plain below Edgehill, upon rising ground about half a mile west of Radway. The slope where he deployed was steep enough to be reckoned a hill that, on his left, had at least one ditch before it. He anchored his right upon bushes and briars (or hedges), and his left on a hedge that, at some point, turned towards the east to flank the prospective fighting area. Perhaps there was also a hedge that crossed part of his front or to the rear of his line, running roughly north-south.

We will examine the argument for these two hedges in the next chapter but before that we need to examine the notion that the battle took place between two enclosed areas. Let us look firstly at the so-called hedges on Parliament's right. Miller states that apart from those surrounding Radway the only hedges this side of the field lay half a mile in front of Little Kineton. Ludlow describes them as hedges, while James II calls them bushes.[25] Both men wrote their accounts many years after the action. Ludlow apparently wrote in exile and presumably isolation from others while James II gathered his information from a variety of participants. Ludlow had to rely upon his memory alone and we must concede that from his position in the cavalry reserve he could not have had a good view of that area. However, there is still work to be done on the extent of farmed land in the area and Glenn Foard of the Battlefields Trust is planning to research both map and written evidence of cultivation. Although Foard leans towards the belief that this area was hedged with a series of old fields belonging to Tysoe, we believe it reasonable to subscribe to the more general picture that Wilmot had to face pockets of dragoons scattered along and among ditches, a small brook, thorn bushes, furze and brushwood, rather than lining a neat arrangement of hedges. Like all who write history we await more discoveries but, bushes or hedges, they certainly provided cover for dragoons and difficult country for Wilmot's Horse.

On the opposite flank there is some support for the idea of several enclosures, both shown on de Gomme's map and recorded by Lord Bernard Stuart when he mentioned 'five or six hedges and ditches'. We are not told exactly when Stuart requested permission to join the fray but it would appear that he did so after the field deployment had begun. So, coming late into the line and being afforded the position of honour on the right, it may well be that he found his troops in the fields to the north of Radway.

However, looking at de Gomme's drawing it would appear that in being positioned on the right his troop was indeed put directly in line with a couple of crossways hedges which might, or might not have been part of a small, hedged field system. Yet Stuart is describing the whole charge which actually went all the way to Kineton. The five or six hedges and ditches he had to leap were probably those of Radway fields, those drawn by de Gomme and those known to be in the rear of Ramsey's line that were encountered in the pursuit, not the advance to contact. Most of Rupert's Brigade appear to have been drawn up further south and, therefore, had a line of advance over open heathland.

To reiterate, we know that Essex drew up in a plainer order than the Royalist Swedish system, and that he did so in battalia. He adopted the familiar pattern of Foot in the centre, flanked by Horse with artillery spread along his line. He was stronger in Horse on his left wing than on his right because not all of his troops had arrived on the battlefield. Ramsey had the left and was forced to deploy further to his left as the day wore on in order to prevent his troops being outflanked. Meldrum had the van which held the right of the Foot with Charles Essex's Brigade next to them in the middle. Ballard had the rear, a part of which had to march uphill to enter the fighting line, while the regiment that formed on his left, Holles's, was positioned directly behind part of Ramsey's Horse. Musketeers were interlarded among the Horse on the left and also lined the hedge on their flank. Three guns were also sited in this area. Essex placed his heaviest guns on his right and covered them with two of Meldrum's Regiments and some Horse. He strengthened this right flank further by ordering his dragoons into the bushes. Thus, we may gain a reasonably accurate picture of the Parliamentary deployment and, by studying the military manuals and the systems under which Essex had previously fought, we can deduce a considerable amount of additional detail.

Two problems remain. Firstly, the position of the right wing of Horse. Although we know that, in theory, it was three regiments strong – the Lord General's, Balfour's and Fielding's – and we also know, from Fiennes, that Fielding's were drawn up behind the other two, (Fiennes should be reliable, as his troop was part of Balfour's Regiment). However, although Fiennes's troop was there, several other troops had not yet arrived. Cromwell's and perhaps two other troops were missing from the Lord General's Regiment while Balfour's may have been several troops short, including John Fiennes's and Kightley's. We only know of four troops belonging to Fielding's that were definitely present and it may be worth looking at exactly what can be gleaned from primary sources regarding which troops formed which regiments in the Parliamentarian Horse at the time of Edgehill. More than this would be guesswork and assumption. In table 5.2 we set out the results of our current investigations. Some allocations have been changed from previously published sources as new information has come to light. Names listed indented and italicized indicate those in field command of a superior officer's troop, C indicates cuirassier, while (K or cP) indicates that the troop captain was either killed or captured at Powick Bridge.

Table 5.2: Parliamentary Horse

The Right Wing

Balfour's	Bedford's[26]	Essex's
Sir William Balfour's C	Earl of Bedford's C	Essex's Lifeguard C
John Meldrum	*William Anselman*	*Philip Stapleton*
Nathaniel Fiennes's	John Flemming's	Earl of Essex's
Lord Grey of Wark's	Adrian Scrope's	*Nathaniel Draper*
Sir Arthur Haselrig's		John Gunter's
Walter Long's		Robert, Lord Brooke's
Sgt. Maj. William Pretty's?		James Sheffield's
Francis Dowett's		Oliver Cromwell's
		Edward Wingate's
		Henry Ireton's?
		Thomas Temple's

The Left Wing

Fielding's	Goodwin's	Ramsey's
Bazil, Lord Fielding's	Arthur Goodwin's	Sir James Ramsey's
Robert Burghill's	Sigismund Alexander's	*John Farmer*
John Hale's	Richard Grenville's	William Balfour's
Samuel Luke's	Sir Thomas Sanders'	Edward Clarke's
	Thomas Tyrill's?	Crohn's
	Philip, Lord Wharton's	
	Robert Viver's	

Sandys's[27]	Waller's	Willoughby's
Edwin Sandys's (kP)	Sir William Waller's	Lord Willoughby's
John Cockayne	Horatio Carey's	Edward Ayscough's
Edward Berry's (kP)	Sir Faithful Fortesque's	?Fiennes
Edward Saunders	Anthony Milemay's	? Brookbank
Alexander Douglas's (kP)		? Harrison
Thomas Lidcott's (cP)		
Robert Stradling?		
George Austin's (cP)		
William Royston?		

Urry's[28]
John Urry's
Arthur Evelyn's
Simon Rudgely's

Troops from Essex's Army lists who are known to have fought at Edgehill but proof of regimental allocation remains undiscovered:

John Dalbier's	
William Frampton	
John Fiennes's	*poss. Balfour's*
Fernandoe Hastings'	
Edward Kightley's	*poss. Essex's*
John Mordaunt, Earl of Peterborough's	
Oliver, Lord St. John's	
Valentine Walton's	*poss. Fielding's*
Christopher Wray's	*poss. Willoughby's*

Other troops possibly at Edgehill but proof still undiscovered:

Frances Fiennes's	Thomas Hammond's	Hercules Langrish's
Henry Milemay's	Francis Thompson's	

Over the years there has been considerable debate about Essex's reserve of Horse. We accept that he formed it and, as it was normal practice, we can expect Essex to not only do so but also to place it behind his Foot in the accepted position. The Official Royalist Account mentions it, referring to 'the Reserve of the Rebel's Horse'.[29] Deciding how it was constituted depends again upon examining the evidence of what each unit did during the action and speculating about the whole command structure. However, the placing of the apostrophe is interesting. It reads as if 'rebel' is singular and they are referring to the reserve of Horse belonging to *the* head rebel; that is Essex. If it belongs to Essex then it was recognizable, presumably by its cornets and thus it includes his Lifeguard and his own troop of Horse. We shall examine this in more depth in chapter 9 below but worth considering here is the idea of who actually held the various commands. There is a school of thought that puts Bazil, Lord Fielding, son of the Earl of Denbigh, in command of the right wing.[30] However, as we know Sir James Ramsey had the left, we are forced to ask that if Fielding had the right, what did both the Lord General of the Horse and the Lieutenant General of Horse command? To suggest between them they only had the reserve is asking a great deal of social status above rank. Fiennes lists the commanding officers on the right wing and, although he erroneously includes Cromwell, he states that Balfour himself was there. He does not name Bedford, who is only mentioned by other writers once the reserve and the troops from the right wing jointly attack the Royalist infantry. It would be very strange that, if present, the experienced lieutenant general of Horse did not command. That the inexperienced Bedford may have taken the reserve is acceptable, especially as we believe that it was comprised of the army's elite mounted troops and, by placing him in the second line, he is also able to exert tactical control without being expected to lead what was very likely to be one of the first conflicts. So, it is more than probable that Sir William Balfour, as lieutenant general of Horse, had the right wing while Fielding led his own regiment.

The second problem lies with the starting position of Ballard's Brigade. To place Ballard's in the rear neatly behind Charles Essex's Brigade is the easy solution. It is however, too neat. Being 'in the reare' means he was the rearguard which in action took the left of the line, as opposed to those 'in the van' taking the right. If one walks the field in line with the supposed position of the hedge it can be seen that, despite the reconfiguration of the land caused by the construction of the storage depot, the ground of the ridge falls away northwards into a gentle fold yet rises again towards the Kineton road creating a sort of refused eminence which, although not discernable on an ordnance survey map, has a marked gradient. To continue the line would have put Ballard forward of this rise and into a depression, depriving his men of any advantage of higher ground. There is also a small water course in the bottom of the fold today which, in 1642, might well have been more substantial. We are told that Ramsey's Horse was forward of the line and that Ballard's units extended out to the left behind them. If Holles's Regiment was in the second line of Ballard's checkerboard deployment and on his extreme left then they would indeed be directly behind some of the Horse. Again we must understand that Essex had ample time to deploy his troops and even his adversaries compliment his skill in deploying them to the best advantage.[31] In the light of Essex having seen the preponderance of Royalist Horse deploying on the right, and knowing that Rupert was in all probability going to lead them, perhaps arranging for his left

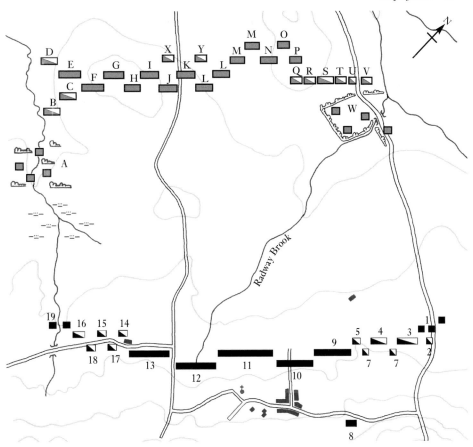

The deployment of both armies. During the morning Ramsey drew out his left. Unfortunately we have no evidence as to how he did this or how far he extended, possibly across the road.

The Army of Parliament

Balfour's Wing
A Browne & Wardlawe
B Balfour
C The Lord General
D Fielding

Meldrum's Brigade
E Fairfax
F Meldrum
G Constable
H Robartes

C. Essex's Brigade
I Essex
J Mandeville
K Wharton
L Cholmley

Ballard's Brigade
M The Lord General
N Brooke
O Ballard
P Holles

Ramsay's Wing
Holles's Muskets
   interlarded
Q Ramsay
R Waller
S Goodwin
T Sandys
U Bedford
V Urry
W Ballard's Muskets

Bedford's Reserve
X Stapleton
Y Bedford/Balfour

The King's Army

Prince Rupert's Wing
1 Usher/Washington
2 Lifeguard (Stuart)
3 The Prince of Wales
4 Prince Rupert
5 Prince Maurice
6 Lifeguard (Killigrew)
7 Byron
8 Heavy Guns & Legge's Firelocks

Astley's centre
9 Gerard
10 Belasyse
11 Fielding
12 Byron
13 Wentworth

Wilmot's Wing
14 Carnarvon
15 Grandison
16 Wilmot
17 Aston
18 Digby
19 Grey & Dunscombe

Other guns are spread along both lines

brigade to be slightly refused on to higher ground was a deliberate defensive placing? This premise becomes all the more plausible when one sees the rising ground which could take some of the impetus out of a horse charge. If Ballard had to advance, angling to his right as best he could, his right-hand battalia would have to pass through this depression, up the slight reverse, and continue to the northern end of the rising ground. This slope, which increases as it goes south, is still discernable by walking through Grave Ground Coppice. Ballard's Brigade, especially the Lord General's two grand divisions, would indeed have 'marched up the Hill' in order to come up into the fighting line and begin to shut down the majority of the gap left by Charles Essex's runaways.[32] It is necessary to walk the ground itself to understand that there is no need to place them directly behind Charles Essex's to find a slope up which to march.

It could be argued that Essex expected Hampden's and Grantham's Regiments to arrive earlier than they did having initially intended to form a reserve line of two brigades but, again, we have problems. Despite Fiennes calling them 'Hampden's brigado', the two Foot regiments and one Horse regiment escorting the main part of the Trayne did not constitute a brigade in the contemporary understanding of the term. Two regiments could be brigaded together for specific tasks but it would be very strange if they were identified as a designated brigade. In addition one is asking for innovative tactical thinking on Essex's part to create four basic divisions. Just as the King and Lindsey had allocated the Royalist army into three tercios (or battles) at Shrewsbury we believe Essex had done the same, probably at Worcester.[33] Having decided the deployment would fall into the standard three battles he then tried to implement it as best he could with what was available to him on the day. We contend that Essex followed the accepted English pattern of copying the Dutch which Henry Hexham's drill manual says should be divided 'into three parts called Brigadoes or Tercias... the Vantguard, the Battell & the Reareguard'.[34] When they deployed upon the field the Dutch aligned each brigade next to each other, with each brigade being checkerboarded so as to form a first and second line. Here again we can see no reason why Essex and his experienced commanders would adopt any formation other than the Dutch, the one in which they were experienced and in which they had trained their regiments. Meldrum would have taken the van to the right, and Charles Essex formed his main battle alongside him. There is nothing to lead us down the path that ascribes Ballard's rear battle to a position anywhere else in the line than where it should be – on the left. It may well have been refused and thus able to realign and come up to replace Charles Essex's when the threat of Rupert outflanking them was removed. To suggest that Essex would place one brigade directly behind another is to give him the luxury of numbers afforded by later English Civil War armies. It also fits too neatly with the events of the action and demands a degree of hindsight. Essex had no reason to suspect that four of his regiments would break and run, especially if they had a hedge with prepared gaps upon which they could fall back. If any regiment was fragile it was unlikely to be Cholmley's Bluecoats who were not only the largest in the Parliamentary army but had already earned a reputation for their quarrelsome truculence.

There is a further aspect to consider. When the regiments of Charles Essex's Brigade routed they were charged by Lucas, Walsh and Smith, who captured many colours, especially from Wharton's. If there had been a second line brigade of ordered Foot directly behind them, would not their officers have gathered the colours and withdrawn them to safety into its midst? If they had had such support would they have run? Given that they did run, why is there no reference to them breaking through or disrupting Ballard's Brigade? The only disruption recorded is that of Holles's contact with the Horse. If they recorded that, then why not mention something as dramatic as one third of their own Foot running through them? We just have to accept that the placing of Ballard, neatly behind the brigade that is to break, is just too tidy and too convenient for both the story and for later drawers of maps.

Having amassed the basic information regarding who was with whom, we now need to look at the terrain, both what remains of the ground itself and at the oldest map of the region we can find, to try to appreciate what the field probably looked like and where these units stood. Walking the field is an absolute necessity, especially for appreciating lines of sight, distances and the relation of various locations to the battle line. Edgehill is a challenge because of the storage depot and the related destruction of the landscape. It is made more difficult because, regrettably, there is no detailed map for our period. Although the Warwickshire Record Office does hold maps that predate the battle, there is nothing useful until we reach Henry Beighton's 1725 map of Warwickshire.[35] This item will be covered in more detail in the following chapter but, suffice to say that, apart from substantiating the claim of the presence of water courses on both sides of the deployment area and the supposed alignment of the conflict, it aids us little in understanding the deployment. All subsequent maps are post enclosure and again there are few useful maps drawn of this area before the beginning of Ordnance Survey.

The final remaining piece of the jigsaw is supplied by identifying what we know of the discovery and location of battlefield artefacts. Unfortunately, this is not as precise an exercise as we would wish due to the working method of those who have unearthed finds in the past and failed to record their exact situation. It does, however, add a further layer of vital information for consideration and as full a record as we could piece together can be found in appendix B below.

We now come to the task of constructing a Parliamentarian Order of Battle. It is important to note that, due to the paucity of evidence, much of what has been written is speculative. Names of troops and regiments are drawn from various sources including diaries and personal accounts, pay lists, garrison postings and letters. Gradually it is possible to build up images of which troops fought in which regiments and where each unit fought in various engagements. While there is de Gomme's battle plan for the Royalist army, no such drawing has, so far, been discovered for the Parliamentarian army. Until such a precious document is unearthed all we can offer is a debated and agreed consensus.

Parliamentarian Order of Battle

Right Wing   Lieutenant General of Horse, Sir William Balfour. 15? troops of Horse + 12 troops of dragoons

Flank Guard Colonel John Browne's Regiment of dragoons   537 in six troops
      1 Colonel John Browne's
      2 Sergeant Major Gilbert Blair's
      3 Captain Sir John Browne's
      4 Captain Robert Mewer's
      5 Captain William Buchan's
      6 Captain Robert Marine's

Right Wing continued

Colonel James Wardlawe's Regiment of dragoons	500? in six troops
1 Colonel James Wardlawe's	
2 Lieutenant Colonel George Dundas's	
3 Captain Alexander Nerne's	
4 Captain John Barne's	
5 Captain James Stenchion's	
6 Captain Archibald Hamilton's	

First Line

The Lord General's Regiment of Horse	360 in 6 troops
1 Sergeant Major John Gunter's	
2 Lord Brooke's Troop	
3 Captain James Sheffield's	
4 Captain Henry Ireton's	
5 Captain Edward Wingate's	
6 Captain Thomas Temple's	
Sir William Balfour's Regiment of Horse	360 in 6 troops
1 Sergeant Major William Pretty's	
2 Lord Grey of Groby's	
3 Captain Nathaniel Fiennes's	
4 Sir Arthur Haselrig's	
5 Captain Walter Long's	
6 Captain Francis Dowett's	

Second Line

Basil, Lord Fielding's Regiment of Horse	360 in six troops
1 Colonel Lord Fielding's	
2 ?	
3 Major Robert Burghill's	
4 Captain John Hale's	
5 Captain Samuel Luke's	
6 ?	

Centre   Acting Sergeant Major General Thomas Ballard

Front & Second Line Composed by checkerboarding alternate battalia

Right Colonel Sir John Meldrum's Brigade	2,650 in four regiments
1 Sir John Meldrum's Regiment	700
2 Sir William Fairfax's Regiment	750
3 Sir William Constable's Regiment	700
4 Lord Robartes's Regiment	500
Centre Colonel Charles Essex's Brigade	2,828 in four regiments
1 Colonel Charles Essex's Regiment	600
2 Lord Wharton's Regiment	500
3 Lord Mandeville's Regiment	600
4 Sir Henry Cholmley's Regiment	1,128
Left Colonel Thomas Ballard's Brigade	3,604 {700 det} in four regiments
1 The Lord General's Regiment of Foot, Earl of Essex's[36]	958
2 Colonel Thomas Ballard's Regiment	776 (300 det)

Centre continued

3 Lord Brooke's Regiment	740
4 Colonel Denzil Holles' Regiment	1,130 (400 det)

Third Line

Reserve of Horse Lord Lieutenant General of Horse William Russell, Earl of Bedford

300 in four troops – Stapleton's & Balfour's were double troops

1 Sir Philip Stapleton's (Essex's Lifeguard)
2 Captain Nathaniel Draper's (Essex's harquebusier)
3 Sir William Balfour's
4 The Earl of Bedford's Lifeguard

Left Wing Commissary General Sir James Ramsey

24+[37] troops + Commanded muskets from Ballard's 300
Commanded muskets from Holles's 400

Front & Second Line Composed by pairing advanced and support troops

Unknown position of Sir James Ramsey's Regiment of Horse — 240 in four troops?
1 Sir James Ramsey's
2 Sergeant Major William Balfour's
3 Captain Edward Clarke's
4 Captain ? Crohn's
5 ?

On the right Sir William Waller's Regiment of Horse — 240 in six troops?
1 Sir William Waller's
2 Sergeant Major Horatio Carey's
3 Captain Anthony Milemay's
4 Sir Faithfull Fortesque's
5 ?

On the left Col Arthur Goodwin's Regiment of Horse — 360 in six troops?
1 Colonel Arthur Goodwin's
2 Sergeant Major Sigismund Alexander's
3 Captain Robert Vivers's
4 Captain Thomas Sanders's
5 Captain Richard Grenville's
6 Captain Philip, Lord Wharton's

Unknown position Colonel Edwin Sandys' Regiment of Horse — 240 in four troops?
1 Colonel Edwin Sandy's
2 Sergeant Major Edward Berry's
3 Captain George Austin's
4 Captain Thomas Lidcott's

Unknown position Earl of Bedford's Regiment of Horse — 120 in 2 troops?
1 Captain John Flemming's
2 Captain Adrian Scrope's

Unknown position of Colonel John Urry's Regiment of Horse — 360 in four troops?
1 Colonel John Urry's
2 Captain Arthur Evelyn's
3 Captain Simon Rudgely's
4 ?

Left Wing continued

Along the Line

The artillery: 16 guns from a trayne of 29 of which 6 were mortars and would not have been on the field and 7 were still being brought up. Any combination from the list below is possible although we favour weighting it towards the lighter pieces.

> 2 x long-barrelled 12-pounders
> 2 x short-barrelled 12-pounders
> 4 x 6-pounders
> 11 x short drake 3-pounders

Arriving late

Captain Oliver Cromwell's Troop of The Lord General's Regiment of Horse
John Fiennes's Troop
Captain Edward Kightley's Troop
Sergeant Major Alexander Douglas's Troop (part)
Lord Willoughby of Parham's Regiment of Horse
Colonel John Hampden's Regiment of Foot

Arriving on 24 October

Lord Rochford's Regiment of Foot	710
Colonel Thomas Grantham's Regiment of Foot	800 ?

Elsewhere during the action

Two companies on detachment are known to have been posted, but from which regiment and where they were remains unclear.

Troops of Horse whose regimental allocation is unknown or unconfirmed

On the right with Balfour:

> 1
> 2
> 3

On the left with either Bedford or Sandy's

> 1 Sir James Ramsey's
> 2 Lord Hastings's
> 3

On either wing

> 1 Lord Wharton's
> 2 Captain Joseph Fleming's
> 3 Sir Samuel Luke's

In addition there were 251 firelocks under Captains Devereux, Turner and Tyndal that were originally members of the Lord General's Regiment. However, when they left Worcester they were converted to dragoons.[38] They took casualties at Edgehill but we have no evidence that enables us state with any degree of certainty where or under whom they fought, although it is possible they were guarding the artillery as part of the force which came up late in the day with Hampden. There was also a company of firelocks missing from Essex's army who marched into Gloucester on 21 October having escorted the Pontoon Train from London.

Chapter Six

The Field

... a great broad Field, under that Hill, called the Vale of the Red Horse.
Official Parliamentarian Account.

The Royalist rendezvous was on the distinctive landmark of Edgehill. With their objective clearly visible for miles around, it was unlikely that any element of the King's army could fail to understand their orders or get lost. Seemingly, Prince Rupert was the first senior Royalist officer to arrive at the rendezvous as his men began to occupy the high ground on the Arlescote end of the ridge at about 8:00 a.m. The King did not leave Edgecote until mid-morning so it was past midday when he reached Edgehill village to see Essex's army already deployed on the plain below the escarpment. The Rev. G Miller, writing in 1888 stated that the King viewed the field with a telescope from an eminence called Knoll End before calling his famous and, with hindsight, disastrous 'Council of Warre'. Local tradition has this meeting taking place in a house on the present site of The Castle Inn; although it may be that, in reality, Charles had his carriage or indeed his tent placed there.[1] The view from The Castle Inn is excellent and in 1642 it would have been even more dramatic. We must try to imagine the land without the trees! The whole area was one of heathland; the greater part of it, both hillside and plain, open moorland with patches of scrub of gorse and brushwood. The ground on the plain was generally soft and in some places boggy, but the land around the village of Radway was high enough for cultivation.

So too was the slight hill or small ridge held by Essex that tends to run across the field at roughly ninety degrees to the modern road, although it is far from continuous. There are folds in the land not great enough for Ordnance Survey contours but significant as slopes. It is higher at its southern end where The Oaks coppice now stands and there is a marked dip between the northern end of Grave Ground coppice and a slightly refused rise nearer the road.

This is a rise amid the wet headwater rivulets of the Dene, and the slightly higher land was under the plough because its elevation resulted in improved water run-off and drainage and seed would be less prone to suffer wet rot. In fact a small stream, Radway brook, ran diagonally across the whole field and then along the foot of the rise before bending westward towards Kineton through a shallow, fairly wide depression that even today has the typical tussocks and sedge of marshland. Thanks to modern drainage and the proliferation of small farms, coppices and hedges and scrubland clearances, it is hard to visualize the field as it would have been, but to envisage the battle one must try.

Much work remains to be undertaken on this aspect, but we can make a few useful

Ramsey's Hedge? The southern part of a hedgeline that is in a plausible position to be the one lined by Parliamentarian-commanded musketeers.

general comments. There were few buildings on the moor. Lonely farms set amid their own acres were not a feature of farming until the enclosures of the eighteenth century had become 'England's new prison bars' and places like Battle Farm or Thistle Farm were not, in all probability, in existence. When looking for evidence of what was under cultivation in 1642, the modern visitor must not be deceived by the remains of ridge and furrow farming. This was a method to counter England's erratic weather patterns that remained in use well after the battle. When driving through this area, especially up the Fosse Way, there is plenty of evidence of this type of cultivation. It is not evidence of feudal demarcation zones, nor of medieval field systems. This method of clearing and breaking land for cultivation was popular for a long time both before and after 1642. Finding evidence of ridge and furrow only tells us that the land was farmed in a certain way before the great enclosures of the eighteenth century. It is unlikely that the land around Radway in the mid-seventeenth century was a wide expanse of medieval, hedge-ringed, ploughed fields – the small local population could not have worked them.

Communities tended to live together grouped in villages that decamped into the fields during the daylight hours to work and returned home at dusk. Ridge and furrow farming marked the cultivated sections because, although no longer a feudal ground allocation in strip farming, this system maximized yield through wet and dry seasons. While family groups may have tilled fields rather than strips, the obsession with land ownership, with possessions marked by fences and hedges was not yet prevalent. There was little travel, few strangers, and men did not feel the urge to shout 'Get off my land' at their neighbours. There may have been garden and field hedges around the buildings

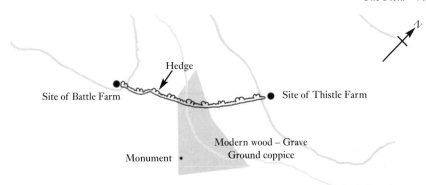

A conjectural diagram to show where Miller's hedge supposedly ran, based upon an OS map of the 1930s and evidence from Miller and drawings by Burne and Young.

of the three villages involved, such as one around Kings Leys Barn, but, according to Miller, there was only one hedge on the field itself, perhaps marking the parish boundary between Kineton and Radway.[2] Miller's hedge, a portion of which the nineteenth-century author claims to have found, ran between sites once occupied by Battle Farm and Thistle Farm, partly along what became the right of Essex's line.[3] However, there is reason to believe that there were actually two hedges – what we call Miller's hedge and Ramsey's hedge. The latter appears frequently in most modern accounts and in them influences the action. Roberts and Tincey mention a hedge but do not show it on their maps, while Davies did not publish a map.[4] Holmes and Young together seem to agree with Miller's location but do not give any further details.[5] However, Young positions another hedge, north of the Kineton to Banbury road, on the diagrammatic map in his work Edgehill 1642.[6] This tends to be in keeping with the drawing by Bernard de Gomme which shows a series of right-angled turns and part of what appears to be a field complex directly across the extreme right of Rupert's deployment.

Having examined the ground and the period maps available, the evidence suggests there were hedges in both locations. Miller's hedge, the central location of which he substantiates with reference to both landscape archaeology and significant numbers of finds, cannot be the one which the Official Royalist Account says 'crost the field', as that writer describes that hedge as 'upon their Left Wing' and under which 'the Rebels had placed some Musketeers.' This hedge is way over to the left and presumably ran parallel to the small stream and on the forward slope of the 'ridge', before it curved or turned towards the Royalist lines. Neither the length, nor height, nor width, nor composition of either hedge is mentioned.

If Miller's hedge was there, and if indeed the Parliamentarian Foot fell back upon it at one stage as suggested by Burne, then presumably it had gaps in it to allow the passage of troops. Essex did have plenty of time during the morning to cut such gaps. However, we believe the thinking regarding this hedge by many is influenced by simplistic preconceptions of geographical features; namely that the crests of hills and ridges run central to the rise which is quite rare. From looking at old Ordnance Survey maps and field patterns one can see that the slopes of Essex's ridge were steeper on the Kineton side than those which faced Radway and that its crest or highline was much nearer its military reverse slope. This means the Royalist army had a long incline to climb towards the waiting Parliamentarian ranks. Regrettably the Depot works destroyed much of this ground but this point can be substantiated by examining the southern end of the feature, over in the Oaks. However, although Burne's main locating features, Battle and Thistle Farms, have gone, along with the hedge itself, they can be placed using old maps, and the first positioned on or near the crest and the second on the reverse slope. Although these farms were not there during the battle, the hedge supposedly was and would thus have run partially along the crest of the defensive position before dropping down the back slope. Rather than have the Parliamentarians fall back, which no contemporary source mentions, it would seem more likely that at least part of their line used the hedge as a basis for such retrenchment as they could, which would account for the archaeological evidence discovered by Miller. This part of their line was probably that allocated to the left of Meldrum's Brigade and one is tempted to wonder if, having a hedge behind rather than in front of them, the young soldiers, known from Wharton to have been in Charles Essex's Brigade, did not feel more exposed than their neighbours. This crest line appears to have flattened out and devolved into several tongues as it went northward. It is on part of one of these slight eminences that we place Ballard's Brigade. Plotted fall-of-shot maps confirm this angle of Essex's line and indicate shooting taking place at fairly close quarters north of Grave Ground coppice where we believe Ballard's fought.[7] However, all this assumes Miller's hedge was there in 1642 and that Miller is right about the one hedge.

Unfortunately we do not believe him implicitly because the diagrammatic battle map of the Royalist deployment drawn by Bernard de Gomme actually includes the 'rebel-held' hedges on Ramsey's wing which we, for convenience, call Ramsey's hedge. This is, according to de Gomme, the edge of a small complex of fields which, it would seem, was used by Ramsey to anchor his left. Whether they were part of the same 'one hedge' seems unlikely for that would mean a defensive soft cover line across most of the field which a contemporary would most likely have mentioned. It would mean that the whole deployment had to conform to a hedgeline which would be very unusual, for Essex did not usually do the unusual. It would also impede the movement of troops in an age when open ground was much preferred for the execution of virtually all drill manoeuvres.

We opt for placing a hedge roughly on the line of the crest and the reverse slope of Essex's ridge, and another running across the front of the leftmost portion of Ramsey's hill with part of it angling east towards the Royalist lines. In this way one hedge can provide a vital obstacle to prevent Fielding's Brigade exploiting the central gap created by the flight of Charles Essex's Brigade, with the other providing a degree of cover for many of the commanded musketeers, once overrun, to be able to struggle back to rejoin Ballard's Brigade while it marched into position.

While discussing the vegetation it may be interesting to note that Walford comes up with a strange idea when discussing the bushes on the right: 'the thick growth of furze [was] wattled together on the gently sloping upland'.[8] Wherever he found this he does not say, but Essex's men certainly had time to do it if they had the mind, and it would allow for Ludlow's confusion between bushes and hedges. However, plaiting gorse bushes does seem a bizarre and prickly occupation

The rest of the ridge was more open heathland, but the right itself rested on a sloping drop into yet another marshy depression around another small tributary of the Dene.

Despite his critics one must allow that Essex had selected a good position and taken the time to try and deploy conforming to it.

It is extremely difficult to determine much of the detail of the contemporary landscape as map-making in the seventeenth and eighteenth centuries was focused upon simplified route planning rather than providing accurate representations or descriptions of the landscape. The first traceable map of the Kineton area was drawn, printed and published by Christopher Saxton in 1576 and entitled *A Map of Warwickshire and Leicestershire*. It was not very detailed, showing only the river Dene and a mill in the region. Another printer, known as WB, produced a set of playing card maps in 1590, while Pieter van den Keerne published another two-counties version in 1599. There was also another map of 1603, but its artist is unknown and it adds very little information. They all appear to be very much alike in style and content to that of Saxton's and it would appear that map-makers often copied from those of previous generations. The map in Dugdale's *Antiquities of Warwickshire*, 1656, is also very similar to those mentioned above. In his study of maps of the area Harvey states that Saxton's map was still in service in 1776 with various additions and changes.[9]

William Kip is known to have updated Saxton's map in 1607 and this served as a model for John Speed's map of 1610 which, although it included 'an engraving of the battle', is very representational and adds little to our understanding of the ground. John Bill produced a map of Warwickshire in 1626 and so did George Humble in 1627 but the latter appears very similar to that of van den Keerne. To the uneducated eye it seems a good copy. The most recent map of the road system which could have been used by the commanders during the campaign would have been that of Jacob Florenz von Langeren, published in 1635, but it too adds nothing to what was available before and is remarkable for its lack of detail. Rivers are marked but streams are not and, while forests merit inclusion, hedges and cultivated areas do not. The anonymous map of 1603 enjoyed a popular revival after the battle, being reprinted by Peter Stent between 1643 and 1667, and then by John Overton between 1668 and 1707. Overton even issued a further reprint in 1714.

It is not until Dugdale's work was republished in the 1730s that a marked improvement appears with the inclusion of a map taken from Henry Beighton's *Field Book* for 1732. Beighton actually includes trees and references to the battle, and draws and labels locations for the action, the Kingsmill monument and the sites of several commanding officers' tents. He does not reveal, however, any evidence to support what he has drawn but there are similarities between Beighton's work and that of Speed. It would seem that Dugdale and Beighton did not enjoy respect from their contemporaries for Thomas Habington wrote to Sir Simon Archer concerning their work: 'You doe well not to rely upon Heraldes petegrees which are often farced with untruthes'.[10]

John Cary published his *New and Correct English Atlas* in 1787 but detail was still scarce until William Yates and Son issued their *One Inch Map of Warwickshire* in 1787, but this was post-enclosure and 145 years after the battle. Subsequent maps, including Charles Smith's *New English Atlas containing A New Map of the County of Warwickshire* of 1804 and the *One Inch Map of Warwickshire* by C and J Greenwood in 1822, all appear to be founded upon information collected and collated by the pioneers, and it is not until the arrival of the Ordnance Survey of 1862 that we see any detail of the region recorded on Sheet 53, 1st edition, Old Series 201. Looking at the works of those who described regions for travellers or visitors can also reveal information but, once again, there is a paucity of material relating to the battlefield. Francis Smith's *Warwickshire Delineated*, published in 1821, includes a sketch map of the roadways but little else, but does say 'vestiges of the battle are often turned up by the plough, as pieces of armour, spear-heads, buckles and human bones'.[11] However, he falls back upon Dugdale, complete with invented incidents, for his description of the battle.

Before leaving the problems of describing the field it is necessary to refer to another that the authors have encountered. Military historians tend to use terms such as 'the left' or 'the right' when locating particular events to battlefield locations, but this can become ambiguous and confusing as each time the phrase is employed it needs qualifying by stating whose left or whose right is being described. Unfortunately, Edgehill has no easily attributable features which can be used to clarify the flanks of the battlefield, such as making reference to the Tockwith flank at Marston Moor. Therefore, throughout our narrative, we have often used the basic compass reference as used by the early map-makers, and thus we call that part of the field where Ramsey's and Rupert's wings fought the north flank and, where Balfour's and Wilmot's men drew up, the south flank. Following this simple directional labelling, Kineton lies to the west of the field and Banbury to the east. Like those who drew the maps by which the armies navigated, we trust simplification will aid rather than confuse understanding.

Chapter Seven

The Opening Moves

The great shot was exchanged on both sides. Ludlow.

By the early afternoon on that Sunday, 23 October, both armies stood arrayed in the field. This must have been a strange time as, despite the various adjustments of position that must have been carried out, the majority of units seem to have stood patiently awaiting the battle to come. No doubt 'Divines' moved among the battalia preaching their own brand of religious encouragement. Up on the hill the Royal Standard fluttered in the breeze.[1] Various orders or instructions were given and morale-boosting efforts were undertaken to lessen the tension and put courage into the hearts of the would-be warriors. Prince Rupert rode from one wing of Horse to the other with orders and words of encouragement while, in the opposing army, General Ramsey spoke at the head of each of his squadrons. Not only did he exhort his men to show magnanimity and resolution, calling upon their ancestors, and assuring them of the justness of their cause, he also told his troopers that the enemy were, 'Papists, Atheists, and Irreligious persons'.[2]

The King himself took part in these pre-battle ceremonies. Gathering his personal entourage of senior officers, advisors and Gentlemen Pensioners about him, he rode, together with his two sons, Charles, Prince of Wales and James, Duke of York, along the Royalist line. Bulstrode says he went 'to every Brigade of Horse and to all the Tertias of Foot' and that he 'encouraged them to do their Duty', speaking 'with great Courage and Cheerfulness'.[3] He is reputed to have said, 'Matters are now to be declared with swords, not by words', and a transcription of one of his speeches is in appendix E.[4] Little real command and control was exercised in these displays, but they certainly have the appearance of leadership which could and did inspire the men. Bulstrode claimed that Charles's appearance certainly had the desired effect and caused 'Huzza's thro' the whole Army'.[5] To incite an entire army to cheer was no mean feat. However he may have had an altogether different agenda – to induce the Parliamentarians to strike the first blow.

We have no explanation as to exactly why the battle started. However we do know that the Parliamentarian guns fired first at about two o'clock – the time being close enough to the King's progress for Peter Young, in his account of the battle, to suggest 'it may be that it was this royal progress and storm of cheering that provoked Essex to open fire'.[6] Although possibly scoring a political point, this 'he struck the first blow' argument smacks a little of the age of elegant Fontenoy or even the pre-World War II

Bullet Hill. The fields in the distance above the bales and below the tree line is where the Royalist gunners are believed to have set up their six largest guns in a battery. There is a flat expanse about half-way up the slope.

school playground. Essex had deployed his army during the morning and appeared content to await developments. He resisted the opportunity to attack his enemy while it deployed before Radway, preferring to remain on his rise of higher ground. As the morning turned into afternoon his chances of assembling all his forces were increasing. We have no records of messengers arriving but it is feasible that he was kept aware of the marching progress of his missing regiments and guns. Time was on Parliament's side so he would have been wise to resist all Royalist attempts to prompt him into action. However, Ludlow states that 'Our General having commanded to fire upon the enemy, it was done twice'.[7] One must question why Essex opened fire when he was still waiting for a significant portion of his army to rendezvous. The first point may be Ludlow assuming that because the guns fired they had been ordered to do so. While not suggesting anything implausibly dramatic, guns are sometimes fired inadvertently as later happened during one of Waller's parleys at Basing House, men who are nervous and on edge can do strange things and, if one gun fired, it is plausible that other gun captains might have believed that the order had been given to commence firing. Did they, after two rounds, realize their mistake? If so by that time it was too late, for their aim had been 'upon that part of the army wherein, as it was reported, the king was'.[8] Despite Ludlow telling us that Essex commanded the guns to open fire, it is extremely unlikely that he would have ordered them to fire upon the King's person. Whatever the sequence or the reason, the Royalist guns replied and the battle had begun.

Parliament's guns opened fire along their line but the Royalists' main fire came from their six-gun battery on Bullet Hill; their lighter pieces dispersed to the brigades would have been out of range. Rates of fire during this opening bombardment phase can be

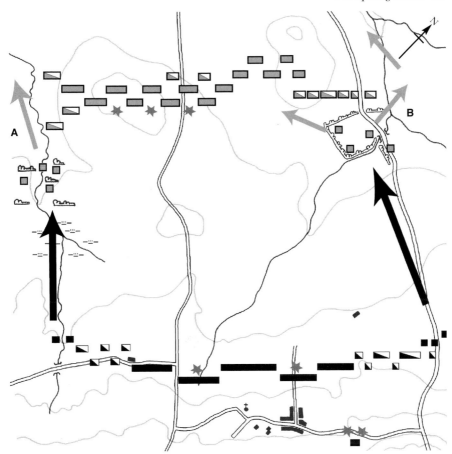

*The battle begins. Both lines of guns open fire and the Royalist dragoons on both wings drive off their opposite numbers, thus clearing the way for their Horse to advance. At **A**, Parliamentarian dragoons run for their horses while more quit the field, and at **B** Ballard's commanded musketeers flee: some make for Kineton while others run for their parent regiment.*

interesting if one interprets the comment 'wee gave them two shoots for one' in 'A True Copy of a Letter' as inferring that Parliament's gunners kept up double the rate of fire sustained by the enemy.[9] It could, however, refer to those opening shots and mean that they got off two rounds before their Royalist counterparts fired back. Notwithstanding the rate of fire per gun, Essex's artillery seems to have had more success in hitting their targets. Most accounts credit the artillery duel as going to the Parliamentarians. There are several reasons why this happened. Firstly, Essex had more pieces of ordnance in action. Exact numbers are not available but he is known to have had more guns available than the King. Secondly his gunners seemed to have been more skilful in laying their shot. A London newsletter, of Royalist sympathies, reported that the King's guns 'shot over' while Kightley reports them dropping short by twenty yards.[10]

The consensus seems to be that the six larger pieces of Royalist artillery deployed on the bottom slopes of Edgehill, firing downhill, had the more difficult task regarding the calculations for charge, distance and trajectory. In contrast to this, Parliament's gunners

An English Civil War saker. A faithful construction of a civil war field gun, commissioned by Hampshire County Council Museum Services and currently on display at Basing House.

were able to bounce their projectiles, their uphill shot allowing the solid balls to strike the sloping ground and skip upwards into blocks of men, unlike shot fired downhill which had a tendency to plunge in. As described in the previous chapter, unimpeded by soft ground or obstacles a ball can bounce several times before running out of kinetic energy. At a certain point in this process it stops bouncing and just rolls along the ground; and even then it can still maim any soldier foolish enough to extend his foot to stop it! The terrain itself also seems to have had a hand in this preliminary work. The plough furrows of softer, turned earth of the cultivated land in front of several of Essex's units absorbed shot more easily than the untilled scrubland of the Edgehill slopes. The London Newsletter again: 'the King had so great an advantage of the hill that it turned to his disadvantage, for being so much upon the descent his cannon either shot over, or if short it would not graze by reason of the ploughed lands; whereas their cannon did some hurt having a mark they could not miss'.[11] Could this also allude to a further reason for Parliament's successful cannonade? The deployment of the Royalist army presented a wider and more easily hit target-rich environment. In conversation, Bob Leedham revealed that Peter Young advanced the view not contained in his excellent book on the Edgehill battle that account writers on both sides kept quiet about the numbers of horses that bolted and men who ran off when the bombardment began.

It is widely believed that the first man injured in the bombardment was the Royalist Lieutenant Francis Bowles of Fielding's Regiment of Foot, whose petition in 1660 is recorded in the State Papers.[12] This exchange of cannon continued for some time – Ludlow says an hour – but that seems a little protracted considering the shortage of remaining daylight for fighting and the impulsive nature of Prince Rupert. Wharton estimated that the Royalist guns killed less than twenty men while Kightley states that the Parliamentarian ordnance 'killed many of their men'.[13] Matters grew so hot among the Royalist ranks that the King's progress along his line was not only halted but his party was made to retire. Bulstrode relates how 'all the Generals went to the King… and

The northern hedges, the extreme left of Ramsey's left wing. The water course can be made out and the ground is still boggy.

desired he would retire to a rising Ground, some distance from thence'.[14] Charles, it would appear, had indicated his intention of accompanying the general advance in some sort of quasi-romantic gesture.

Although regarded by some as the mark of a good leader, willing to risk his life with his men, this move would not only have resigned tactical command and control of the whole battle picture, but it would also have been sheer strategic folly. A king who falls early in battle, no matter how heroically, not only loses his life but risks those of his soldiers in any ensuing panic rout, and, probably more importantly, jeopardizes his officers' and supporters' investments, be they great or small! Besides, Charles was no warrior king, unlike Gustavus Adolphus, and could have contributed little to any ensuing fight. He was prevailed upon to see sense and his entourage fell back to an eminence at the right rear called, since the battle, Bullet Hill. He did not retire out of range of the enemy's larger cannon and this knot of Royal personages, friends and bodyguards would have presented an attractive target in their elevated position.

Battles of the period did make use of open-order skirmish troops but they were usually deployed in advance of the line to provide disrupting fire. Parties of commanded musketeers or dismounted dragoons would seek any available cover as protection from attacks by formed bodies, especially from cavalry against whom they had little defence and could be ridden or cut down easily. If ordered to launch an attack, they had little hope of standing against the volleys of formed musketeers and could not melee with massed pikemen. Thrown forward of the main army with little chance of real success they were dubbed 'the Forlorn Hope'; a term the military were later to apply to those brave souls who, in later siege warfare, lead escalades and stormed into breeches. However, in the field they could ensconce themselves behind or among hedgerows, bushes, ditches or coppices as these were excellent impediments to formed horse. Individual troopers could still jump or navigate them quite easily, although they would place any rider at a disadvantage in close combat. Such obstacles would prevent skirmishers from being ridden down en masse and they could be useful in helping stem a unified attack by reducing any fight to an individual, hand-to-hand, melee.

Indeed, the tactical emphasis of seventeenth-century skirmish troops was usually towards defence with firepower to break up any attack. A favourite deployment was lining hedges that flanked ground over which the enemy had to advance. As well as preventing the turning of the line they could shoot into the flank of attacking bodies who marched across their front, putting in enfilading shots down the ranks often at close range. Their limited numbers, dispersed firing formation, poor training and sometimes cheap weapons, meant their effect was seldom devastating, but it could be effective and worthwhile if it disrupted an attack sufficiently to break its cohesion or unnerve its morale.

Essex had deployed his skirmish troops well. The two regiments of dragoons of Browne and Wardlawe he placed on his south flank among a network of bushes and ditches with their right protected by a small stream, and on his north flank he stationed 700 commanded musketeers. A body of 400, presumably from Holles's, was arrayed in blocks in the intervals between the troops of horse, while another 300, probably from Ballard's, were placed 'under a hedge that crost the field where the encounter was to be made, that flanked upon their left wing'.[15] De Gomme's map shows a series of hedges which form a sort of right-angled hedgeline protecting the extreme left of the front of Ramsey's Horse and the ground any attack upon would have had to cross. In line with established practice, Ramsey had these barriers lined with firepower to harass the enemy Horse attack frontally and to pour in enfilading fire should they advance. The Royalist Horse on both wings would, therefore, receive close range small arms fire unless they eliminated these men. To this end, the initial bombardment was to be followed by the clash of the forlorn hopes as 'the King's Dragooners', men of Usher's Regiment, commanded by their Lieutenant Colonel Henry Washington, worked their way forward and engaged Ballard's 300 musketeers in a bitter fire fight, first along the enfilading hedge and then frontally assaulting the one which crossed the field; often firing at point blank range and having to hack or force their way through the winter branches and briars.[16]

In the seventeenth-century hedges were not the lines of neatly clipped, low bushes that we see today. Where they existed, they formed essential elements of the agrarian landscape, standing as tall, thick animal barriers that had been methodically layered and, at intervals, interlaced with fruit-bearing brambles. Some, especially those marking the Radway fields or surrounding the barns, may have been kept cropped by grazing or deliberate pruning and were perhaps somewhat smaller than the one clearly visible by the Royalist from the top of Edgehill. There were usually gaps to allow passage and these would be gated with stout branches that were easily opened, but would act as a restricting defile for a moving line of troopers. If riders did not use such gaps, traversing a hedge was not simply a case of pushing through a line of bushes but scrambling over a snagging, tearing, stoutly constructed, and often prickly, wall. It is to their great credit that many of the Royalist troopers jumped the hedges that they came up against but, it has to be said, probably quite a few did not.

Usher's three troops of Royalist dragoons were probably not armed with carbines. The Royalist ordnance accounts state that the artillery train carried match for the dragoons which appears to indicate that, like the Foot, they carried matchlocks. This meant that both they and the weapons of the Parliamentarian musketeers had the same range but, their ability to fight spread out into open order would quickly have placed the dragoons at an advantage during the opening clashes and gone some way towards negating their numerical inferiority. In the event, Washington's men were successful in clearing the Parliamentarian skirmishers. The Official Royalist Account subsequently stated that 'they very well performed', and we may hazard a guess as to why.[17] Lining that right-angled collection of hedges resulted in the left flank of the Parliamentary line being directly in front of the enemy – Ballard's commanded musketeers were outflanked from the very start of the engagement. It would be logical for Washington to use one troop to work up the length of the main hedgeline, front and back, while two troops remained in the open, pinning the cross hedges, only advancing when their right flank was secure. Alternatively, one troop could have been used to right-hook the position thereby taking Ballard's men in the rear. Once the main hedgeline had been cleared, the Royalists could then turn the Parliamentarian left. As regimental musketeers, Ballard's were trained to operate according to the drill book as a standard body, eight deep rotating their ranks and reloading out of the firing line while their colleagues continued to shoot. Finding themselves in a situation where they were expected to hold an outflanked position, in an unusual deployment, with nobody behind them, against albeit rudi-mentarily trained soldiers operating as skirmish troops, one can understand why the Parliamentarians lost this unequal contest.

However, this Royalist success was not without loss. Captain Gawdye, one of the regiment's officers, was shot twice in the thigh and wounded so badly that he gave up his commission shortly afterwards.[18] The men that they had driven off streamed back, away from their hedges, most heading for the safety Kineton but others returning to the shelter of their parent regiments who were far back over to their right rear. Some perhaps pushed their way through the brigades of Horse and other commanded parties of musketeers standing between them and their colours.

On the opposite wing of the army, on the south flank, a similar story unfolded. Sir Arthur Aston lead the attack of two Royalist dragoon regiments, Grey's and Duncombe's, against two of Parliament's dragoon regiments, those of Browne and Wardlawe. This time the attack was made over ditches and through briars and brush-wood. At first, the men waiting among the obstacles would probably have felt quietly confident, watching their opposite numbers ride up, dismount and struggle towards them, having to undertake apparently hard, wet and cold work. The numbers involved were unequal, about two to one in favour of the Parliamentarians, who perhaps also had much better, if shorter ranged, weapons. Initially it seemed that the attack came to halt and was forced to retire but a renewed effort was made, possibly in conjunction with some of Wilmot's Horse encircling the flank of the whole position. It would appear that an early version of the later infantry tactic of fire and movement enabled the Royalist troops to take the ground and, despite Browne and Wardlawe having held defensive terrain, the Royalist troops took the upper hand and forced their enemies to withdraw. In Clarendon's dramatic imagery, 'Sir Arthur Aston, with great courage and dexterity, beat off those musketeers with his dragoons; and then the right wing of their Horse was as easily routed and dispersed as their left, and those followed the chase as furiously as the other'.[19]

The Parliamentarians fled, their route apparently taking them back west to Kineton where they arrived, not only before the pursuing Horse that was chasing them, but also before Rupert's men who were coincidentally chasing Ramsey's fleeing troopers as discussed in the following chapter. Captain Edward Kightley, a Parliamentary troop

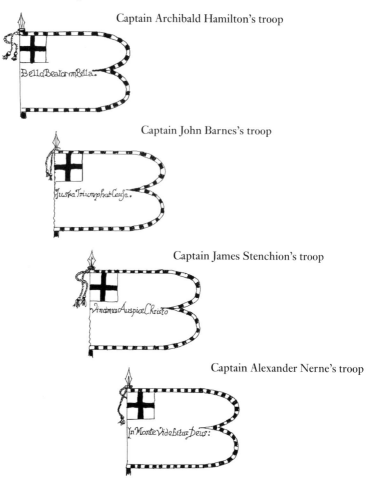

Captain Archibald Hamilton's troop

Captain John Barnes's troop

Captain James Stenchion's troop

Captain Alexander Nerne's troop

Dragoon guidons carried by Colonel James Wardlawe's Regiment of Dragoons at Edgehill (blue with gold lettering).

commander who lost his own waggon and baggage in the confusion, was of the belief that 'our own foote and Dragooners were the greatest Pillagers' of their own baggage train.[20]

The casualty figures may afford an interesting aside on this latter incident. It is likely that the pillagers were from Wardlawe's as they appear not to have suffered as much as Browne's. Could it be that, after being driven out of their cover by the Royalist dragoons, Wardlawe's horses were nearer to the front than Browne's and were able to reach them before Wilmot's attack arrived while Browne's paid the penalty of all dismounted troops caught by enemy Horse?

The artillery duel may have gone in favour of Parliament's army, but the opening fight between opposing skirmishers had definitely been won by the Royalists. The Parliamentarian guns were still able to bring their fire to bear on any advancing troops but the men assigned to disrupt attacks had gone, and so too had the flank guards. Essex's position was now worryingly exposed.

... the left Wing of our Horse ... was suddainly put to a flight. Bifield

Although rallying and responding to the new situation would have taken some time, Usher's and Aston's men probably soon became more than a nuisance. The Parliamentarian Horse on both flanks witnessed their own advance guard and flank cover break and flee, and would have had no orders to return fire at the enemy dragoons who were beginning to shoot at them. They would have felt exposed if not decidedly uneasy; especially those on the end of the line who would have been more aware of any outflanking manoeuvre and very wary of any enemy troops working to get behind them. Even more unsettling was the curious incidence of a defection in the field.

From Ramsey's wing of Horse on the Parliamentary army's left flank one officer, Quartermaster John van der Gerish, braving Washington's fire, cantered forward directly towards Prince Rupert and, as we learn from Rupert's own diary, removed his scarf and not only changed sides but relayed information that his whole troop from Waller's Regiment of Horse, under the command of the ironically named Sir Faithfull Fortesque, was intending to do the same! He told Rupert that Fortesque would signal his men's changing allegiance by firing his pistol into the ground. Rupert sent this news to his own troop commanders to avoid confusion, but his diary records that the time was too short for an appropriate message to reach either Byron's Regiment or Sir William Killigrew's Troop.

Rupert's front line, from right to left, consisted of twenty-one troops forming the King's Lifeguard, the Prince of Wales's Regiment, Prince Rupert's and, lastly, Prince Maurice's Regiments.[1] In the second line stood six troops of Sir John Byron's Regiment. Lord Bernard Stuart, who commanded the 300-strong King's Lifeguard of Horse, requested and was granted the place of honour, the extreme right of the front line and, although a grand heroic gesture, this effectively stripped the Royalist army of a dedicated cavalry reserve. Both wings had their second line to reinforce them if pressed, which could be repositioned to counter any unforeseen problem or to exploit situations if the opportunities presented themselves. There was practically nothing remaining in reserve for emergencies except the King's personal guard of fifty gentlemen, too small a force to be effective in all but a last ditch defence of the King's Majesty. De Gomme shows Killigrew's Troop of the Lifeguard of Horse and Legge's Firelocks with the King on Bullet Hill, but the Firelocks were there to protect the guns. Sir William Killigrew may have begun the battle with his sovereign but, as the momentum of the

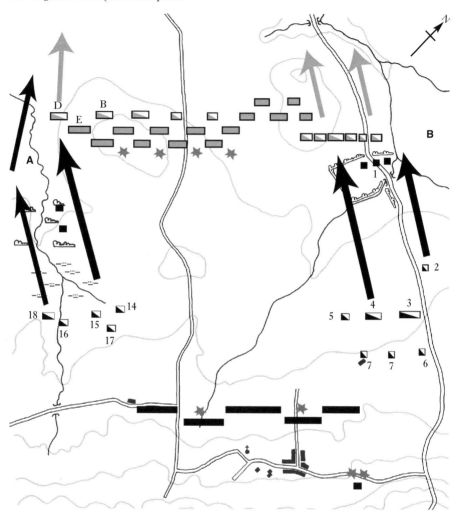

The Royalist Horse attacks. Balfour withdraws the front line of his Horse to the cover of the Parliamentarian Foot. Rupert on the Royalist right and Wilmot on the left move forward to attack. Rupert charges into Ramsey and after a bitter struggle breaks them. At **A** *Wilmot's command veers left, and crashes into and sweeps away Fielding's regiment and Fairfax's Foot while its extreme left hooks Essex's flank and rides into his rear. At* **B** *Ramsey's Horse fires, fights then breaks, scattering in all directions.*

14 Carnarvon	B Balfour	1 Royalist dragoons occupy hedge
15 Grandison	C The Lord General	2 Lifeguard (Stuart)
16 Wilmot	D Fielding	3 The Prince of Wales
17 Aston	E Fairfax	4 Prince Rupert
18 Digby		5 Prince Maurice
19 Royalist dragoons occupy bushes		6 Lifeguard (Killigrew)
		7 Byron

action increased, he seems to have allowed his troop to become embroiled in Rupert's attack.[2]

It is worth exploring why such a decision to commit the Lifeguard was taken. The answer comes from Sir Philip Warwick who rode with them:

> for a vanity possest that Troop, (upon a little provocation, or for a word of distaste the day before, or being called, The Troop of Show) to desire this honour of being engaged in the first charge: and I had the honour to be one of the number … when we valued the estates of the whole troop, we reckoned there was 100,000 £ per ann. in that Body, staked that day in that engagement against men of very disproportionable quality.[3]

Here we see the curiously combined inherent strength and weakness of the Royalist cavalry – such overweening arrogance was a great boost to morale but it was too personal to permit clear judgement and receptiveness to orders. Rupert's men may have had trouble restraining their horses but the Prince would have had greater difficulty in restraining their riders.

The attack of the Royalist Horse was then set in motion. Bulstrode, serving with the Earl of Northampton's Troop in the Prince of Wales Regiment, tells us that Rupert personally delivered orders that they were 'to march as close as possible, keeping their Ranks with Sword in Hand, to receive the Enemy's Shot without firing Carbin or Pistol, till we broke in amongst the Enemy'.[4]

There is some debate about the decision or instruction to advance. Rupert's diary says they were ordered to march 'when ye Canon went off' but whether this was geared to the opening bombardment or to a signal from a specific gun or group of guns, we cannot tell.[5] Rupert certainly did not move until Washington had cleared the hedges which rules out the latter advancing during the bombardment phase. Perhaps it was the news of the intended defection that prompted Rupert, or even a six-gun battery signal as suggested by Peter Young.[6] It would appear that the Royalist heavy guns also fired at a pre-arranged time as an agreed signal for a general advance. This may have entailed the guns firing in unison as opposed to sequentially down the line. Whatever the instigation, on Rupert's command, probably relayed by trumpet, the whole of the right wing moved forward in ranks of three files. However, it is hard to believe that being composed of horses unaccustomed to the sounds of battle this forward movement had nothing to do with the tremendous noise the six-gun battery made. From James II's account we get the full picture: 'the Royalists march'd up with all the gallantry and resolution imaginable… while they advanced the Enemy's cannon continually played upon them as did the small Divisions of their Foot… neither of which did in the least discompose them so much as to mend their pace'.[7] This is the slow march advance under fire of disciplined troops, keeping abreast and filling gaps in the ranks torn by cannon balls and musket shot. It was also a testimony to the skill of the horsemen because controlling horses with that degree of, never-before heard, noise behind them would have been very difficult.

Awaiting them stood Ramsey's Horse, bodies of Holles's commanded musketeers and several guns. Both the formations of Horse and Foot were deep, in order to maintain steady rate of fire by successive ranks. Consequently their frontages were narrowed to the width of only nine troopers or six musketeers. As we have already seen, having

The 'Golden Cavalier'
monument of Edward St John,.
a troop commander in Byron's
regiment at Edgehill, in
Lydiard Tregoze Church, near
Swindon.

St John's troop of Horse, from
the base of the monument; the
only known example of a
contemporary depiction of a
Civil War troop of horse.

perceived the build-up of Rupert's wing opposite him, Ramsey was 'inforced to draw out our Left Wing'.[8] He had sufficient time for this manoeuvre, but the effect was to spread the line and weaken the ability to stem Rupert's attack.

The Official Parliamentary Account states that Ramsey had twenty-four troops of Horse but, unfortunately, we cannot determine all of their names or their affiliations. Thus far we have identified a considerable number of named troops known to have fought at Edgehill but, as yet, many of these remain unaffiliated. We believe that there may well have been more than twenty-four troops on Parliament's left but we cannot yet be certain. We do know that they tried to stop the onslaught with their firearms. Both mounted and foot soldiers poured fire into the enemy with their carbines and muskets, while the gunners working feverishly with worm, sponge, ladle and rammer loaded with single ball and whatever close-range case shot they had to hand. Lord Bernard Stuart, commanding the King's Lifeguard, later related in a letter how the Parliamentarians stood still, making the Royalists come to them, forcing their enemy to approach to within close range of the guns and, further, firing their pieces as often as time and efficiency would allow. Fortunately for the Royalists the gunners' accuracy seemed less than efficient, for, when the horsemen 'came within Canon Shot of the Enemy, they discharged at us three Pieces of Cannon from their left Wing… which Cannon mounted over our Troops without doing any Hurt, except that their second shot killed a Quarter-Master in the Rear of the Duke of York's Troop'.[9] The gunners were firing high, most probably, in their haste, failing to depress their barrels as the distance closed or hammer in their quoins as far as possible at point-blank range. Stuart also tells us about the ground the advance went over, 'we were fain to charge them uphill and leap over some 5 or 6 hedges and ditches'.[10] Although, as we have seen, he was probably exaggerating, formed cavalry become very disordered over this type of terrain, and even though many of those riding would have been expert horsemen, quite used to jumping while hunting, to go into action like this would have been yet another major problem with which to contend.

Fortesque's dramatic defection supposedly occurred during a lull in this prolonged firing. His troop advanced from the Parliamentarian line and trotted towards the on-coming Royalist troopers, whereupon Sir Faithfull did as he had promised and, upon his firing his pistol into the ground, the men turned about and joined the attack upon their erstwhile comrades. Several it would seem did not take the time to remove their tawny scarves which denoted their allegiance to Essex's army.

The pace of the attack increased. The response from the Parliamentarian Horse was almost immediate. Standing their ground they presented their weapons and fired. Fire now came from all along Ramsey's line as 'they gave fire with their cannon lined amongst their horse, dragoneers, carbines and pistols, but finding they did nothing dismay the King's horse and that they came more roundly to them'. Meanwhile, another trumpet had, presumably, unleashed the final order to fall-on.[11]

This charge must have rolled forward, going into the 'good round trot' or canter. Cannon balls would undoubtedly have been unleashed at them as they advanced and some must have fallen. Indeed not every Royalist trooper would have been an exper-ienced hunting gentleman and several may well have fallen off, particularly as a result of the tumultuous noise frightening their mounts or the obstacles they may have met. The little stream, or Radway brook, which was definitely there, poses a problem in that none of those who charged mention it. Its meandering path would have obliquely cut

Radway brook, sometimes called Ramsey's stream because he had this brook to his front and Rupert's wing of Horse must have crossed this obstacle somewhere along its length.

the line of troops and caused some disruption as it remains a significant obstacle to riders to this day. In September the stream would have been in low flow but, by the end of October, there had been a sustained period of bad weather and the stream would have been full and the surrounding ground may well have been extremely boggy making it, at the very least, a feature likely to cause considerable disorder to advancing cavalry. Later, towards the end of the day, it was sufficient to halt the progress of the battle when it formed a protective ditch behind which the King's retiring infantry reformed their line to make a stand. However, during Rupert's charge, the whole of the right wing seems to have taken this stream and then spurred on up the slope towards the waiting dense ranks of musketeers and carbine-armed troopers.

The old tactical convention of using Horse as mobile firing platforms, which had been highly successful on the Continent, was about to be proven to have become outdated and of little value in the face of determined, charging horse. As previously shown, it is probable that Rupert's cavalry at Edgehill did not go in at the full gallop. Although several individuals might well have done so, the general practice during a charge was to engage the enemy at a pace somewhere approaching a canter. It was believed that this would maximize the full effect of a concentrated moving mass, especially upon a stationary enemy. Although the final advance into contact was fast for the period, it had also to allow the ranks disordered by fire and obstacles to regroup and reform on the move. Reordering an entire troop on the move was, more than likely, out of the question.

Seeing this wave of men advancing towards them, the majority of Ramsey's troops fired too soon. Ramsey's *Vindication* records that the men fired their 'long peeces afarre of and without distance', that is to say that they fired at a target that lay beyond the effective range of their carbines. The *London Newsletter* quotes forty yards![12] Some troops would have drawn pistols and even trotted forward *en bloc* to fire, but even these seem to have fired too soon or their shot had little effect. It was a similar tale with the interlarded muskets. If the Horse had opened up with their carbines one could expect the men armed with the longer range muskets to have added their shot to the barrage. The attackers rode through it. The oncoming Royalists must now have seemed unstoppable and some individuals broke and fled. Nathaniel Fiennes alleges that a Captain Robert Vivers of Goodwin's Regiment was the first man to run. The Rev. Marshall recorded that 'our left wing, upon the second firing, fled basely'.[13]

It is interesting to note his mention of a second firing. Presumably that portion of the line, be they Horse or interlarded Foot, had time to fire and retire thereby allowing the second rank to fire before the Royalist Horse was too close to be stopped. Bulstrode, who charged with Rupert, reported that 'Prince Rupert led our right Wing so furiously, that, after a small Resistance, we forced their left Wing and were Masters of their Cannon'.[14] Once the break had started it was very difficult, almost impossible, to stop.

Ramsey's men had seen their covering musketeers beaten and fleeing to the rear, their flank had been uncovered and they had endured Washington's flanking fire. They then witnessed this steady, rolling advance performed by the men who had beaten them at Powick Bridge, led as then by a known battlefield champion. Very few of them had much experience, their training had been minimal and here they were facing the best mounted troops in the land, whose standards included those of the King's own Lifeguard. 'There was not the same quality of courage in the horse'.[15] They had watched them advance through their cannons' fire and over hedgerows which would have stopped other troops. They had seen them ignore the supporting fire of their own interspersed musketeers whose role it was to stop them and they had witnessed a troop of their own men deserting to this same enemy. Now, without bothering with the accustomed rein-in to deliver shot, the Royalist Horse continued to advance.

James II relates how, as the Royalist troops spurred into contact, 'they came up close to the Enemy's Cavalry, which after having spent their first fire, immediately turn'd their backs'.[16] However, before we add our account to the pantheon of popular images that show the Parliamentarian Horse firing and fleeing, we ought to examine the incident more closely. The Official Royalist Account claims that 'the Charge began between the 2 Wings of Horse; those of the Rebels not standing our Charge a quarter of an hour'.[17] Whether this implies that both Royalist wings charged, or that Rupert's and Parliament's Horse charged each other, is unclear but what is stated is that it was not the rollover generally accepted. It would appear Ramsey's men did fight, and they fought for nearly fifteen minutes. This was not the instant dissolve of an entire wing as described by previous writers. Twenty-four troops amounted to almost 1,500 men and it is most unlikely that they would all have panicked. Neither would they all have lost their nerve at the same time or even have been hit by the Royal Horse at the same time. In some places the shot must have knocked riders and horses over who, in turn, brought down the horses following behind. Some charging men must have veered away from the noise and flying lead. The charge could not have gone in 'Hollywood style' and the break would have been neither universal nor immediate. Over-zealous enthusiasm for the romance surrounding Prince Rupert appears to have coloured many people's judgement and done a great disservice to those brave men under Ramsey's command who, against the odds and using outdated tactics, still did their duty. We cannot tell how many sat and traded blows but pockets of resistance appear to have given a good account of themselves. Ten to fifteen minutes is a long time to spend in melee. From the hospital casualty figures it can be seen that Waller's Regiment sustained proportionately more injuries than the other commands on Ramsey's wing, but whether this was because they fought on or were unlucky during the pursuit we cannot determine. If they were among those who fought, they must have, eventually, been overwhelmed or realised the situation was hopeless and, once they had been forced back, the affair turned into a rout. It is also said that they abandoned the musketeers – can we deduce from this then that these foot soldiers also fought a protracted melee before breaking? Routs spread, they do not occur as spontaneously as some historians propound for dramatic effect and, even then, the fighting continues.

The combat took its toll. On the Royalist side, the Lord d'Aubigny was mortally wounded, Lord Taafe wounded in the mouth and Dr John Nurse killed; for Parliament Lord St John was mortally wounded before being overpowered and taken and Waller had his horse killed under him. However, all Parliamentarian accounts generally agree that 'the left Wing of our Horse being charged by the King's right Wing, was suddainly put to a flight'.[18] Despite desperate fighting by individuals and odd troops, within fifteen minutes the whole of Ramsey's left wing of horse, commanded muskets and artillery collapsed, dispersed and ran.

The Royalists pursued them. The men on foot must have been easy prey to the slashing swords, if they were not ridden down – a painful and much-bruising experience but preferable to a sword cut. One is also tempted to speculate whether those among them who believed that horses would not tread on fallen men actually put the theory to practical test although, it should be noted that, unseated jockeys tell tales of sustaining severe wounds as a result of flying hooves. Rupert himself appears to have led this pursuit that, later, Bulstrode deemed to have been an error of judgement for which he laid the blame squarely at Rupert's door, 'the Prince being extreamly eager of this Advantage (which he knew better how to take than to keep) was not content with their Canon and keeping their Ground, but eagerly pursued the enemy, who fled on the other side of Keinton towards Warwick'.[19] His tactical criticism did not, however, prevent his own Prince of Wales's Regiment from joining in the chase.

The manner in which the whole of Rupert's cavalry joined in the pursuit has been a favourite talking point for military historians over the years. Burne and Young were both great defenders of Rupert, explaining the difficulties of restraining cavalry to a readership that they assumed had no conception of the problems of cavalry leadership.[20] Rupert can be criticized for charging off the field, but it must be noted that he did nothing that the average cavalry commander would not normally undertake. It was the way things were done in that age. The intention was to disperse the foe and chase them, thereby preventing them from taking any further action in the battle. Indeed, if pursuing cavalry troops could be physically rallied, it would normally be for the purpose of preventing the arrival of additional enemy reinforcements, to mount an organized pursuit or to secure the enemy's baggage, horse lines and artillery carriage park. The very fact that the enemy knew that their Horse had been beaten would undermine their morale, have them constantly watching their rear and then, convinced that they had lost their lines of communication as well as their war chest, they would throw down their arms and capitulate. Well, that was the theory.

To drive off the enemy horse, reform and switch attention elsewhere was unusual and it took the lesson of Edgehill to demonstrate the value of reforming and returning as later achieved by both Wilmot and Byron at the battle of Roundway Down in July 1643. Rupert should be criticized however for assuming the men understood the role of the second line. Although his diary berates them for not doing what was, with hindsight, required, there is no record of him either giving orders to hold and await developments or explaining what action his troopers should take in the event of a rollover victory. Clarendon states that Byron's six troops 'seeing none of the enemy's horse left, thought there was nothing more to be done but to pursue those that fled'.[21] They joined the chase too, which effectively robbed the army of half of its remaining cavalry reserve. To be fair Clarendon adds that they 'could not be contained by their commander, but with spurs and loose reins followed the chase' but it is likely these officers were using their own initiative as all of Rupert's other orders had been 'punctually observed'![22] Probably spurred on by the sound of the big guns behind them, while those engaged in the initial contact were slowed down, Byron's second line seems to have caught up with Rupert's first line. The horse is a herd animal and there would be a natural tendency for them to run together in times of danger. This is useful in helping to understand why Byron's command too went off; they had all become inseparably mixed together, both Royalist and Parliamentarian, and before condemning either Byron's or Ramsey's men for riding off, it is worth considering that once the herd of horses began to run, many troopers on both sides had little choice but to remain with them.

Many of the dispersed Parliamentary soldiers would have fled directly to their rear, sweeping away remnants of any supporting troops still in position after Ramsey had extended his line, and turning the whole of that wing of the battlefield into a mass of fleeing and pursuing men. Fleeing men tend to make for the nearest haven of safety, in this instance the gardens and houses of Kineton. The majority fled in that direction with the fleeing Horse naturally outstripping the Foot. However, many saw the infantry regiments standing to their right rear as bastions of safety, especially those on foot, for whom the buildings of Kineton were just too far to run pursued by speeding Horse intent upon cutting them down. Of the running Foot, those of the 300 from Ballard's Regiment would probably have made for the gap between the first and second infantry lines in order to reach their friends, while whatever remained of the 400 musketeers taken from Denzil Holles's Regiment would have seen their own regiment, detached as it was on the extreme left of the infantry, as their nearest objective. Wherever the retreating troops were heading, the effect was to produce a mass of running horses and men who bore down on Holles's exposed Regiment. Holles himself stood firm in the face of this onslaught and 'did what possibly he could do to make them stand; and at least prevailed with three Troops to wheel a little about, and rally'.[23] Unfortunately this was not sufficient. Afraid to close ranks and forbid their frightened comrades to enter, Holles's pikemen stood in confusion while their own troopers broke through them and their musketeers crowded back on to them. Shaken and disordered as they must have been, these Londoners did not run.

Ramsey had tried to rally his troopers but the Horse continued their flight sweeping him away with them 'himself being engaged among the Squadrons of the Enemies Horse, was carried violently out of the Field'.[24] He estimated that he was personally carried along 'two miles at least' and only broke free by jumping his horse over a ditch where his pursuers were loathe to follow. There were naturally many incidents during the pursuit that are recalled in detail by those who featured in and later recounted them. We owe the existence of Bulstrode's detailed account to his own Colonel, Sir Thomas Byron, who shot dead a Parliamentarian trooper who, having first struck Bulstrode on the head, was about to deliver a second, killing blow with a poleaxe. Fate also put a cruel twist to the Fortescue tale. The men of the second line, including Byron's and Killigrew's, who, it may be remembered, had not been informed of the pending defection, seeing several riding among their first line wearing tawny scarves (which they had been negligent or thrifty about casting away) cut them down from behind.

Rupert must be granted some compassion regarding the difficulty of controlling Horse. Over the centuries, English cavalry has enjoyed something of a reputation for always getting carried away and continuing to gallop at anything until their horses were exhausted. Various writers have attributed this to a fox-hunting mentality; even Wellington had his fair share of problems. Rupert's men were exceptionally brave but many were inexperienced. They had not been under arms for more than a few months. Many had enjoyed a runaway success at Powick Bridge and were keen to emulate that victory. Their desire to strike down a rebel for their king must have been somewhat akin to young RAF pilots in 1940 'bagging a Hun'. In modern parlance they were too 'gung ho' and needed tighter control and channelling of that useful spirit. Add to this the fearful noise of the guns and one can appreciate their trials in attempting to persuade a horse, no matter its breeding and bravery, to move towards that terrifying sound. Undoubtedly, Rupert should have performed better but there is some justification for claiming that Byron was the villain of the piece. His decision to join the pursuit was a disaster for the Royalist cause. Leaving aside any sympathy for his desire to participate,

Cornets at Edgehill: the north flank. The Kings Lifeguard, Sir Charles Gerard's, Fortesque's, Ingoldsby's, Waller's and Urry's.

Cornets at Edgehill: the south flank. The Earl of Carnarvon's, Dowett's, Fiennes's, Fielding's, Haselrig's and Luke's.

Cornets at Edgehill: the centre. Essex's, Bedford's, both Balfours' (although the son was with Ramsey), Gunter's and Brooke's.

Top: The armies on the field. A computer-generated conjecture of the armies in position on the field at Edgehill. We have removed the ammunition sheds, lots of the hedges and superimposed 1/300 scale models, but due to problems of scale, we have had to resort to representation.

Below: Edgehill from Bullet Hill. One of the finest views of an English battlefield.

Officers at Edgehill. A Royalist field officer by his red scarf and modish Dutch garb, while the ensign has more of an old-fashioned country look .

Soldiers at Edgehill. A Parliamentarian pikeman and Royalist musketeer.

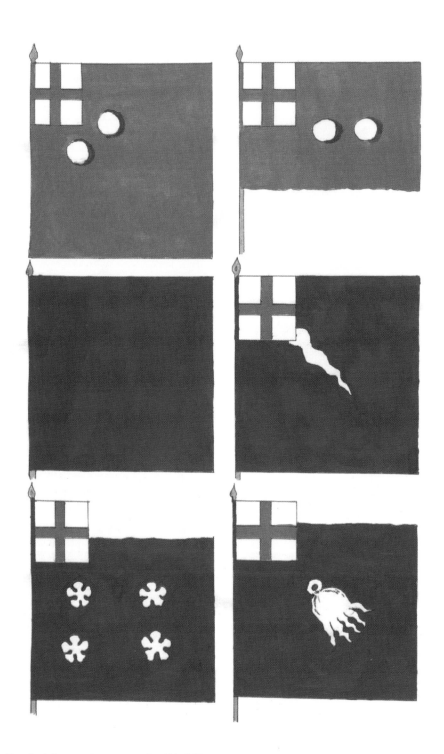

Royalist infantry colours captured at Edgehill.

and also acknowledging that it was unlikely that he could prevent his command's continued involvement in the action once the two lines had coalesced, he failed in his duty as commander of the second line. That being said, he was under the direct orders of Rupert who should have issued him specific instructions, ensured that he was positioned far enough to the rear so that his troops could not easily catch up, and generally overseen his performance. The brave, romantic Prince has been indulged for far too long, the responsibility was Rupert's and he apparently ignored it!

The route for both the pursued and their pursuers was funnelled by the river Dene which grew progressively wider and deeper as it flowed westward, fed by a number of tributaries. It crossed the Banbury Road several times before skirting Kineton to the south. These were fords and places that parts of Essex's baggage would have adopted as battlefield outposts. Unofficial followers were the bane and the lifeblood of period armies and it is not unreasonable to see these fords as places that were sufficiently far forward to be near the action, suitably accessible for wheeled transport and provided with the basic necessity of fresh water. The modern Edgehill authority, Bob Leedham, maintains that these fords were blocked by civilians, women anxious to be near their menfolk, ammunition carts and even locals out sight-seeing.[25] With the river Dene hemming in their flight on their right, and their escape exit fords blocked, the retreating troops would have been channelled towards the south and pushed on to the major Kineton Ford. This is the site that the archaeologists Oliver and Pollard's recent discoveries indicate may have been a horse encampment during the previous night and this finding is supported by the Rev. Miller's statement that skeletons were found in the region of the ford when the 'new road' was put through in the 1880s.[26]

The majority of the routing horsemen and their pursuers reached Kineton and beyond, some even went as far as Chadshunt.[27] The pursuers must have been hacking at their victims all the way but, when they got into the town, they discovered a new sport, the Parliamentarian baggage train. Allowing the terrified Parliamentary horsemen to ride on, many of the Royalist soldiers fell to despoiling coaches, carriages, carts and wagons. This was not securing the enemy's material of war as advocated by the military theorists of the day but plunder and booty-taking. Young asserts that it would be absurd to believe that the Earls of Dover and of Denbigh as well as Lord Capel and all of the Lifeguard would sink to pillaging but great estates have to be maintained. The valiant horsemen who had achieved such a splendid victory now forgot their comrades who were still fighting and fell to lining their pockets. The carriages of Essex's senior officers fell into their rapacious hands. Some sources state that Essex's own coach was also ransacked, along with part of his war chest and his privy purse containing £2,000, although others recount that his baggage was not taken until Tuesday morning.[28] These carriages, effectively mobile homes, were stripped of military funds, personal cash and property. Captain Kightley was later to complain that his wagon and his money had been stolen. The looters even appropriated the horses.[29] Everything was fair game and many gentlemen troopers literally took their fortune in their own hands. Rupert himself had stopped before reaching Kineton and tried to rally his dispersed command. He had been partially successful in gathering three troops to him, but little could be seen of the overall situation and even less done to affect anything at that moment, and any such action took time. The pursuit petered out in a rampage of self-interest. This allowed a surprising number of Parliamentarian troopers to escape with their horses and arms and failed to bar the way or even notice the arrival of Essex's reinforcements.

However, some of Rupert's men did encounter them. Davies states 'their headlong career was only checked when they met a parliamentary force under John Hampden hastening to the battlefield' although he does not quote his source for this statement.[30] Nathaniel Fiennes's account states that his brother 'gave them a stop, discharging five pieces of Cannon against them, he slew some of them'.[31]

Late for the start of the action, Captain John Fiennes, who had been quartered in Evesham, brought his troop near enough to the field in time to witness the collapse of the left wing. Some distance west of Kineton, he appears to have been partially successful in attempting to halt the rout of Vivers's Troop from Goodwin's Regiment while, fortunately, managing to persuade his own men to stand fast. Having gathered together a significant number of soldiers, including the newly arrived troops of Cromwell and Kightley, he deployed his force on a hill and covered the town. This scenario was recorded by his brother, Nathaniel, who went on to tell how John subsequently took his polyglot command towards Kineton where, in the face of a Royalist attack, 'he made a stand'.[32] John Fiennes had personal knowledge of the Kineton area as he had been there in September however, unable to influence matters further, he then deployed his scouts in an attempt to discover the whereabouts of Hamden's reinforcements and, having gained that intelligence, set off with the troops under his command to join the approaching formation in their march to Kineton.[33] Had he been rash, he would have charged into the town and into action, and likely lost those he had steadied and effected nothing save a few minutes' distraction from the pillaging. Instead, he bided his time, held his men from flight and provided a formed body to cover further routed men as they fled the field. This was neither a daring nor heroic deed, but his formed unit must have discouraged the Royalists from venturing westwards out of Kineton and saved many Parliamentarian lives. He also provided a rallying point for other late arrivals and covered the approach of Essex's reinforcements before joining them. The north flank had been a disaster for the army of Parliament, but the damage had been stopped and the effect of the rout contained.

Chapter Nine
The South

I could never speak with any of our Army, that either saw any such number of horse, or could tell what they did, unless they went directly to Keynton to plunder the Carriages without charging our Army at all. Captain N Fiennes.

Some writers suggest that, whereas Ramsey had drawn up on the north flank with some twenty-four troops, on the south flank, Colonel Fielding, with the command of his own regiment of six troops, awaited the Royalist onslaught alone. This is somewhat implausible and contrary to everything eyewitness Nathaniel Fiennes relates.[1] It is also extremely unlikely that Essex's battle plan would allow such an imbalance and we have already argued the illogicality of such officers of senior rank as Bedford and Balfour, being passed over for command of the right wing. If we accept that Balfour was in command of that section of the Parliamentary army, then it becomes even more likely that both the Lord General's and Balfour's Regiments of Horse were allocated to and deployed as part of that wing but, when the Horse were dispersed to quarters, several troops had not yet arrived leaving the right far weaker than Essex believed it to be.

It was further weakened by Essex's decision to form a cavalry reserve under Bedford from his heavy cavalry troops. By withdrawing his own troop of Lifeguard and Balfour's troop of cuirassiers, both heavy cavalry, and joining them to Bedford's troop of cuirassiers and Draper's harquebusiers, he formed a substantial body of well-armoured shock troops capable of plugging any gap or making a decisive strike, albeit at the unintended expense of Balfour's command. Students of history soon learn that contemporary writers note what is unusual and Bulstrode's Royalist account refers to some of Essex's Horse being behind his Foot, but does not tell us the size of the Horse units deployed there.[2] Nor does the account tell us that the right wing was almost bare of Horse, which it certainly would have been if the whole of the Lord General's and Balfour's Regiments had been allocated to the reserve. This would have been very unusual and we would maintain that this is not mentioned by anyone because it was not the case. The bringing together of all the cuirassier troops and supplementing them with yet a further unit of heavy cavalry to make up numbers is a sound thing to do. Richard Holmes argues that this was good thinking by Essex who understood the nature of his cavalry and the essential differences, both tactical and movement, between cuirassiers and the usual, lighter, Horse.[3]

His right wing, however, was not held as strongly as Essex would have wished or intended. We estimate that Fielding had his full six troops present; the Lord General's Regiment also had six, although missing at least Cromwell's and probably Kightley's troops. Balfour's Regiment also had six, but was missing at least one, that of John

Essex's right flank is now covered by the Oaks Plantation. The height of the rising ground can be seen in the bottom left corner. Grave Ground coppice is visible on the left, and Miller's hedge ran from the site of Battle Farm, approximately where the single white building in the centre is situated, to the left.

Fiennes. Although the usual establishment of a regiment of Horse was six troops, those of senior general officers could have more, and frequently their personal lifeguards were also double-sized troops. By deploying these two larger regiments on his right Essex, on paper, was attempting to compensate for the presence of only three regiments with Balfour compared to a theoretical five or six with Ramsey. It may be that, in theory, Willoughby's were also part of Balfour's wing, although the arrangement favouring Ramsey may also have been part of a deliberate bolstering of the left in order to contain the expected onslaught from Rupert. Essex added further protection to his right flank by sending there both of his available dragoon regiments; those of Browne and Wardlawe, who were present in substantial numbers in the expectation that they would perform their fire and skirmish role among the gorse and briars. This allocation gave Balfour eighteen troops of Horse plus twelve troops of dragoons, thirty in total.[4] Nevertheless, Essex appreciated that a weakness existed and, consequently, ordered that 'the best of our field pieces were planted upon our right wing'.[5] The terrain too was all in Balfour's favour. The extreme right flank rested upon another tributary of the Dene, slightly deeper than Radway brook on Ramsey's wing, but surrounded like its counter-part by boggy, broken ground which was supposedly covered with tussocks, gorse and scrub – fairly difficult for close order troops be they Horse or Foot, but natural dragoon country. Today this ground is occupied by the southern part of a small coppice known as The Oaks, but walking through it one can still find natural water courses as well as man-made ditches to facilitate drainage of what must have been, in its lower reaches, a wet part of the heath. Together, the slope and a liberal scattering of gorse form a reason-

Wilmot's ground. The trees in the background belong to the modern Oaks Plantation but you can see how the ground they stand on rises significantly. It was on those slopes that Essex anchored his right wing of Horse.

able anchor position for dragoons and, if there were a few scrubland trees and brush-wood present, they would have provided cover and a place to tether horses. However, it was the ground before them that offered the greatest advantage. It too was crossed with ditches and boggy water-courses, some small and narrow, others deep and wide and, although there may not have been hedges, some would have had bushes growing beside them while others would have been open and wet. Designers of modern National Hunt courses often use wet ditches or open water obstacles because of their inherent deterrent effect upon horses. This was most inhospitable cavalry country and far more formidable than that in front of Parliament's left flank where, as we have seen, Bernard Stuart's uphill charge was limited to several ditches, a difficult stream and one hedge.

Balfour had started the battle with a small force but was arrayed in a substantially strong position. He had infiltrated natural obstacles to his front with dragoons, and had others cover the stream on his right flank. However, both commands had been driven off by their opposite numbers and, instead of remounting and reforming as a supporting unit, they had fled in considerable confusion to the rear. Instead of a secure flank he now had Royalist dragoons beginning to work around it, just as Ramsey was encountering similar problems of his own on his left.

Opposite Balfour and waiting to move stood the fifteen troops of Lord Wilmot's front line. These were Lord Wilmot's own Regiment, Lord Grandison's and the Earl of Carnarvon's. Behind them were placed the seven troops that formed Lord Digby's Regiment and Sir Thomas Aston's, plus Grey's and Duncombe's six troops of dragoons, under the command of Sir Arthur Aston. It is interesting to note that the Royalists on this wing all appear to have owned property in the south of England. If there were to be a disaster, then they would at least be able to return home. There is some suggestion that Rupert had transferred the Earl of Northampton's Troop from Wilmot's command to his own right wing, deliberately strengthening his attack at the expense of Wilmot.

There is also some debate about Wilmot's ground and the number of hedges his men had to cross. Deploying in the area of what is today Westcote Farm he might have found himself among the fields around Radway, but these were clustered on the lower slopes of the escarpment and, as an experienced officer, he would probably have chosen the more open heath. A lot of credence has been put on Ludlow's reference to 'hedges on our right wing' but he was probably writing of the array of furze bushes that abounded on the forward slopes of the little hill.[6] We know from Clarendon that Wilmot's men did encounter hedgerows, but Miller's investigations in the nineteenth century place these as the enclosures around Little Kineton. As a result, Wilmot's attack was broken up, but not before he had driven into the rear of the Parliamentarian position.[7]

As with the advance on the Royalist right, there is debate about Wilmot's decision, or received instructions from Rupert, to commence his advance on the left. Yet again there is mention of the cannon being a signal and, yet again, we know Wilmot, like Rupert, did not move on Balfour until Aston had cleared the opposing dragoons from the interposed obstacles. Aston did not find this as easy a task as Washington did on the right, being initially 'repulsed by our dragoons without any loss to our side'.[8] They persevered and eventually caused the Parliamentarian dragoons to fall back. We presume they would have then secured their position and occupied the bushes, seeking ways to bring their fire to bear. It is interesting to note, at this juncture, a theory advanced by Bob Leedham concerning the direction of the wind. His research has revealed that the vicar at Alcester, some twenty miles from Kineton, reported that he and his congregation heard thunder that day, whereas tenant farmers at Manor Farm in Fenny Compton, only two miles from the battlefield, who were being paid by Oxford University to complete a weather journal, mentioned nothing similar. From this, Leedham deduces that, contrary to previous assumptions, the wind was more easterly than south-westerly at the start of the action. In which case Wilmot would have had no trouble hearing any signal gunfire.

In all likelihood Wilmot began his march forward at about the same time as the Prince, or perhaps slightly later having been prompted by seeing his advance if the smoke from the bombardment permitted it. His Foot advanced in ranks composed of files of three in two major lines, coming under cannon shot as they went forward. However, as previously described, his ground was far worse than on the Royalist's right wing. He would have had to pick his way forward, moving in spurts, spurring forward at obstacles and then slowing down to reform. Cannon balls occasionally ploughed into their ranks but the wet ground would have countered a lot of the bounce, and the forward positioning of Balfour's front line must have caused aiming difficulties. Although several men and horses would have fallen to the artillery, with Aston's dragoons having already cleared the way, the troopers did not have to contend with carbine fire sporadically emptying saddles.

The direction taken by Wilmot's Brigade over this difficult ground now plays a crucial role throughout the remainder of the battle. If we accept Miller's assertion that King John's Lane was not upgraded into a road until the eighteenth century then we need to look for an alternative main route down the escarpment for Wilmot's Horse. Some would have descended via that track, but it is very steep for horses even post improvement. The most likely descent would be by the main Stratford to Banbury road that runs past Sun Rising. There was plenty of time for this command to take that long loop of a route to their deployment ground on the Royalist left. Some small groups could have come down the open slope but we must think in terms of moving large numbers of men and horses effectively. Getting down the hill in penny-packets would result in the disruption of the formation previously achieved on the plateau. To move effectively without destroying their order, the Sun Rising route seems plausible. However, it would have had its drawbacks in pulling Wilmot out to the left. Several Victorian historians place his left flank on that road. Walford even sites Digby's second line well up the hill.[9] Having fought as a captain of Horse with the Dutch and served as Commissary General against the Scots, Wilmot understood mounted arm tactics and this was a tempting opportunity few cavalry commanders could resist. He would have begun his advance against Essex's right fully aware that he could engage and overlap on the outside flank, hook the position and fall upon the enemy's rear echelon while his second line turned to attack the flank of the Foot. This would be an ideal scenario but Wilmot was subsequently criticized for his actions at Edgehill in claims that stated he was ever a politician rather than a warrior. However, if this was his appreciation of the tactical situation, it would appear sound, at least to a cavalryman's eyes.

The initial target of his attack would have been Balfour's two forward Regiments, the Lord General's and his own. However, they had other problems. The Royalist Foot had begun its march and Wentworth's Brigade would have been advancing steadily towards Meldrum's, perhaps slightly overlapping them? Faced with the prospect of having to fight Wilmot and also contend with part of Wentworth's units, Balfour must have realized the situation was against him. His command was just too weak, he was so far forward of his guns that he partially masked them as well as reducing their effective arc. His Foot would need additional support if it was to stand. He may also have retained a niggling concern for the resolve of the Lord General's Regiment, for many had panicked at Powick. A decision was taken. Insofar as 'their right wing of Horse, which were not all come up, they drew that part of them which was present behind their Foot, seeing they were not strong enough to encounter with the King's left wing'.[10] At which stage this occurred we cannot be sure but it would seem that something, possibly Wilmot's advance, triggered this reaction. It might have been during the deployment phases or it could have been Aston's dragoons opening desultory fire into them from front and flank. No matter what caused it, the Lord General's and Balfour's Regiments of Horse went north, to their left, behind Meldrum's, and out of the target zone of Wilmot's charge.

We believe this coincided with Wilmot's attack veering south through a combination of factors. One is the tactical temptation already discussed; another would be their tending to shy away both from compact gorse bushes which can be high, stout and tear at horse flesh unmercifully, and from the cannon fire, now able to blast without having to carefully lay their shot. Thirdly, there was the need to avoid riding down their own dismounted dragoons and, finally, there was the lie of the land. Riding up a slope is straightforward, but in riding across a horse tends, inevitably, to moves sideways down the slope and, although it continues to move forward, the animal drifts off the original planned course. Equally, some of the land at Edgehill is what Gloucestershire farmers call 'crosswise ground', by which they mean it somehow pulls a tractor in a particular direction. Much of this type of ground is characterized by slopes that contain springs or watercourses. The author has driven on such land and spoken to horsemen who have

The breaking of Fairfax's.

experienced it. A significant portion of the slope at Hastings has this illogical effect as does this gentle hillside at Edgehill. Discounting this phenomenon, there are sufficient grounds to consider the likelihood that a significant part of Wilmot's command gradually edged away to his left and around the flank. Yet another reason for this is the very wet and boggy ground where a tributary of the Dene rises; horses do not like marshes. The idea that a substantial part of the wing failed to make contact with their enemy is borne out by Fiennes when he speaks of the numbers of troops Wilmot had in his command: 'I could never speak with any of our Army, that either saw any such number of Horse, or could tell what they did, unlesse they went directly to Keynton to plunder the Carriages without charging our Army at all'.[11] Had both Parliamentarian regiments been engaged, broken and pursued, then surely Fiennes would have mentioned it? Even if he personally escaped such a disaster, he or even Ludlow would have found an excuse for the rest of their own regiments' running. Furthermore had they run it is doubtful that Wharton, who made excuses for his own Foot having run, would have said of the officers of the Horse upon the right wing: 'they did give extraordinary service'.[12] We would not go so far as Davies to say that Wilmot 'had missed Balfour's and Stapleton's (i.e., the Lord General's) altogether'. It is likely, but we think it was more of case of both sides acting in such a way that a collision did not occur.

In any case, not all of Wilmot's troops could have made contact. There was insufficient space as the tributary of the Dene on that south side of the field would have hemmed them in. Part of his line probably went south of the water while the remainder would have swept forward, at an angle and crashed into Fielding's Regiment as it stood in the erstwhile second line. Outflanked and overwhelmed, it is likely that Fielding's troopers then gave ground and broke. Young suggests they put up less resistance than their counterparts on the north flank but offers nothing to substantiate the claim.[13] This directly contradicts Miller who maintains that he found bullets, skeletons and cannon balls in the area of Lower Westcote which lies forward of what is now the Oaks, indicating a hard fight.[14] The musket balls he describes could have come from the dragoons, as discoveries made since Miller's work indicate that the majority of dragoons carried matchlock muskets at this stage of the war, but their presence may also offer the conclusion that Sir William Fairfax's Regiment, posted on the extreme right of the line, and dropped back as part of the second line, may have become involved in this action and, without agreeing with Fiennes who says that Wilmot was driven back, it would appear that Wilmot, like Aston, was indeed initially checked. In spite of this, we know that Wilmot's troopers eventually gained the upper hand, broke Fielding's and pursued them as they fled.

There are no detailed accounts of how Wilmot gained the fight on this side of the field but, in character, it may well have progressed in much the same fashion as that which had taken place on the opposite wing. Initially Balfour had roughly the same number of troops to oppose Wilmot's front line but, by dropping two regiments behind the Foot, he effectively reduced the Horse on the right wing to six troops. If Fielding's Parliamentarians tried to remain stationary, firing their carbines and pistols before drawing swords and with the impact upon their static unit by a mobile enemy force numbering more than twice its number, it is not surprising to learn that they were overwhelmed and broken. In all probability they also suffered a deterioration in their morale having seen the front line of moved out of the way.

This collapse would have been a disaster for the dragoons who, presumably, were still making for their horses, or had recently mounted. Unfortunately, they would have been caught up in the melee and their retirement converted into flight. Wilmot would have had substantially more men than Fielding, even if many of the dragoons had managed to stay and fight. In any engagement, the outcome is influenced by the numbers that can be brought to bear. We are left to imagine a dramatic picture of a swirling mass of horsemen sweeping from the field and, as with Ramsey, Fielding was also carried away amid the close-packed ranks of his fleeing troopers.

Not all were swept away to the rear. Once again the hitherto popular conception that, when a formation breaks, every constituent part of it leaves the field has to be challenged. Men would break in all directions, in a manner reminiscent of a dramatic break of a snooker triangle, and it would seem reasonable to suspect that a number of them joined their General and his cuirassiers in the reserve.

This left-hook surge of Wilmot's seems to fit the scenario of another disaster for Parliament on this wing. Fairfax's Foot had fired, and having probably aided the checking of the Wilmot's advance and having tried to support Fielding in melee, was ridden into and broken. It too got swept way in the ensuing maelstrom. No full account of this part of the battle survives so, once again, it is necessary to piece a picture together from what fragments are known.[15] Thomas Whitney, one of Fairfax's lieutenants, procured a horse from among the large numbers having lost their riders, deserted his command and bolted from the field.[16] It was said he did not stop until he reached London! Most of Fairfax's infantry swiftly followed his lead and ran. Perhaps they ran because they were shaken by the sight of Browne's and Wardlawe's dragoons retiring followed soon afterwards by Fielding's Regiment. Perhaps they were broken through by some of Fielding's desperate troopers or even charged by Wilmot's triumphant Royalists. It was probably a combination of everything. What is certain is that they broke, that their movement was sudden and totally unexpected. Only seven of their number appear in the hospital lists, a figure that tends to support Young's idea that they did not put up much of a hand-to-hand fight.

Wilmot's second line was commanded by Lord Digby, and he too spurred forward with his command to join the chase. This was all that remained of anything approaching a Royalist cavalry reserve. Being younger and less experienced than Byron may be a partial excuse for his unsoldierly conduct, but Digby appears to have made no attempt to stop the pursuit. In fact he led it, like his superior, galloping in disorder in pursuit of a fleeing foe. What a waste. It would also appear that while the front line was being checked around the Little Kineton enclosures, possibly by a hastily organized defence formed from a combination of fleeing men, late arrivals and advance parties drawn from what has been erroneously termed Hampden's 'brigade', Digby did not use his command to support them. Neither does he appear to have followed his leader, but somehow veered towards Kineton Ford. Following Fielding's men he sped on and clattered into Little Kineton and then right, over the ford into Kineton itself, where his men enthusiastically cut down defenceless wagon drivers and civilian baggage personnel and, perhaps because of the distance travelled, arriving after Rupert's and Byron's men had had their pick of the spoils, Digby's cavaliers began burning carriages and wagons that would have been a priceless acquisition for the Royalist artillery train, had they been properly secured and removed.[17] Kightley, whose battle was mostly fought around Kineton, tells us 'the enemy killed the Waggoners, women and little boys of twelve years of age'.[18] This is corroborated by the Rev. Master Stephen Marshall who also tells of the Royalists who 'fell to plunder our Waggons and killing the servants which attended them, even unto women and children'.[19] This might be propaganda but many modern writers seem to ignore it and even Young offers no defence for this mindless behaviour. Perhaps we have here the first Civil War perpetrator of war crimes?[20]

The Parliamentarian right had been scattered, but so too had the Royalist left. Wilmot's command had been broken up into piecemeal *ad hoc* units. Wilmot himself had been checked at Little Kineton enclosures and indeed was gradually being pushed back during the time that Digby had gone off looting. There was, however, one senior officer on the Royalist left who managed to keep a command together and realized what needed to be done. The Lieutenant Colonel of Carnarvon's Regiment of Horse, Sir Charles Lucas, reined in and tried to halt the speeding general pursuit. He was already known as a hard disciplinarian whose men obeyed rather than liked him. Clarendon described him as 'a gallant man to look upon and to follow' and, by his reputation, he managed to rally about 200 troopers from across three regiments. Pre-dating Cromwell's tactical reforms and aided by three other notable personalities, Lord Grandison, one of his captains, John Smith, and Wilmot's own captain-lieutenant, Robert Walsh, he formed these men into a provisional fighting force and resolved to bring them back into the action, an manoeuvre that, as Young points out, he repeated on a grander scale two years later on Marston Moor.[21]

With most of his Horse routed, his line turned on both sides, his baggage lost, his line of communications severed, Kineton in enemy hands to his rear and parties of enemy Horse forming behind his flanks, it looked all over for Essex and it seemed that nothing worse could befall him; but the worst was to come.

Chapter Ten
The Centre – Attack

'March on boys!' Traditionally ascribed to Sir Jacob Astley.

While we are fairly certain King Charles sat with his entourage and the Gentlemen Pensioners on Bullet Hill, we cannot be certain where the Earl of Essex started his battle. He may have been with his own regiment of 'orangecoats' in Ballard's Brigade, but he also spent part of the day, which part we do not know, with his troop of Horse in the reserve. He had made the best dispositions he could with what forces he had at his disposal and had chosen his ground well, although the compromise of having Ballard's Regiment on his left flank refused may have been unsettling. Wherever he stood, Essex was in the ranks of awaiting the assault of the five brigades of the Royalists' centre unaware of the catastrophes that were about to befall both of his cavalry wings.

There is confusion concerning the orders for the Royalist infantry to advance, and it is necessary to speculate regarding the existence of prearranged timings in an age when watches were uncommon. Their synchronization was most unlikely and signals by guns could be lost in a general bombardment. The actions of staff officers, who, in an age prior to the Duke of Marlborough's reforms, functioned as field runners, were unrecorded while the observation of movement was difficult once smoke had wreathed the various formations. By whatever means his orders were transmitted, the Royalist sergeant-major general, Sir Jacob Astley, started the whole of the Royalist Foot rolling forward in a dramatic manner shortly after both wings of the Horse had been set in motion. He knelt, uttering in prayer the words that have, ever since, been adopted by English soldiers about to go into action – 'Oh Lord, Thou knowest howe busy I must be this day. If I forget Thee, do not Thou forget me'. Then, rising to his feet, he raised his sword and cried, 'March on boys![1]

A preparative roll must have sounded from the drums of each of the five brigades followed shortly by each unit stepping off in their own time to begin their advance upon the Parliamentarian line 'with a slow and steady pace and a daring resolution' and with Sir Edmund Verney, striding out in the midst of Byron's Brigade, carrying the great Banner Royal, sometimes mistakenly called the Royal Standard (see page 135 below).[2] It is likely that the Foot moved off later than the Horse because, with guns positioned to their front, it was necessary to wait until the latter had finished firing. They would not relish suffering the effect of hang-fires discharging into their rear! Once the guns had been declared unloaded, the Royalist Foot would have needed to negotiate the gun positions which, in the event, were unlikely to have been so neatly deployed as to

The Royalist Foot's starting position. This field is to left of centre of the Royal line and probably marks the position of Byron's brigade wherein floated the Banner Royal.

coincide exactly with the intervals between the infantry formations. Perhaps one or two of the lighter pieces, such as the two robinets, were dragged along towards the front but this cannot be substantiated, unless their short range fire is included in the general, but vague, comment that alluded to the advance talking place 'after some playing with the cannon on both sides'.[3]

It would have been impossible to co-ordinate the stepping off of individual regiments, let alone those of an entire brigade, although some degree of cohesion may have been achieved with the help of the drums beating a regular rhythm, their cadence swinging into the period march-pace of around seventy to the minute. There appears no evidence to suggest any attempt was made to have the men march in step although there would be a natural tendency for the body to fall in with the beat and rhythm of the drum. Covering the ground between the fighting lines was probably the soldiers' most practised manoeuvre, as arriving in front of the enemy with the ranks in order was important to the manner of fighting whether it be for 'firing taking ground', exchanging 'salvees' or coming to 'push of pike'. Unlike the Horse, without order and control the fighting ability of a unit of Foot was seriously impaired. Cannon and smoothbore muskets took time to use and the amount of shot to be endured during an advance was nowhere near as heavy as it was later to become with technological advances in rifling, firing mechanisms and automatic reloading. The slow, steady pace may have meant that they took longer to reach the point of contact but it was necessary for the men to maintain their formation. There has been a long debate about the ability or otherwise of Civil War units to march in step, but one only has to walk with other people to naturally fall into their stride pattern and timing. As part of a group marching to the beat of drums it would be difficult not to keep in step, and it is probable that each division did just that. The further the formation continued to march, with field officers dressing their ranks, so would the effect of the merging rhythm of the various company drummers have told on the soldiers' corporate feeling of togetherness. Nevertheless, it has to be said that although whole regiments marching to the same step may have been achieved, there is no recorded evidence to prove or disprove the fact either way. Neither was any chanting noted, but it is hard to imagine the men remained silent. It was only much later that English armies established a reputation for being quiet prior to an engagement.

The ground they crossed was not easy. Open scrubland and the occasional ploughed field are notoriously difficult to negotiate, especially after such weather as occurred during the wet autumn of 1642, but the slow, methodical pace must have helped, and active NCOs would have kept the order and formation by yelling and pushing their men into straighter files and more compact ranks. We have no record of how they held their pikes during this march but they are likely to have been held 'at shoulder', angling them backwards to lessen the possibility of splinters should they be shattered by flying ball.

This moving mass must have been a daunting sight for those men in the Parliamentarian front ranks. The steady forward movement, the regular drums, the tall pikes and the sheer number of fluttering colours, including the dramatic Banner Royal, all contributing to the spectacle. The front three brigades had been deployed with wide gaps between them to allow the two in the second line to come up; it must have been awe-inspiring. There has been a tendency to see this attack as a solid block but its sheer size and complex checkerboard arrangement, the inexperience of the men, the short time units had been together, the distance covered, the various pieces of difficult ground traversed, and the different regimental drumbeats must all have broken the cohesion. The attack did not relentlessly roll forward and into the awaiting line. It actually halted, a fact missed by other historians. The officers who wrote the Official Parliamentary Account described the moment as 'their Foot, which appeared to us, divided into nine great bodies, came up all in Front, and after some playing with the cannon on both sides, that part of it which was on their Left, and towards our Right Wing, came on very gallantly to the Charge'.[4]

The front three brigades must have stopped in order to allow the rear two to catch up. We note that there was apparently no musket fire so they probably halted just outside effective range of about 100 yards and, while the Parliamentarian cannon, and perhaps the lighter Royalist pieces, continued firing, they probably realigned their ranks, regained their order and adjusted their formation. Stopping to reform prior to coming within musket range was common contemporary practice.[5] Although it remained a typical checkerboard deployment of the period, the Swedish formation was designed to array the troops in grand divisions for protection against enemy Horse but, by the time the Royalist Foot closed upon their opposition, Rupert's and Wilmot's cavalry had achieved their primary role, leaving the flanks bare of Parliamentarian cavalry. The time had come to form the fighting line ready for the Foot to Foot contact. The Parliamentary account records that the Royalist infantry advanced in 'nine great bodies', a statement that has hitherto caused considerable discussion among students of the battle. Davies, in particular, argues hard for the whole army being drawn up in only three brigades. It is important to establish the time that this impression was formed, and examination of the ground may shed some light upon the conundrum. If the ground covered by the

The Royalist advance: Royalist infantry brigades advanced across these fields towards Essex's little rising hill. On the right is King John's lane – a farm track which helped angle the advance. Byron's and Fielding's were in the foreground with Belasyse's and Gerard's hidden over the modern hedgeline.

advance is walked over today, it will be noted that the ostensibly flat fields are, in reality, set on a marked slope. During their initial advance, the Royalist second line would have been hidden from the Parliamentarian position and the de Gomme drawing, viewed from the point of view of the defending Parliamentary officers, indicates that they would have only seen the front three brigades. As each of the brigades would appear to have formed three bodies, a central block of pikes flanked by two musket wings, it becomes clear how those who wrote the account counted nine bodies. The Parliamentary account goes on to say that the enemy then 'came up *all* in Front', an indication that Byron and Belasyse brought their brigades up and into the gaps between Wentworth and Fielding, and also between Fielding and Gerard, thereby forming one long fighting line.[6] There is no conflict between these two reports, they simply recount an on-going movement.

Ahead of them, on the hill to their front, the same operation must have been going on among the Parliamentary troops as both Meldrum's and Charles Essex's two lines coalesced to fight, although they no longer had Fairfax's to come into the line. It is not clear what Ballard's Brigade did at this stage. Holles's were probably still disordered and in a very shaky state but there must have been a general order or understanding that the army would move and co-ordinate to form a fighting line at the same time. In all probability Ballard, with a careful watch towards his rear for returning Royalist Horse, drew his regiments into their fighting formation, realized he had the overlap and thus had time to wait for Holles, and perhaps even slowly angled his alignment.

In the centre the five Royalist brigades, six ranks deep, stood waiting for the order to advance further. The musket bodies opened long-range fire with the result that noise, flame and smoke filled the air. Roughly opposite them two enemy brigades, composed of eight ranks of Meldrum's and Charles Essex's Regiments, did the same. It must have seemed an agonizingly long time for the pikemen poised in their silent ranks. When the

order for the Royalists to move forward again was given, they may have stepped off together on their advance to contact but, when it came to the charge or 'fall on', the left, composed of Wentworth's and Byron's Brigades, struck first.

Contemporary practice, as required by seventeenth-century foot drill, did not allow for a sudden dash forward with the troops screaming and yelling while running at top speed. Direct contact with the enemy formation began with a steady advance and a measured tread, with great emphasis being placed upon control and compact order. The advance into contact began with the muskets loaded and primed and the pikes held at 'the advance', the men having been warned to be aware and ready to counter any threat. The body moved forward with the muskets firing by rank, gaining ground and with the pike keeping abreast of their colleagues, those 'smoky, rude mechanicals'. The opposing Parliamentarian musketeers would have replied, firing and maintaining ground. The attackers would next arrive at a critical distance from their enemy, perhaps twenty or so yards, at which point, both sides might endeavour to fire by salvo. This may well have been preceded by a further musketry exchange as the advance halted for the Royalists to fire again, but there is no evidence of this. However, the attackers may have shot their final volley in salvo as the drums played the preparative and signalled the troops to fall on! This was the true charge, a faster pace than the advance, with the sixteen-foot pikes levelled in order to stab and the muskets raised ready to club. The shouting would undoubtedly have started on both sides, with the pace increasing and the men pressing in closer together, until the two huge bodies crashed into each other; the impetus of Wentworth's and Byron's charge 'very gallantly' delivered being 'as gallantly received' by Meldrum's stolid line digging in to absorb it.[7] This clash took place along the line of the hedge identified by the Rev. Miller. Although we have no confirming evidence to demonstrate that a hedge was indeed present in this area, confirmation that the fighting occurred here is available as a result of the wealth of archaeological evidence recovered by Miller on this site.[8]

This first charge and push 'was very well disputed a long time'.[9] The fact that Parliament gradually obtained the upper hand may suggest that the Royalists' deployment was

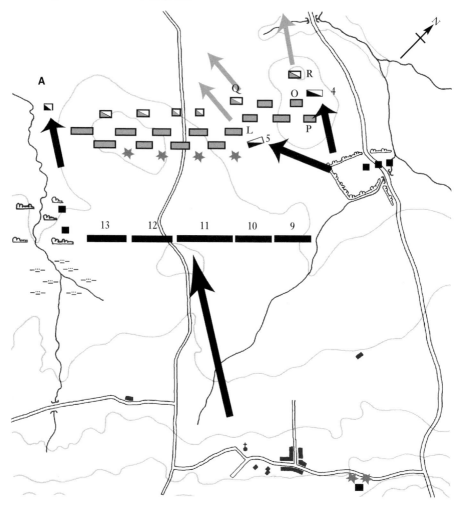

*The Royalist Foot attacks. Astley leads the five Royalist brigades forward. They form their fighting line and begin to engage in a firefight. Routing Parliamentary Horse followed by their pursuers break through the regiments of Holles and Cholmley. Holles's Londoners stand but Cholmley's bluecoats run causing a ripple effect along the line. The majority of the brigade of five battalia crumbles and runs. At **A** Aston's regiment covers the Royalist pursuit.*

L Cholmley's 2nd division	4 Prince Rupert (?)	11 Fielding
P Holles	5 Prince Maurice	12 Byron
Q Ramsey(?)	9 Gerard	13 Wentworth
R Waller	10 Belasyse	

maintained, with over a quarter of their strength acting simply as helpless spectators. The Parliamentarian regiments appear to have out-gunned their Royalist counterparts and, being eight deep, they would not have had to enter the firing line so frequently. In addition to which, their guns, which did not have to move to get clear fields of fire, would have been firing at close range. These are possible contributory factors as to why this outnumbered line held. If the Royalists had also run short of shot, their collars of bottles being almost empty, and their powder replenishment (budge barrels) back on their start line, the Parliamentarian musketeers would still have several charges each and could probably have maintained a more effective rate of fire into the Royalists' line during the lulls between clashes.[9]

This is a very important and pertinent factor that has previously been ignored, missed or glossed over by many writers and will be amplified later in this chapter. It would seem that these contacts were not actions in which the participants were continuously locked together in combat 'for each as if by mutual consent retired some few paces… continuing to fire at one another… that nothing less than so many witnesses as were there present could make it credible'.[10] The lines engaged, fought, then drew apart, rested then re-engaged. It would be interesting to determine just how far they did retire because, although James II says 'a few paces', Ludlow says that they remained within musket shot.[11] After a short respite to draw breath and restore some order, the pikemen crashed together again, in a desperate attempt to break the will of their enemies. The Royalists could have afforded to rest some units and allow fresher ones into the melee in their place. A 'push of pike' became a physical shoving match between divisions, or even grand divisions, of pikemen with each man in the front rank peering out under his lowered helmet brim to direct his steel pike-head into arms, untasseted thighs or into their opponent's armpit and through into his lungs. The rear ranks may have stabbed their pikes at the heaving mass of enemy but their essential role was one of leaning-on, adding weight to the push while attempting to gain the advantage of impetus. No matter how fit or well-trained, men cannot sustain hard, physical effort for more than about twenty minutes, so repeatedly breaking apart for a short rest appears to have been the normal practice. In addition to this it is apparent that several of these rests occurred all along the line giving the battle several lulls, including one that was lengthy.[12] It was during these rests and lulls that the musketeers would replenish their powder from budge barrels and then return once again to pouring more shot into their enemies' ranks.[13] The rests over, the deadly push-of-war began again but, because of numbers, the Parliamentarians had no option but to commit the same men time and time again, although their numbers would have begun to steadily decrease. The fighting in this sector evolved into a bloody stalemate.

It has to be questioned why Fielding's, Belasyse's and Gerard's Brigades, having formed a single line, did not commit themselves to a charge or even come to push of pike at the same time as the two brigades on their left. A simple explanation would be that their immediate enemy had gone! The usual view is that virtually the whole of Charles Essex's Brigade broke and fled at the sight of this massive body readying itself for the final fall on. Godfrey Davies suggests that they broke as soon as Ramsey's Horse ran, but there is no evidence for this and his comments appear somewhat too simplistic, if not partisan.[14] We can work out when the break started, and it was not when the Royalists were marching up, which was when the Horse broke. The Official Parliamentary Account states 'our Battalia at the very first wholly disbanded and ran away without ever striking stroke, or so much as being Charged by the Enemy'.[15] Particular note has to be taken of what these words used actually say. The passage states that they ran without 'striking a stroke', that is without making a lunge with a pike, a cut with a sword or a swing of a butt. Nothing is said about firing having ceased. It is

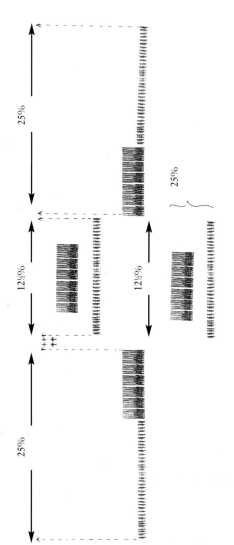

The deployment of Byron's Brigade. The Swedish system's lozenge arrangement of brigade battalia was conceived to provide all-round defence and was especially effective against Horse. However, if committed to a frontal attack only 62½% of its files could fight, the remaining 37½% acting as a support. Replacing divisions which were tired or had exhausted their ammunition with those supporting bodies involved in complicated drill manoeuvres which the Royalist Foot at Edgehill had not been trained to perform.

Beaumont's (320), Lord general Lindsey's (840) and the King's Lifeguard of Foot (670) constituted Byron's Brigade. Drawn up 6 deep they formed 304 files of pike and musket in approximately equal numbers. They were then arrayed in 4 battalia of 456 men in 76 files in the drill book's classic lozenge pattern with 38 files of each arm to each battalia.

important when reading these documents to note equally what is not said as well as what is said. This account does not say 'without firing a shot'. If Charles Essex's Brigade had broken early without cause the several Royalist account writers would surely have said so in their reports, and made a lot more of it in subsequent propaganda. James II's account states that 'when the Royalist Army was advanced with musket shot of the enemy, the Foot on both sides began to fire, the King's still coming on and the Rebells continuing only to keep their ground'. In other words the advance had taken place and fire had been exchanged. Bulstrode does not mention the break, while both Belasyse, who must have seen it, and the Official Royalist Account both attribute Charles Essex's Brigade's rout, in part, to the success of their Horse.[16] We think that it may be assumed that, like Meldrum's, Charles Essex's Brigade stood and fired shot into the advancing Royalists. It was unfortunate for Essex that the rearward under Ballard was refused and not drawn up in line on their flank where it should have been under normal circumstances.

Here then is a situation in which the Royalist musketeers fired 'by gaining ground' and the Parliamentarian musketeers fired 'by maintaining ground'. While their attention was focused on their front, and their musketeers were firing, some of the commanded musketeers, driven from their position among Ramsey's horse, would have run into them, especially Cholmley's two battalia who were nearest. Musketeers usually fired with an interval of about six feet between files and either three or six feet between ranks. Theirs was a fairly open formation and the gaps would have appeared highly attractive passages promising protection to fugitives. However, as Holles earlier experienced, it was not only the musketeers but also Ramsey's troopers who ran back among their own Foot.[17] As stated previously, not all Ramsey's troops would have taken the Royalist charge stationary. Some would have been moving forward so that, when they broke, they would have selected their own particular line of perceived safety and least resistance. For some this would have meant heading towards the safety of their comrades in arms. We know that the Horse melee split in all directions, for even one of those chasing the runaways, Bulstrode, who was on the left of Rupert's wing near Charles Essex's flank, admits that his own Prince of Wales's Regiment was dispersed.

Cholmley's Regiment was on the left flank of Charles Essex's Brigade, possibly divided into two grand divisions, and his muskets soon had fugitive foot and horse among them. The latter would have been followed by the cavaliers who were eagerly pursuing them.[18] A compact body of musketeers should be able to resist cavalry to a certain degree but, disrupted by the fleeing men and then hit in the flank by Horse at full tilt, the open order firing formations of both battalia would have quickly crumpled from the left. Even with the unit tightly formed together, and their left wing of muskets made up of several hundred men, its cohesion would have dissolved in minutes. As more and more enemy Horse arrived, those not cut down would have been driven into the pikes, who losing their order, command and control must have failed to react to this unexpected assault from the side. Whether the pikes were positioned at the charge, ready to receive their share of hand to hand combat, or at the advance would be immaterial if the orders were not given. Some re-enactor pikemen would argue that it is possible for whole bodies to adopt the position 'charge your pikes to the flank' in seconds, but they presume a unit has both the space, the command and the control, to do so. Crowded by their own musketeers they would have been jostled and pushed back.

A Civil War regiment in fighting formation. The model in the Kineton Depot Officers' Mess.
Although the number of ranks seem at odds with what we believe were the arrays for Edgehill, this
model gives an impressive interpretation of the size of a single unit and the space it covered.

In such a struggling mass it is doubtful that they would have had the freedom of movement to swing their right hands through their upward arc and, even those who could have done so, would have found levelling their points to horse-breast height difficult. Additionally, the pike was effective as a weapon when used in a unified body, but sporadic resistance by individuals would have achieved little. In truth, whether they could or could not turn is immaterial, it appears that they did not. Cholmley's Regiment could not protect itself. Panic set in and the regiment broke and ran. Pursued by Rupert's horsemen, probably Prince Maurice's Regiment from its position in the line, some would have gone to the rear but many would, understandably have fled away from the threat – that is to the right – and into the muskets of Mandeville's to begin the whole sorry process over again. Mandeville's broke, followed by Wharton's, and then, surely to his own mortification, so did Charles Essex's Regiment.[19]

Fired at from the front, aware that the order to fall on was about to be given, with some of their own cavalry breaking through them, their own men already running to the rear while enemy horsemen gradually crumbled away the brigade's flank, what remained of the brigade broke and ran. Although 'Colonel Charles Essex himself, and others, those who Commanded these Regiments in Chief, did as much as Men could do to stay them' nothing could stop them.[20] Although 'his Lordship beseeched them, yea cudgeled them' all four regiments, except some eighty of Cholmley's, ran for their lives.[21] Run the regiments certainly did, leaving Charles Essex's father, Sir William, severely wounded and captured. Charles Essex himself, along with a small body of men and several of his officers, ran to join Meldrum's Brigade where he continued his fight until he was tragically killed later in the action. Unless new evidence comes to light we will never know what happened. We have tried to formulate an informed opinion on this subject but concede that the whole incident could, conceivably, be attributed to what Clausewitz calls 'friction' inasmuch as, despite all training and planning, circumstances and experience, in action, for no apparent reason, inexplicable events happen.

Many writers have invited their readers to regard the outcome of this event in simplistic terms by writing off the men of Charles Essex's four Regiments. That just cannot have been the case. Admittedly the formation was defunct, but not all the men would or could have been scattered to the winds. Some would have run to their right and joined Meldrum's Regiments for safety, while others would have sought refuge in Ballard's ranks. A good proportion would have run off and, as we have seen, Cholmley's and Wharton's did so in large numbers. Nevertheless, a good many of them would have attached themselves to the still-ordered units if only to save their own lives. It must have been an inconvenience to those who had to push and shove them into ranks and files, but they would most certainly have been useful in countering the numbers still to be faced. Those who ran for Kineton were not as safe as they thought. The lists of wounded recorded in Warwick and Coventry provide clear evidence of the hurt that befell these fleeing men.[22]

There is no indication that Essex took any action to stop this general collapse of his left flank. His brigade and regimental commanders did but their officers' reactions were mixed. While Wharton excused his soldiers on the grounds that many of them were 'only young souldiers' he and others firmly believed that the officers were to blame for the debacle.[23] Indeed, he repeated the oft-murmured treachery theory in claiming that 'the Souldiers swear that their Commanders ran first, and bid their souldiers run too' although he also took the trouble to single out one particular officer, Captain Hunt of Chomley's Regiment, for praise as an officer who had refused to flee.[24] A more reasonable interpretation would appear to be that the rout occurred as the culmination of the circumstances described above.

This was the crisis of Parliament's battle. Both wings of Horse had fled, the guns had been overrun, a third of the line had broken and the remainder looked likely to be overlapped and taken in flank. A lesser army would have thrown down its arms to a man and run away. A not-so-conscientious field commander would have run for his horse and quit the field, as did Waller at Roundway Down, but Essex dug in and committed his remaining Foot, the men of Ballard's Brigade, to closing the gap. Young describes Ballard as 'it's profane commander' leaving us with an image of an imposing figure who swore like a trooper as he urged his four Regiments steadily forward into the attack. To achieve their goal the brigade had to undertake a demanding piece of military field craft. Their left was probably still in turmoil as Holles's Regiment reordered after being ridden through but, in their attempt to close the gap left by the demise of Charles Essex's Brigade, they must have performed a partial wheel to the right, marched forward for a distance and then wheeled again, this time to the left, to bring them across the intervening depression in the ground to reach the spot recently vacated by the fleeing troops.

No recorded commentary describing this manoeuvre survives, but it is the only possible way that the regiments could depart from their starting position on the rise and reach their eventual place in the line roughly adjoining Meldrum's.[25] They could not close the gap completely however. The distance was too far and they had Belasyse's and Gerard's Brigades opposing their progress. To ask them to complete the full manoeuvre would be expecting too much, and would also close the gap required by the reserve cavalry to advance and charge in a compact body against Fielding's Brigade. As has been suggested earlier, Ballard could have altered his alignment at the time that his unit deployed into the fighting line, but we cannot be sure. Johnson gives some indication of this move when he comments that 'they were wheeled up' although he fails to quote his source.[26] Battalia wheeling and marching on the right-oblique, by throwing forward the left shoulder, was perhaps too complex a drill movement this early in the war. It would be asking even more from them to be ordered to wheel by line of divisions. No matter the technical detail of how they accomplished it, this was a tremendous feat and bears witness to the quality and training of Parliament's soldiers.

Brushing aside the stragglers of Charles Essex's in flight, Ballard's Brigade would have faced in turn Gerard's, then Belasyse's and finally Fielding's, as it came into line. Ballard had commanded 2,900 men in eight ranks while the Royalists had 6,400 in six (although, thanks again to the Swedish system, only 3,700 were in the actual fighting line). These brave men turned to the attack against their enemy despite being, significantly outnumbered, facing the likelihood of themselves being overlapped, with a slow, deliberate advance, firing as they moved, until they finally charged into contact. The archaeological finds of Captain Grant confirm that this fighting took place in an area north of Grave Ground coppice. There is nothing to suggest that the Royalists moved to meet them, so it seems that they were able to move into an alignment with Meldrum's Brigade, cover his left flank from a battalia attack and begin to narrow down the central gap (probably also covered by both the reserve and some of the Horse from the right wing, possibly, the Lord General's).

The greatest problem facing them was the need to remove the potential for Gerard's Brigade to turn their left flank, therefore Holles's would probably have been allocated the task of containing the regiments over on the Royalists' right. It is now necessary to calculate how far along the line Ballard's Brigade could have engaged their enemy, but calculating their numbers is made considerably more difficult due to the fate of the overrun commanded musketeers. Many would have stood around in bewildered or defiant groups as the Horse rushed past them. Indeed, some may have fled even before the charge and others would have been cut down, but sheer differences in speed would mean they would soon have been overtaken, cut at or ignored, and then left behind. Others must have endured this terrifying prospect twice as Byron's second line swept through them. Any suggestion that all 700 ran in one direction towards Kineton cannot be sustained. Of those running, a good proportion must have fled back to the safety of their own brigade, although, in doing so, the fleetest of foot would have attracted the attentions of the enemy Horse. Some must have run off, crawled under the hedge, been killed or severely wounded but, given time, the majority had very little option but to return to their parent body. Those who retired into Holles's Regiment would have been part of their amazing re-ordering but overall the reintroduction of several hundred men into the brigade would have extended the line. Was this unheralded reinforcement a hidden blessing that gave Ballard sufficient men to hold his part of the line?

The lack of enemy Horse may have afforded Ballard the luxury of opening his battalia's intervals in an attempt to extend the line but we cannot be sure. Using this precept and our rough approximations it is possible to project that Holles's, although overlapped, would very likely have engaged amalgamated enemy blocks composed of companies drawn from Gerard's, Dyve's, and perhaps some of Dutton's, while Ballard's and elements of Brooke's Regiments would have opposed Dutton's and Blagge's. Lord Brooke's probably also faced-off mixed companies of Belasyse's and Pennyman's, while the Lord General's tried to fight as much of Fielding's as they could. If part of the line benefited from a continuation of Miller's hedge as a defensive feature, they would have been very grateful for it. Once again we must also note that, if the Parliamentarian musket to pike ratio was higher than two to one, they would have occupied more ground and the effect of the overlaps would have been considerably reduced.

However far Meldrum's and Ballard's lines were stretched, the fact remains that a substantial part of Fielding's Brigade faced little or no opposition. It is also highly probable that a hole had appeared in the centre of Essex's line, a gap that was, thankfully, covered by the Earl's judicious placement of his cavalry reserve as well as the fortuitous movement of more cavalry from the right wing. Equally important was the influence exerted by the near presence of their two parent units who were somewhere in the vicinity. Undoubtedly, Essex's creation of this force, consisting mainly of cuirassiers, to shore up his incomplete army line apparently saved the day, as Fielding's Regiment suddenly halted and stood still.

The ideal solution for the Royalists would have been for Fielding's units to have advanced upon the Horse. This could have been achieved by his ordering the two flank regiments of his command to both perform right and left outward wheels in 'line of divisions' while the central body of their Swedish formation expanded its front by halving files or bringing forward their rear divisions, to act as cover. The rear placed body could have acted as a reserve and provided support where required, even going forward into the front line as the outer two units gained ground and widened the gap. Such a manoeuvre would have broken Essex's line, enveloped its flanks and probably rolled it up in two directions!

It is always easy to develop such theories with the benefit of hindsight. It would have taken an experienced commander of great initiative to instigate such a movement as well as men with considerably more training and confidence in their abilities to accomplish the necessary evolutions and effect such a broad departure from normal contemporary practice. The Swedish system owed a lot to the old, unwieldy, Spanish tercio and, to be fair, the Royalist officers would have had little chance of succeeding as, when companies were drawn together from disparate regiments to form the blocks of their Swedish style brigade, their normal field command and control would have been so seriously disrupted that the manoeuvre appears even less likely, if not impossible. Essex's men may have been fortunate but, even so, they still only managed to engage four of the five Royalist brigades. Virtually unopposed, Fielding's five Regiments were free to act as a flank guard for the units engaged on either side of them, and added the shot of their outermost muskets to the firefight. Like Meldrum's, Ballard's line would also have gaps in it, gaps which the Royalist Foot could have used to their advantage if only their battle order had been different.

The struggle between the two lines of opposing Foot was fierce with pikes stabbing at faces, arms, thighs and at the chest of any rear-ranker unlucky enough to enter the front rank without a breastplate. Muskets would be fired wherever they could at point blank range, their soft lead bullets punching holes through breastplates, and certainly through flesh, leaving gaping wounds. The firearms could also be used as effective skull-crushing clubs, sometimes in conjunction with a drawn short sword or a flailed bandoleer. This is not the battalion line melee of the early seventeenth century because, up and down the entire line, groups of men would engage furiously, pull back and let other groups set to. Although the unified charge into contact could be delivered, in the fury of the once-joined melee it would be impossible to co-ordinate the actions of each division. The fighting itself was very fierce as the attack drove forward against Meldrum's line. Regrettably the Rev. Miller, who says that he walked the ground many times, left no plotted maps of his discoveries for us to refer to. He reported that he discovered a great deal of battlefield debris in the vicinity of the hedge and also that he discovered the grave pits that are all, unfortunately, now lost beneath the Ministry of Defence's earth and monument-moving alterations. Miller maintains that his finds provided evidence of an initial Royalist surge, but counter to this another Victorian source, one Major Ross, who also failed to leave plotted evidence, stated that he had made discoveries that discounted any theory that the Royalists made an inroad into Essex's line.[27] If the existence of the reported plethora of finds made in front of Miller's hedge line is accepted, then the information must be interpreted as signifying an initial Royalist gain, that their advance impetus took effect and that they were able to drive Meldrum's back up the slope. The action was so hard that many anticipated that one side or the other would break and run fairly quickly but this did not happen. In spite of the Royalists gaining an early advantage, it appears that Parliament's deeper formations proved themselves to be a match for the Royalists' numbers and much-vaunted, if probably overstated, *élan*. If we also accept the theory that there were occasional lulls in the fighting, and only super-humans can withstand continuous effort without a rest, it would seem from the end positions gained that the Parliamentarians had the edge, the momentum changed and the whole line gradually began to move back, away from the Parliamentarian start line and towards the base of Edgehill.

This statement cannot be allowed to pass without discussing the probable factors which enabled Essex's men to gradually drive their opponents before them. If the first exchanges and fierce clash of arms occurred on the forward slope of the small ridge, then the recent discoveries of Oliver and Pollard indicate a second location where the fighting lines remained static and for a lengthy period of time.[28] This area lies in the flat fields south of the Depot's perimeter fence, about 200 yards east from where the fighting began. To be forced back a couple of hundred yards must indicate that the Royalist troops bore the worst of the fighting.

It was not a single reason but a combination of factors that led to the Parliamentarian supremacy. As mentioned earlier the Parliamentary musketeers fired less frequently than their Royalist counterparts due to the depth of their files. If the interval between firings was thirty seconds then the Parliamentarian block would empty its bottles in forty-eight minutes whereas the Royalists would have ceased firing twelve minutes before them. Some may argue that the number of musketeers was roughly the same in which case the number of balls fired was the same and this factor would, therefore, have made no difference to the overall casualty figures. This may be so, but many battlefield historians would argue that battles are won in the mind, by the state of the unit and individual's morale. If an opponent continues to shoot at you when you cannot answer back, morale suffers and discipline plays a significant part in determining the outcome. Is it possible to confirm that the number of musketeers was equal? Early in the war Parliament controlled the arsenals of the Tower, Windsor, Farnham and Portsmouth as well as those of the north, like Kingston upon Hull, that had been denied to the King. The gunsmiths of the Minories, notably the London Gun Company, and in other parts of London and the south-east were well paid to deliver quantities of muskets, and government contractors were able to purchase foreign-made weapons in large numbers. Equipment lists indicate that, in October 1642, Essex received 2,690 imported muskets and nearly 4,000 imported rests. It is therefore very likely that Parliament enjoyed numerical supremacy in the number of muskets available to the combatants.

Turning to ammunition supply, here again the manufacturing base was firmly in Parliament's hands and, although the powder mills at Rotherhide and in Surrey, especially Guildford, and the bullet making sheds in the Minories were not as well stocked in early 1642 as Essex would have liked, they remained under Parliament's control as did the London bandolier manufacturers. By mid 1642 all of these factories had swung into action turning out the required munitions, some 1,600 muskets and 2,000 bandoliers per month from London alone. Added to this, quality control could be maintained over the vast deliveries of match produced in what we now call the Home Counties. Parliament's supply, organization and production levels may not have been good at the start of the war but were always far superior to that of the King. Purchasing authority over the manufacture of all four components of the firing process, weapon, ignition, projectile and propellant led to better opportunities for standardization with a resultant improvement in the fit of ball to muzzle, less windage, more range and greater accuracy. Add to this a supply system that provided sufficient quantities of bandoliers to permit stockpiling of replacements and it is possible to begin to appreciate the

The push of pike: although a re-enactment photograph it does capture the desperate chaos of a pike melee.

advantages commanded by Essex. He certainly experienced shortages but he seems to have triumphed over maintenance and supply problems more readily than did the King. These factors may well have been the direct result of the appointment of the adept administrator, Lord Peterborough but may also have owed much to two very shrewd London businessmen, Aldermen Andrews and Estwick. These men were appointed Parliament's official purchasers responsible for managing the arms import trade between England and both Protestant Holland and Catholic France with equal proficiency.

Very little is known about if, how or when the musketeers in the fighting line received more powder and ball. If, despite his rather inept second-in-command, Du-Bois, the very able Peterborough had also turned his mind to resupplying men in action with either budge barrels brought close to the rear of the fighting line, or with replacement collars, they would not have had to withdraw as far from the firing line to replenish as the Royalists were obliged to do. It is probable that the Parliamentary army fought with a greater number of musketeers than their opponents, fighting in the formation in which they were trained, using newer, better quality muskets, with more and improved powder, accurately measured charges, closer fitting balls, and a superior re-supply system. Couple this to the effect on morale of maintained and sustained rates of fire and we begin to understand why Parliament won this phase of the musketry battle.

As for the pikes, we have seen that the first three ranks of the pike were those most likely to cause impalement damage. Men in subsequent ranks would step forward as required to replace casualties and, when necessary, lean forward and contribute to the overall weight and momentum of their block. Armed with the same, unbending and forward thrusting weapon, the leading three ranks of either side in a pike push would inflict roughly equal numbers of casualties upon their opponents. Overlapping files on the flanks needed space to wheel in order to bring their weapons to bear upon the sides of a block, but they would be very hesitant about doing so in front of formed muskets at point blank range, especially as such a wheel would mean them exposing their flank in turn. An overlap might have been difficult for the man on the overlapped front corner but, beyond that, and any associated morale effect, it would have been unlikely to produce anything of greater significant practical consequence. With a numerical width advantage negated, it would appear that, again, adherence to the eight deep Dutch system had its rewards.

Given the difficulty of trying to disentangle the various constituent Royalist companies of the fighting blocks, we are obliged to look at the numerical proportions of comparative strengths in a hypothetical clash of pike. We have already speculated that Constable's would, most likely, have opposed an amalgamation of Gerard's and Beaumont's Regiments. Initially this would appear to have been a two against one victory but, knowing what we do of the formations used, attention must now turn to examine what exactly this entailed:

Table 10.1   Comparative pike strengths

	Pike Files	Available Men
Royalist regiments		
G Gerard	29	174
Beaumont	17	84
Total	46	258
Parliamentarian regiment		
Constable's	30	240

Source: S Peachey and A Turton, *Old Robin's Foot* (Leigh on Sea, Partizan Press, 1987), appendix 4, p. 58 and calculations by P Young from BL, Add MS 34713, f 1.

There would obviously be an overlap but, in general terms, the blocks would balance. In the central portion the additional depth enjoyed by Constable's would have resulted in about 180 Royalists attempting to hold 240 Parliamentarians and, inevitably, the former would have been forced to give ground despite their overlap. If their officers had obeyed their orders, more pikemen would have been available to them in the Swedish-style rearguard unit. If we allow that rear block to join the main block it would be their weight leaning on that stemmed the thrust, but that assumes that the additional weight could be directed to the correct point of pressure. The Royalist line engaging head-on, would overlap Constable's by nine or ten files per flank. Although a useful body of pike, it could have been readily kept in check by musketeers, or even obliged to retire in the face of the latter's close shot.

If the rear ranks were not thrown in then it can been seen just how relatively easy it would have been for Constable's Regiment to drive Gerard's and Beaumont's backwards. Had the rear ranks been added to the pike push then the Royalist troops would gradually have gained the advantage. We have already established that the Royalists were fighting in an unfamiliar formation. Their officers would not have understood the correct methods for employing their men in their current deployment and the men would find themselves standing in positions for which they had not been trained. Although the action of thrusting a pike would be the same in any formation, the knowledge that they were in an unfamiliar situation and any thoughts that the officers were also unsure of how to control their fighting blocks would have seriously undermined the unit's morale. A knowledge of when and where to commit the rear blocks was just one of the many minor tactical aspects required to fight efficiently in the Swedish fashion. Various surviving memoirs and letters indicate that Essex had instigated a comprehensive training regime during the weeks and months prior to the battle. There is no evidence to show that training on anything like a similar scale and frequency was pursued by the Royalists under Lindsey's direction, and what had been provided was negated by the change from the Dutch to the Swedish formation.[29]

Supply arrangements also impinge upon the efficiency of the pike's performance. The sixteen-foot long, steel-tipped, ash pikes were common to both armies. As previously mentioned, Essex had drawn his initial supplies of weapons and armour from the great London storehouses at the Tower, Greenwich and Woolwich, and also from the three major outlying arsenals at Kingston, Portsmouth and Hull. Imports were also purchased from overseas, particularly from Holland and France. Additionally, he could also make requisitions on the equipment of the London Trained Bands. Undoubtedly some of the King's forces would have had armour but theirs would mostly certainly have been provided from private collections, the stores of various town Trained Bands or indeed from out of church porches, much of which would have been old and worn and possibly not refurbished since Queen Elizabeth's day. The percentage of unarmoured pikemen in the Royalist army must have been much higher than in that of Parliament. Clarendon makes the point that, at Edgehill, Essex's Foot were 'completely armed' while in the Royalist Foot 'there was not one pikeman had a coselet, and very few musketeers who had swords'.[30] The Hounslow sword-maker Jencks may have decamped to Oxford with many of his workforce but they did not take their stock or their heavy equipment and raw materials with them. Clarendon also states that three or four hundred of the Royalists' Foot were armed only with a cudgel. Despite their bravery, the Royalists would become increasingly less well equipped as Parliament's control of the nation's purse strings, repositories and manufacturing areas exerted a powerful influence upon events in battle. The October 1642 delivery of imported arms to Parliament's stores at the Tower of London recorded the arrival of 2,331 sets of infantry armour as well as 5,580 pikes. These would immediately have been made available to Essex.[31] While a broad study of the arms and equipment shows that shortages existed on both sides, for the purposes of this battle, it appears inevitable that Parliament's troops benefited from their ability to field a greater depth of pikemen who fought in a formation for which they had been trained, under officers who were sure of what they were doing, and that they were protected by more and better armour. In addition to these factors a favourable sloping ground, albeit a gentle incline, and it is, perhaps, possible to gain a clearer understanding of how Parliament was able to win this phase of the pike battle.

These facts and figures may now help us understand how Meldrum's and Ballard's Brigades gradually and sporadically drove Gerard's, Belasyse's, Byron's and Wentworth's Regiments before them, back to the field where Oliver and Pollard's team found so much of what they called 'battle detritus'. Although Fielding's Brigade was only threatened by the Parliamentary Lord General's two battalia, it would also have been forced to fall back in order to maintain the continuity of the Royalist line and protect the inside flanks of the other engaged brigades from the hovering Parliamentarian cavalry reserve. In the infantry combat the Royalists were certainly thrown back and yet, despite this, their numbers would eventually tell, unless something dramatic was done to tip the balance.[32]

The Earl of Essex had recovered the situation for the time being. By committing Ballard's Foot he had prevented Meldrum's from being overwhelmed. Dogged, determined, close-quarter fighting had swung the fate of the day into a delicately poised equilibrium. The battle might now still have gone either way but the Royalists retained an advantage. If Rupert's or Wilmot's second lines of Horse had been able to drive into the exposed flanks of Ballard's or Meldrum's the fighting would have ended there and then with a resounding victory for the King. Instead it was Essex's cavalry who were to make a decisive contribution.

Chapter Eleven

The Centre – Counterattack

With Great resolution . . . charged into the enemy's quarters. Ludlow.

Whether he had been biding his time, explaining his intention to his superior, the Lieutenant General of Horse, reordering his own command after their move, or trying to peer through the smoke to get a clear understanding of the situation, Sir William Balfour now gave orders to the two bodies of Parliamentary reserve. Using the gap between Meldrum's and Ballard's, he advanced half of the reserve, led by The Lord General's Lifeguard Troop, consisting of fifty gentlemen and fifty troopers commanded by Sir Phillip Stapleton, followed by Nathaniel Draper's troop of about fifty or sixty men. Whether or not they remained six deep we are not told. This first body numbered around 150 men. Confronting them were the Royalist Foot of Sir Nicholas Byron's Brigade, in the middle of which Sir Edmund Verney carried the Banner Royal. Many of the Lord General's Lifeguard were well armoured gentlemen in complete cuirassier suits while Draper's harquebusiers were also from the Lord General's Horse. Both troops were mounted on good horses from their own stables and constituted a formidable body. However, such was the quality of Byron's Foot that, despite the nature of their opposition, they were the first to move. According to Ludlow they 'came on within musket shot of us', a statement that tells us just how close the factions came to one another during these lulls in the action.[1] Ludlow continued: 'upon which we observing no Horse to encounter withal, charged them with some loss from their pikes, tho very little from their shot'. This might corroborate the idea that the Royalists ran low or even out of powder and bullet earlier than their Parliamentarian opposition.[2] Despite suffering minimal damage, Stapleton's were unable to break them and therefore retreated to their former station.

Stapleton was buying time for Meldrum's hard-pressed Foot. Meanwhile Balfour had returned to bring up the second half of the reserve and deployed it more or less opposite the largely uncommitted Fielding's Brigade. Once again, he would have formed them in a line of troops. Bedford's horsemen were well-trained and also equipped as cuirassiers, as were many of his, Balfour's, own double-size troop.

One of the mysteries associated with the battle of Edgehill is the problem of how to determine when the two regiments from the Parliamentarian right wing became mixed with the reserve. We know that all of the units appear to have been involved in one or other of the various combats fought by this large body of Horse, but teasing out the exact story is very difficult from the limited and, at times, confused evidence that remains. It appears that Balfour may have returned to the area behind the Foot yet again to advance part of his own regiment, at least Fiennes's troop, to augment the reserve. Another of its sub-units appear to have covered Meldrum's right flank, shoring them up as the Royalists attempted to drive them back. The central body of Horse thus formed probably numbered over 200 men and, having formed for a charge, they awaited the order to advance.

Miller, the amateur archaeologist and historian, based his conclusions on a combination of what he read and, more importantly, what he found.[3] Regrettably, he did not compile any notes regarding the precise locations of his finds, or even make detailed lists of the artifacts themselves. If he did they have yet to be traced. We may deplore his lack of scientific method in poorly detailing his findings in writing, but we should not summarily discount his views. He favours the idea that some Royalist success against Meldrum's, who did not have the hedge for an advantage, initiated a movement in Byron's part of the line. It may also have been that, according to our calculations, the right of Byron's Brigade appeared to have little opposition, in which case they would have been able to drive forward more easily. Both scenarios indicate a wheeling movement to the left. This scenario is corroborated by Davies who commented that 'there seems to be no doubt that Byron was deflected to the left' and describes Byron's Brigade as having 'its flank exposed as it moved forwards across the field to attack Meldrum'.[4] This would have caused the line to become stretched and a gap to open which Fielding would have had to cover. We hesitate to go as far as Davies who claimed that 'there seems to be no doubt'. No known source relates whether Fielding's Brigade had been engaged, although one expects that only parts of it had been fighting the Lord General's. It could be argued that it was the freshest of the Royalist Foot, in the best order, and the most capable of resisting a frontal attack by Horse, but it had faced a difficult task in trying to keep the line connected. Given that Belasyse's and Gerard's had halted in front of Ballard's, and that Byron's was going forward against Meldrum's, the distance between these two blocks was widening. Did Fielding attempt to extend his line only to run into trouble as he was changing formation? Did his brigade try to advance, or wheel and march forward, to cover Byron's flank, thereby allowing one regiment to get too far ahead, or did it uncover its own flank in the process? Whatever it did, the result was the opening of intervals in its formation.

This was the opportunity Balfour had been waiting for. Advancing on an angle into the flank and front of the disjointed formation, Balfour's heavy cuirassiers initially walked, then increased the pace into a trot (most probably taking fire from the muskets) and, at last, 'with great resolution, …charged into the enemy's quarters'.[5] Fielding's Brigade consisted of Stradling's, Lunsford's, Bolles's, Fitton's and Fielding's own Regiment but companies had been mixed to form the blocks of the lozenge required by the Swedish system. Being new to them the arrangement (not surprisingly) operated inefficiently. The widening intervals turned into gaps. One regiment appears to have been left out on a limb and Balfour's attack was able to single them out. He charged them 'and breaking into it, cut most of it off; and after by the assistance of some of our Foot, he defeated another regiment'.[6] This was a bloody action as, in contemporary understanding, the phrase 'to cut off' meant 'to destroy' or 'to cut up', (cf. the modern expression 'cut off in one's prime'), rather than to detach or prevent from gaining assistance. Balfour's half of Bedford's reserve had beaten and ruined two Foot regiments.

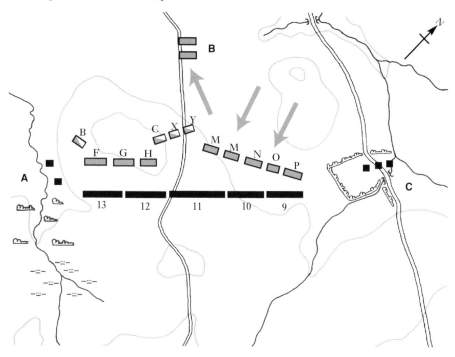

*The battle rages: while Bedford's reserve of heavy cuirassiers covers the gap in the line, Ballard's brigade partially wheels and marches across the fold in the ridge and up the slope to try to narrow it. It has to fight its way into position. At **A** the Royalist dragoons are held in check by Balfour's; at **B** the remnants of C Essex's Brigade leave the field and at **C** the Royalist dragoons retire.*

B Balfour	N Brooke	9 Gerard
C The Lord General	O Ballard	10 Belasyse
F Meldrum	P Holles	11 Fielding
G Constable	X Stapleton	12 Byron
H Robartes	Y Bedford/Balfour	13 Wentworth
M The Lord General		

Witnesses do not name which Foot regiment first gave ground but it had green colours and would appear to have offered scant resistance.[7] On the right Stradling's lieutenant colonel, William Herbert, was killed and one of his colours taken. Soon the whole brigade gave way and Balfour's troopers were able to drive them from the fighting line, back to where they had started their march and where their own light cannon were positioned. Here many of them threw down their arms and ran away, presumably scrambling up the hill, although it is plausible that many fled for the protection of the houses and gardens of Radway.

The Royal Military Academy, Sandhurst, has always placed great emphasis upon the need for officers to ensure that their men were adequately fed as a means of bolstering efficiency and morale. It is therefore interesting to speculate whether Fielding's men were among those 'many companies who had scarce eaten bread in eight and forty hours'.[8] In their flight they carried the men working the light guns along with

The clash of pike.

them while several Parliamentarian troopers, who demonstrated a cool presence of mind, dismounted and hammered nails into the touch-holes of the barrels, rendering them useless.[9] The remaining troops cut down some of the fleeing men but, unlike the men who followed Rupert and Wilmot in what resembled a sort of undisciplined fox-hunt, the majority rallied, rounded up prisoners of quality, including Colonels Fielding, Stradling and Lunsford, and gathered up abandoned colours and personal trophies. Most of them then made their way back to their own lines, heading for the gap through which they had charged and the safety of the reforming ranks of Stapleton's half of the reserve.

The loss of Fielding's central Brigade, coupled with the threat of enemy Horse on their flank, must have had a detrimental effect upon Byron's and Belasyse's Brigades and, in response, it seems that they gave ground somewhat, thereby continuing the gradual retirement of the fighting line back to the Royalists' start point. The rear companies of their Swedish formations perhaps retired to reorder, and their forward sub-units subsequently dressed back onto them.

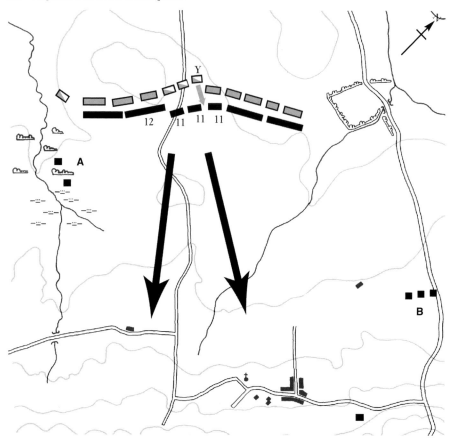

*A hole in the Royalist centre. Wentworth and Byron drive forward causing Fielding to try something to bridge a gap opening in the Royalist line. Seizing the opportunity, Balfour launches Bedford's reserve into Fielding's brigade which breaks and runs before it. At **A** the Royalist dragoons begin to retire, and at **B** they begin to fall back.*

Y Bedford/Balfour	11 Fielding
	12 Byron

Balfour and some of his men chose not to rally back but, although it could be argued that they were as undisciplined as Rupert's troopers, they actually undertook a positive tactical move. Following their bold commander, they inclined to their left and headed for the Royalist's main six-gun battery on the slopes of Edgehill, very near to the spot where the King sat watching the breaking of his centre!

Having seen his own Horse leave the field, albeit in victory, King Charles must have become somewhat apprehensive to observe that, with a breaking centre, his own regiment of fifty Gentlemen Pensioners were the only Royalist cavalry left under command. With great courage, he again moved to hazard his own life by going forward into the fighting line 'to incourage them by his presence, and thereby to prevent their intire defeat'.[10] This he did, but not before requesting Sir William Howard and his Pensioners to escort his sons, Wales and York, from the field. He had earlier attempted to persuade firstly the Earl of Richmond and then the Earl of Dorset to undertake this duty but both refused, with Dorset, somewhat indignantly, exclaiming 'he would not be thought a Coward for the sake of any King's Sons in Christendom!'[11] Howard led the two boys and Edward Hyde down from Bullet Hill and its battery and off the field to Arlescote House, intending, we are told, to later climb back up to Edgehill itself. The King, accompanied only by the two fiercely loyal and proud Earls and a few other gentlemen, rode southwest towards the fighting hoping to prevent a debacle. This move was not achieved without incident. One of the accompanying footmen did not make it. He was shot in the face while standing beside the King's horse.

Meanwhile Balfour, probably ignoring a few lone riders and runners, had led his men in a charge against the grand battery of guns and, evidently, penetrated into its flank. There was a brief melee, Legge's Firelocks were scattered and the gunners who did not run away were cut down among their pieces.[12] During this brief action it would appear that Sir George Strode was injured. Balfour's troopers then proceeded to sever the horse traces and the rope traction harnesses, the means by which these heavy cannon could be repositioned manually after the recoil of firing. Fiennes described the episode when he wrote: 'and so we got up to the greatest part of the enemy's ordnance, cutting of the gears of the horses that drew them, and killing the gunners under the carriages'.[13] The Official Parliamentary Account says that Balfour also dismounted and called for nails in order that he might spike the guns but, unfortunately, none of the men near him could find any.[14]

While elements of Balfour's detachment went for the guns, several others rode across the Radway fields, behind the Royalists' lines, and approached the small cluster of riders making their way down Bullet Hill. It was the King's two sons. It appears that Sir William Howard's fifty Gentlemen Pensioners had failed to keep together, although exactly where they went is unknown, although some loyal souls may have taken off after their King. In the evening light, Howard's party misidentified Balfour's men as Royalists, approaching as they did from the back of their own Foot, and rode towards them – sending forward an equerry, Sir Richard Graham, to make sure. Graham was knocked from his horse and left for dead. Howard then spurred his group forward to gain the shelter of a barn that was currently in use as a Royalist dressing station.[15] Sir John Hinton, the King's physician, later recalled how the young Prince of Wales, having spanned his pistol intending to fire, was persuaded that discretion was the better part of valour before the group decided to chance their luck and rode off. There must have been considerably fewer than fifty Parliamentarians in the enterprising group of Horse that continued to circle the area or they would surely have attacked the gilded entourage as it chose to ride out from the shelter of the barn. One man did, but Hinton intercepted him and, in a one to one sword and pistol struggle, managed to unhorse him but, although he struck him with his sword, the unidentified man's full armour, described as 'cap-a-pie', turned his blade. The incident finally ended when another member of the Royalist group, Miles Matthews, rode back from the Pensioners and, while Hinton engaged his opponent, killed the gallant Parliamentarian with a poleaxe.[16] This may well have been a tiny action on such a vast and busy field, but the capture of the Princes would have been a coup for the Parliamentary forces and yet, thanks to Sir John Hinton, they all reached safety. Their would-be captors were left to ride back and rejoin Balfour and the rest of their group who, by now, were unsupported and totally out of command range.

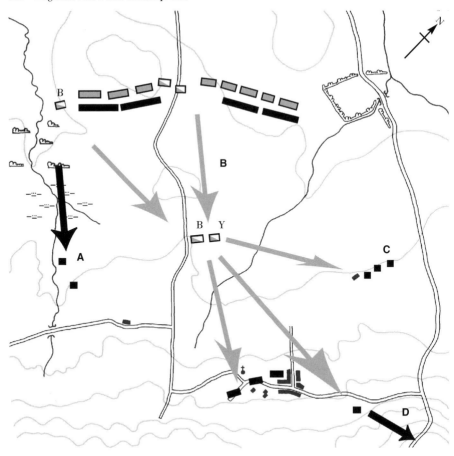

*Balfour charges the guns. While the Foot and the guns hold the Royalists, Balfour leads a dramatic charge across the field, taking the Royalist heavy battery in flank. As most of the Royalist Horse loot baggage in and around Kineton, Lucas who has not left the field, launches several charges into the remnants of Charles Essex's brigade. At **A** the Royalist dragoons are falling back. At **B** some of Balfour's men join his Lifeguard and attack alongside Bedford. At **C** the Royalist dragoons halt and a small party investigates Kings Leys barn. At **D** the Royalist guns are taken in flank and Legge's disperse.*

B Balfour   Y Bedford/Balfour

The infantry battle raged on.[17] Stapleton had reformed his part of the reserve and reunited the troops of the Lord General's Regiment of Horse. This process, which required a high degree of skilful battlefield command, took time. Ludlow details an interesting incident that occurred at this juncture. While awaiting further action, Stapleton noticed that the guns in the Parliamentarian line were no longer manned and naturally assumed that the crews had either been withdrawn or had run away. They had probably run when Fairfax's broke. Several of his troopers volunteered to remain with these prized items and guard them, going so far as to order one of their servants to dismount and endeavour to load and fire one of them.[18] It appears that the time available

A cuirassier. These fully armoured heavy horsemen , made up the majority of Essex's reserve.

was sufficient for one man to complete such an operation as he managed to discharge a round of case-shot at a group of horsemen approaching through the now on-coming twilight. He apparently missed, 'the gun being overloaded and planted on high ground'.[19] Ironically, this was fortunate as his target was some of Balfour's men returning from their action with Fielding's Brigade. The shot injured one man in the hand that he had been holding in the air in an attempt to signal that they were friendly![20]

By distilling all of the various related accounts it appears that this took place during another of those lulls in the fighting, albeit an extended one. We know that both sides had exchanged musketry and had come to push of pike, and yet some sources state that Constable's and Robartes's were now ordered to attack Byron's, with Stapleton's and Balfour's in support.[21] The two foot regiments marched forward bravely, presumably firing as they went, and prepared to fall on as they engaged the Red Regiment (the King's Guard) and the Blue Regiment (Lord General Lindsey's). At this juncture, the irrepressible Rev. Miller infers that this giant melee, like a rugby scrum wheel, began to pivot about a central axis thereby exposing the Royalists' right flank.[22] It is usual among modern historians to discredit Victorian imagination, but Miller's comments appear to be corroborated by evidence that Stapleton assisted the attack by 'marching down to take them in flank'.[23] In order for them to strike the enemy's flank, there must have been one, or at least part of one, presented to Stapleton's as a target. They duly attacked across what must, in all probability, have been the gap left by Fielding's rout. The Royalists were pinned at their front by Foot while the Horse hit them in their flank. After three attempts, enough to suggest that the opportune gap was insufficiently wide or open

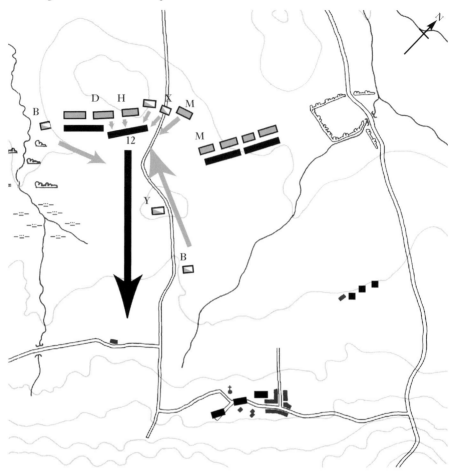

The gap widens. Essex orders a renewed attack on Byron and reinforces it with a battalia of his own regiment. Balfour puts the reformed reserve into Byron's right flank and hooks the remaining right wing Horse around the Royalist line's left, pinning Wentworth's and attacking Byron's rear. Byron's brigade collapses and runs.

B Balfour	M The Lord General	12 Byron
G Constable	X Stapleton	
H Robartes	Y Bedford	

enough to engage with adequate numbers or charge at full–tilt, these tired horsemen eventually broke into the Royalist right wing of musketeers and forced them 'to run in and shrowd themselves within their Pikes, not daring to shoot a shot'.[24]

Hereafter, events become rather confused. The Official Parliamentary Account awards the honour of breaking Byron's Brigade to the Lord General's and Brooke's Regiments of Foot. Although it may well have been that a grand division of the Lord General's were added to the fight, Brooke's were almost certainly engaged further to the left. Perhaps this attribution can be explained by suggesting that, while Constable's and Robartes's Regiments drove their opposition back, half the Lord General's and a part of Brooke's were able to outflank Byron's across the gap left by Fielding's Brigade fleeing the field during an ensuing lull. The preferred option probably attributes Brooke's involvement to the fog of war. Wharton tells us of a 'very extraordinary service performed by my Lord Gray and Sir Arthur Hazelrigg who indeed was a help for to give a great turn to the day by cutting off a Regiment of the Kings which was called The Blew Regiment.'[25] One can envisage the ardent republican Hazelrig's troops driving into Lindsey's and preventing the battalia's mutual support that was so crucial to the Swedish brigade system. It is worth remembering, yet again, that the expression 'to cut off' embraced the notion of being killed or destroyed. This certainly bears out the Imperialist general Raimondo Montecuccoli's adage that 'a small squadron of cavalry, acting promptly, can wreak havoc amongst large infantry battle lines.' As an aside, we must be careful here with translation, because the term squadron could be confusing; English Civil War squadrons were one third of a troop (about eighteen to twenty men) not one third of a regiment (about 120 to 150 men) as later cavalry practice dictated.[26] Among the chaos caused by the breaking of Byron's Brigade Walford suggests that Stapleton himself made a dash at the King, who was watching from what is now called the King's Clump, but a rapid Royalist retreat left him empty-handed.[27]

To corroborate evidence for this lull in proceedings we need to appreciate fully what had happened on the Parliamentarian left, and also to understand why the Earl of Essex issued his order. We know from Lord Wharton's later speech in London that, for part of the fighting, Essex had been with his own regiments, both Horse and Foot.[28] However, he seems to have recovered his overall appreciation of the situation in time to order Constable's and Robartes's to renew their attack. In effect, it appears that a cessation of the melee had allowed Essex to extradite himself and re-establish control of events across his command. Ludlow further complicates the narrative of Constable's and Robartes's attack by claiming that, not only did Stapleton go into Byron's flank, but Balfour charged the rear. Ostensibly, this would mean Balfour's Regiment was in two places at once, both supporting Stapleton and attacking Byron's rear. This situation would, indeed, have been possible if it is also accepted that those in support had returned from breaking Fielding's unit and were now busy reforming, and by attributing the charge into Byron's rear to the horsemen who returned from the escapade behind Royalists' lines on Bullet Hill and around the field dressing station at the barn.

Yet another possibility exists that seems to bear some credence. Both regiments of Horse from the right wing may also have been involved. By this time it would appear that Stapleton's command had increased because the two elements, regiment and reserve, of the Lord General's Regiment of Horse had coalesced into their original unit. Balfour's, however, still appears to have been subdivided albeit engaged in individual troop actions. It is not beyond the realms of plausibility for several troops to have been used to sweep around to the right of Meldrum's Brigade and threaten the flank of Wentworth's, thereby taking some of the pressure off the Foot. Troops performing such a movement could also have enveloped the rear of the line and, indeed, charged into the rear of Byron's Brigade adding weight and numbers to Balfour's returning cuirassiers. Fiennes, who was with Balfour's, had been among the enemy's guns and had certainly participated with great success in a charge against the Royalist Foot during the day. We also know that the troops of his regiment were involved but, alas, there is no proof to clarify exactly where and against whom they fought.

Just as Howard had mistaken Balfour's troopers for Royalist horse, so too did some of the King's Guard as they approached from their rear. Fiennes states that both sides even exchanged handshakes! Error resolved, they fell to killing each other. Fiennes also tells us that 'halfe the Lord General's Regiment [Foot], which His Excellency himself led up, charging into the King's Regiment'.[29] Fiennes also offers his reader an interesting comment on this attack. He too repeats Ludlow's story of the Lord General's 'friendly fire' upon Balfour's men but goes on to add that 'discerning each other to be friends, we joined Companies'. The Horse from the reserve and the right wing was now completely intermixed and would have formed a formidable fighting force amid the great pike melee. The net result upon Byron's Brigade, having been attacked in front, flank and rear, was that the attackers 'forced that Stand of Pikes and wholly broke those two Regiments [the Lord General's and the Lifeguard] and slew and took almost every man of them'.[30]

Thus far we have neglected to comment on the conduct of the Parliamentary Lord General of the Horse, the Earl of Bedford. He may not have been experienced, and indeed may have left much of the tactical command decisions to Balfour, but he was in the thick of the fighting where he performed 'extraordinary service' and 'led very gallantly'.[31]

Byron was wounded and the erstwhile Royalist Lord General, the Earl of Lindsey, who had unwisely gone out too far in front of his own men, had his thigh bone broken by a musket ball. His son, Lord Willoughby, stood over him trying desperately to protect his father with a half pike as the Parliamentarian troopers surged over them.[32] James II tells the dramatic tale of how Willoughby caught one captain of Horse in the face and almost unhorsed him but eventually surrendered himself, 'chusing rather to be taken with his wounded father so that he might be in a condition of rendering him what service was in his power, than to save himself by leaving him in that distress'.[33] This has hitherto been regarded as stereotypical cavalier gallantry but, militarily, it has a darker side. Lord Willoughby's action in running to his father's aid did nothing to assist in preventing the collapse of the King's Lifeguard. Regrettably, even in times of great personal stress it was, and still is, incumbent upon officers to remain with their men and do their duty by giving commands and by providing an inspiration to them - not to run off. Willoughby's actions were tantamount to desertion in the face of the enemy and by choosing to remain with his wounded father, albeit for the best of reasons, he added further dishonour to his proud name by placing family before King, cause and duty by surrendering. Both field Commanders provided better examples as Lieutenant Colonel Sir William Vasavour of the Lifeguard was captured while the lieutenant colonel of the Lord General's Regiment, John Monro, died at his post.

A letter from Edward Sydenham relates another stirring tale in which Sir Edmund Verney, Knight Marshal and bearer of the Banner Royal, was himself involved in a melee. He killed two men, but not before 'one had killed poor Jason (his servant)'. Verney, despite his being unarmoured, without even a buffcoat, and having also 'brocke the point of his standard at push of pike before he fell'.[34] Fall he did but several accounts claim that, in so doing, the Knight Marshal killed two officers of the Parliamentarian Lord General's Regiment.[35] Verney was cut down, either by Lionel Copley or by Ensign Arthur Young of Constable's Regiment who, legend has it, had to sever the Knight Marshal's hand at the wrist in order to free and take the Banner Royal. This important flag should not be confused with the Royal Standard. The former was the main flag of

The Royal Standard is shown at the top, and the Banner Royal below.

the army, its chief banner, which, by depicting the royal arms, represented all it fought for. The Royal Standard, was the long, almost medieval, personal flag of Charles I previously raised by him at Nottingham and which, to the best of our researches, was not flown in the battle, unless it was displayed upon the heights of Edgehill itself.

The Banner Royal was such a significant prize that it did not remain in the hands of the young ensign for long. Ludlow reports that he saw it carried by Lieutenant Colonel Middleton, a reformado officer who had been fighting in the ranks with a pike. He presented it to the Earl of Essex, who, in turn, handed it to his secretary, Robert Chambers to take to the rear, under escort 'with an intention to send it back the next day unto his Majesty'![36]

Meanwhile, those who had marched beneath the flag earlier that day ran for their lives. Despite the desperate nature of the fighting and the amount of bullets fired, the Royalist effort was contained and overcome. Miller's work, however, poorly recorded, remains our best source for identifying the locations of finds and he states that, in 1889, 'the number of bullets that have in the last few years been ploughed up or found in digging the new drain', is, after the lapse of so many years, 'very large'.[37] If only he had plotted them! Broken by the combined attack, Byron's Brigade now fled although some doubt remains as to whether Beaumont's Regiment went with them.

The two right-hand Royalist brigades saved the day. Belasyse himself, pike in hand, led the charge into the fray in an attempt to reverse the situation. They were repulsed but, nevertheless, they stemmed the break, but not without the loss of 'very many gallant officers'. Belasyse himself was wounded. 'He only received a slight hurt upon his head, and had the good fortune to recover, with Sir Jacob Astley, the major general, and some others [of] our Foot upon the left wing, who never came to charge at all, so they stood entire'.[38] Charles Gerard's Brigade, composed of his own regiment and those of Sir Lewis Dyve and Sir Ralph Dutton, seems to have stood firm and provided an essential anchor for the line.

However, the infantry battle had been rekindled. The firing must have become more sporadic as ammunition failed and energy levels dropped, but Parliament had now gained the upper hand. By driving forward, the right of Meldrum's Brigade, most likely consisting now of just Meldrum's own Regiment and the fugitives from Fairfax's, gradually pushed Wentworth's back. They can be envisaged standing astride the track that later came to be known as King John's Lane with the Royalists being driven before their attack, back to the slopes at the foot of the escarpment. Just as it has been argued that not all of Ballard's commanded muskets ran off the field, so portions of Byron's and Fielding's must also have been caught up in this final phase. Balfour's cavalry pursuits had not had the distraction of other Horse to chase and were, therefore, probably quite effective in dispersing them but, nevertheless, some of the remnants of Byron's probably clustered on the short spurs of the escarpment. Had their officers exalted them to make a stand, the steep narrow route up the hill would have been blocked. In the presence of such strong opposition, holding a near impregnable position, the fight on the south side of the field would, most probably, have arrived at a stalemate with Meldrum's Regiment satisfied by taking the ground and Wentworth's content at having prevented the enemy from gaining access to the great ridge.

The aforementioned scenario is speculation but credible. So too is the idea that the braver men among Fielding's troops were probably fortifying Radway as best they could, the more faint-hearted doing likewise in Edgehill, while others were still running. Over on the Parliamentarian left, Ballard's Brigade, possibly now joined by Constable's and Robartes's Regiments now reformed after breaking Byron's, began the drive forward, this time with the luxury of more men. Parliament's superiority told as the Royalist line went back. It appears that, on the Royalist left, Pennyman's Regiment was under heavy pressure and gave more ground than the rest. This is particularly likely if they were outflanked by Robartes's. The whole line seems to have pivoted backwards, refusing their left, but with the fulcrum retiring also. By turning the Royalist line the Parliamentarians gained the wind. This meant that the smoke now blew into the faces of the Royalists making their return volleys even less effective. As this start and stop action crept across the wet heathland the Royalist guns may have sought targets that had come within range, for it is out in the fields in the centre, across the little stream, that Bob Leedham says Peter Young told him that he had discovered cannonballs with the use of an army mine-detector.[39] The gunners would, however, have found hitting Ballard's line difficult because of the smoke and the close proximity of their own men, and they must have experienced, yet again, all of their earlier problems of dropping shot and soft ground. Finally, Belasyse's and Gerard's, having retired in good order and crossed the brook, 'made a stand; and having the assistance of cannon, and a ditch before them, held us play very handsomely'.[40] The Royalist line, its left now almost back to their starting position, grimly held their ground. They retired almost beyond their gun line 'but seeing some of the Cannon in danger to be lost, advanced again, and made the Place good; the Left hand of the Rebel Foot coming on apace to Charge them'.[41] Despite their casualties, the three regiments of Wentworth's command who had begun the Foot fight, Molineux's, Salusbury's and Gilbert Gerrard's, were still in the line, quite possibly accompanied by some, if not most, of Beaumont's. There may have been a cobbled-together command in Radway, but across a substantial gap stood Pennyman's, Belasyse's, Blagge's, Dutton's, Dyve's and Gerard's Regiments – nine, possibly ten, of the seventeen that had marched forward so resolutely earlier that afternoon. Facing them, stood the Parliamentarian regiments of Meldrum, Constable, Robartes, the Lord General, Ballard, Brooke and Holles – seven of the twelve who had first deployed to face the onslaught. It is likely that casualties were not as high as many historians have tended to think, but the exhaustion was very real and so too was shock. However, these factors coupled with minor wounds, such as gashed and slashed limbs, were seldom acceptable reasons to withdraw from the line. Breathing hard, the two weary lines must have looked at each through the sweat, the smoke and the twilight. Those brave Englishmen had fought each other to a standstill and neither would give ground.

In the gap Stapleton's and Balfour's Horse also drew breath. Now His Majesty's Pensioners too had quit the field they were the only Horse left, or were they?

Chapter Twelve
Disengagement

...by this time it grew so dark and our Powder and Bullet so spent that it was not held fit we should Advance upon them. Official Parliamentary Account.

The Royalist Horse had been effectively unable to renew the action for some time but two men had succeeded in rallying some of them. Prince Rupert on the Kineton road and Sir Charles Lucas on a knoll south of Little Kineton flank, were both now set to play their parts in the next stage of the battle, albeit at different levels. Rupert actually prevented three troops from joining in the runaway pursuit, but all of the accounts so far discovered are strangely silent on what he then did with them. Even his diary says nothing about what 'ye P' did after bringing his three troops to a halt. Apparently he rallied them before they reached Kineton, so they were situated somewhere behind the Parliamentary left rear. To remain inactive in such an advantageous position seems unbelievable, especially when such an opportunist commander as Rupert was involved.

Lucas's Knoll. Here on this slight rise Lucas rallied some of his troopers and then launched a series of charges into the routing men who streamed across his front.

Pen & Sword Books Limited
FREEPOST SF5
47 Church Street
BARNSLEY
South Yorkshire
S70 2BR

DISCOVER MORE ABOUT MILITARY HISTORY

Pen & Sword Books have over 400 books currently in print. Our imprints include the Battleground series, Leo Cooper, Military Classics, Select, Pen & Sword Aviation and Pen & Sword Naval. We cover all periods of history on land, sea and air. If you would like to receive more information on any or all of these, please complete the form below and return. (NO STAMP REQUIRED)

Mr/Mrs/Ms ....

Address...

Postcode .... E-mail address ....

Please tick your areas of interest:

Pre World War One ☐	World War Two ☐	Regimental History ☐
Napoleonic ☐	Post World War Two ☐	Military Reference ☐
World War One ☐	Falklands ☐	Military Biography ☐
Battlefield Guides ☐	Battleground Series Club *(free membership)* ☐	

Please send me information on: Books ☐

Website: www.pen-and-sword.co.uk · Email: enquiries@pen-and-sword.co.uk
Telephone: 01226 734555 · Fax: 01226 734438

Scattering the routers.

Some clue to the situation may be gleaned from the Prince's diary where he is critical of Byron for allowing his reserve to engage in a disordered chase. Perhaps the Prince's subsequent actions with his three troops reflect just what he would have preferred Byron to have achieved with his six. Rupert was probably aware that not all of Essex's army was on the field so, having lost control of twenty-four troops, nearly ninety per cent of his command, perhaps he formed the men that he had stopped somewhere short of Kineton into a line of troops, watching for the approach of Parliamentarian reinforcements or a counter-attack? Equally, he may have used his reduced force as a rallying point while awaiting the return of the the remainder of his units, not knowing that many had continued the chase beyond Kineton while others had fallen to plundering both the baggage and the local civilian population. This, however, remains speculation. What is certain, however, is that, as Commander of all the Horse, he neglected Wilmot's wing. He was able to remember this responsibility before the battle when delivering orders and taking part in the preliminary cheer-leading but, in the heat of action, when he should have ridden across to Lucas and co-ordinated some sort of manoeuvre, he appears to have allowed this aspect of his command to totally slip his mind. On a tactical level, following the defeat of the Parliamentarian left wing, Rupert failed to bring any pressure whatsoever to bear on Essex's beleaguered Foot, thereby delivering the day to him.

At least Sir Charles Lucas tried. Lucas was the lieutenant colonel of Carnarvon's Regiment and he had managed to halt and reform about two hundred troopers from a variety of regiments although Walsingham, quoting Chester Herald, William Dugdale, attributed this feat to Captain John Smith of Lord Grandison's Regiment. This force may have been small, but it was numerically strong enough to be effective and Lucas seemed determined to do something to influence the battle. He arrayed his small composite unit so that they threatened the Parliamentarian rear and then began his march forward. The time that Lucas began this manoeuvre can be established because his men immediately ran into the fleeing infantry of Charles Essex's Brigade. Young suggested the latter body included those of William Fairfax's, but this is unlikely as that unit had been broken at the same time as Fielding's cavalry, and their soldiers who had run away would, by that time, have been well away from the area. Young is probably accurate, however, in his assumption that the attack broke down not only as a result of the routed soldiers getting in the way but also due to chance offering the Royalists an easy opportunity to capture enemy colours. Four running, broken regiments would have meant that forty company colours, prized trophies with scant protection save the skill at arms of the now tired and frightened Ensigns who carried them, were within easy reach – a tantalizing target. Add to this the prospect of cutting down fleeing men, many of whom would have discarded their weapons, and the Royalists would surely have been tempted to take the easier option rather than attempt to break into seven regiments of formed enemy foot, albeit from the rear.

Either Lucas or Robert Walsh, captain lieutenant of Lord Wilmot's own troop, commanded during the subsequent actions, as Walsh was later said to have kept 'his command intact'. Walsingham makes Captain Smith the hero of the hour as Smith's party put in three charges during this later phase, with each charge reducing their numbers as the temptation to follow up their beaten foes increased. The first was made against Charles Essex's fleeing regiment, among whom they inflicted several casualties and, having captured all of their enemy's colours, turned a confused rabble slowly making its way rearward into an all-out rout. After the Royalist unit had regrouped, their second charge was made in an attempt to return to the main battle. Walsingham would have his readers believe that a party of Parliamentarian Horse had wheeled off the back of their larger formation and formed up so as to prevent Lucas's men from threatening an attack on the Foot. Ludlow, who was with Stapleton in the Lord General's Regiment, did not mention the incident but Walsh, who claims to have led his troop in this charge, said that these were the men who had charged the King's Lifeguard and carried off the captured colours –which Smith duly retook, along with some of the Parliamentarian's own. Smith also appears to have led a charge into his enemy's line. He routed them easily and his troopers subsequently pursued them with equal ease. Given the practice of the day, the Parliamentarians that were apparently so easily overwhelmed in this second engagement with Lucas's force might well have been a detached party who suffered the misfortune of running into enemy troopers while escorting previously captured colours, including the Banner Royal, from the field. Smith then rallied once more, but this time he could only muster some fourteen men – but these were enough! His third charge was directed into the remains of Wharton's Regiment who, apparently, appeared to coalesce near Kineton. This charge lost Wharton's their colours and destroyed any hopes that might have been entertained of them rallying. Smith himself took the Major's colour which he then handed to a groom called Chichley who had previously fought in the Duke of Richmond's troop and, indeed, had earlier captured one of Charles Essex's colours himself.[1] In the meantime, Walsh had taken his troop into Kineton where they seized two guns and a wagon which they subsequently managed to take back behind their own lines. Unfortunately it is not known by which route he moved nor what he saw on the way.

These piecemeal attacks prevented the Parliamentarian Foot from rallying, but they

The final position of the Royalist Foot. The end came in the evening in these fields when Belasyes' and Gerard's brigades reformed their line behind the ditch, the treeline marking its position is clearly visible.

also wasted the opportunity to achieve the resounding tactical success that a combined rear attack could have delivered. For the Parliamentary cause, Balfour's and the Lord General's Regiments, unimpeded by enemy Horse, wreaked havoc among the Royalist Foot and ordnance and even, perhaps, turned the tables of the battle. Nevertheless, Smith had certainly achieved a propaganda coup and, in doing so, had created a military legend for himself by his recapture of the Banner Royal. A Royalist newsletter reported that the banner was retaken within six minutes but, more realistically, Kightley specifies an hour and a half. Young tells a rattling good tale of its retaking, drawn from Edward Walsingham's account, but the original is so full of drama and descriptive detail it is worth quoting in full!

> But now of all his fourteen there was no more left but himselfe and Chichley...As these two were passing on towards our Army, this Mirrour of Chivalry espies six men, three Curiasiers and three Harquebusiers on horsebacke, guarding a seventh on foot, who was carrying off the Field a Colours rouled up which he conceived to be one of the ordinary Colours of His Majesties Leife-guards, and therefore seeing them so strong, intended to avoide them. Whilst he was thus considering, a boy on horsebacke calls to him saying, Captaine Smith, Captaine Smith, they are carrying away the Standard. He would not suddainly believe the boy, till by great asseverations he had assured him it was the Standard, who forthwith said, 'They shall have me with it if they carry it away'; and desiring Chichley if he saw him much engaged to throw down the other Colours and assist him; presently he charg'd in with his rapier at the footman that carried the Banner, (who was the Secretary to Essex the Rebells General) saying, 'Traitor deliver the Standard', and wounded him into the breast, whilst he was bent forward to

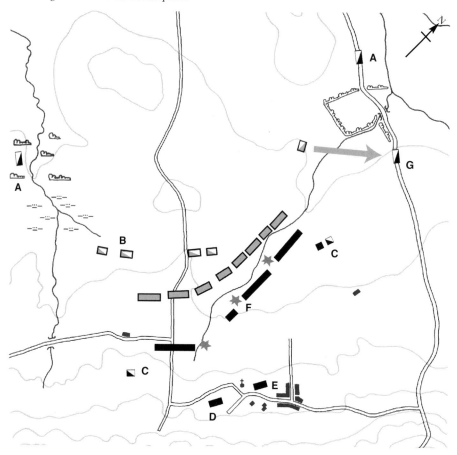

*Fall back and dig in. With Fielding's and Byron's gone, the remaining Royalist Foot lose the push of pike contest. Wentworth is driven back to the gun line at the foot of the escarpment while Belasyes's and Gerard's pivot back and adopt a defensive line on Radway Brook supported by guns, dragoons and some returning Horse. The Reserve makes one last charge but both armies are fought to a standstill. At **A** the Royalist Horse is returning. At **B** scattered elements of Balfour's protect the Parliamentary flank. **C** are Horse and dragoons. At **D** are remnants of Byron's, at **E** remnants of Fielding's. At **F** Royalist guns pushed forward to support the defensive line. At **G** returning Royalist Horse are charged by the Parliamentarian reserve.*

follow his thrust, one of those Curiasiers with a pollax wounded him in the necke through the Collar of his doublet, and the rest gave fire at him with their pistols, but without any further hurt than blowing off some pouder into his face. No sooner was he recovered upright, but he made a thrust at the Curiasier that wounded him, and ran him in at the belly, whereupon he presently fell, at which sight the rest ran away. Then he caused a foot souldier that was near at hand to reach him up the banner, which he brought away with the horse of that Curiasier.[2]

This account is contradicted by two Parliamentarian sources. Firstly, by the Official Parliamentary Account where it was stated that the banner was removed from Secretary

Chambers by 'some of our Troopers' and thereafter lost, no-one knew where and, secondly, by Ludlow who claimed that Smith had disguised himself with an orange-coloured scarf and 'pretending it unfit for a penman should have the honour to carry the standard, took it from him'.[3] Meanwhile, we are to believe that, if Smith's story was not a fabrication to embroider his personal achievements, Chambers's escort stood by all the while and did nothing.

Smith's story continues. He rode to yet another rallying group of Royalist troopers and handed the Banner Royal to Robert Hatton to carry to the King – for this hero had not yet done with daring deeds. Later in the evening gloom he road off to attack yet another small, isolated group of Parliamentarian horsemen, this time a party who were escorting the Royalist brigade commander, Richard Fielding, into captivity, and rescued their prisoner. This may be what swashbuckling cavalier heroes are all about but, whatever the reality of the situation, the King sent for Smith later the next day and knighted him on the field. Walsingham then proceeds to tell how, after being knighted, Smith took yet another party of thirty troopers back out onto the field, away to the Parliamentarian left, and dared the enemy to attack him while he ordered horses spanned into traces so that he could carry away three of his enemy's brass cannon. Finally the valiant hero, now transforming himself into an angel of mercy, assisted Adrian Scrope recover his sore-wounded father.[4]

Irony aside, it may appear churlish to cast doubt upon the deeds of one so brave but, in the words of that popular writer of military history, Donald Featherstone, the phrase 'courage the great pardoner' encapsulates much of what happens when a story is needed to boost morale after a setback.[5] A closer look is necessary to properly evaluate the actions of these rallied 200 horsemen who, if we discount Rupert's enigmatic three troops, were the last disposable force of the Royalist cause that was, by this stage of the battle, in desperate straits. The timing of events seems to suggest that Lucas's attempted intervention came sometime after Byron's Brigade had broken, the Banner Royal having been transferred from Young to Middleton to Chambers, and an escort having been found to take it from the field. Considering the fact that the Parliamentarian Horse was not then engaged, we come to the conclusion that the episode coincides with the prolonged lull discussed earlier. Had Lucas been able to restrain the dashing élan of men such as Smith, curb their piecemeal, albeit successful, attacks and bring his rallied force together as a cohesive shock into the rear of the Parliamentarian fighting line, (Smith proved that the covering cavalry could have been brushed aside), the day could have been decided there and then. Once again we see evidence of the weakness inherent in a mind set that applauds bursts of spectacular, individual feats of glory at the expense of the steady practice of the collective work that epitomises the soldier's trade and wins battles.

In the dim evening light, Essex was about to be reinforced by more of those men who put duty and steadiness above heroics and flamboyance. Fresh units of Parliamentarian Horse began arriving in and around Kineton, probably gathering on the hill where Captain John Fiennes stood with his troop and whose earlier calm actions had probably prevented more slaughter among the Foot. The influx of these arrivals on the outskirts of Kineton ended the pillaging of the baggage and, slowly, the looters withdrew. Not all returned to their Royalist lines for, to be of use, loot has to be taken home. How many men were lost to the King and for how long they were absent cannot be estimated, but their numbers may well have provided a significant factor in the strategic decisions taken in the next few days.

Captain Kightley was another of the late arrivals who had previously heard nothing of the impending battle until it started. Presumably he had heard the guns when some five miles distant. Hastening forward he encountered other latecomers, including the troop formerly commanded by the late Major Alexander Douglas and yet another, un-named troop. Just as Fiennes's men had been disheartened by Ramsey's fleeing troops, when the newly arrived troops came onto the field they encountered about 200 fleeing men of Fielding's. These routing men declared that the day was lost and, suddenly, Kightley found his little 'ad hoc' regiment reduced to thirty-six men when the remainder panicked and were swept away in the rush. Aware that his force was not strong enough to undertake much without great risk to themselves, he drew up in a small field that had a track running through it, and there he contented himself dealing with isolated Royalist soldiers unfortunate enough to venture near his hedge-lined position. It is likely that Kightley's hedges were part of the Kineton enclosures which, along with those around Little Kineton, seem to have afforded a refuge of sorts and a means of stemming the flood of men to the rear. Kightley's men, rather than killing the enemy, appear to have satisfied themselves by pillaging their adversaries, taking their horses and weapons, touching off their powder and sending the men on their way - 'I tooke away about tenne or twelve horse, swords, and armour... the powder which the Enemy had was blowne up in the field'.[6] Eventually their source of plunder probably dried up for Kightley shifted his laden troop to join Fiennes on his hilltop.

One of the last of these disparate troops to arrive on the field was one of the Lord General's Regiment under the command of Captain Oliver Cromwell who, rather than becoming embroiled in the chaos, also took his men to the high ground. The exact location of this hill cannot be ascertained but Cromwell's troop, together with other individuals who had attached themselves to his unit, rallied around Fiennes who now found himself in command of a useful force. The combined body of Horse moved off down the hill and, having been attacked, sensibly turned and rode back to reinforce Hampden's command that was, by now, finally approaching Kineton.

Some of the Royalists had found the new arrivals already. Bulstrode, with the scattered troopers of the Prince of Wales's Regiment relates how they 'pursued also, till we met with two Foot Regiments of Hambden and Hollis and with a Regiment of Horse coming from Warwick to their Army, which made us hasten as fast back as we had pursued'.[7] Indeed they were chased back and it may have been in this pursuit that some of the Parliamentarians under Willoughby were hurt. Bulstrode himself, as he later reported, was nearly killed – 'in this Pursuit I was wounded in the Head by a Person who turned upon me, and struck me with his Pole-axe, and was seconding his Blow, when Sir Thomas Byron being near, he shot him dead with his Pistol'.[8] Local tradition has it that the first encounter occurred a mile up the Warwick Road at a place now known as Rupert's Headland but, regrettably we cannot tell on which side of Kineton this desperate action of Bulstrode's occurred nor how far it was from the town. It is worth noting that recent archeological surveys of other battlefields suggest that such events probably took place over a wider area than has hitherto been believed.

Willoughby's Horse probably pursued their prey past Kineton but there is nothing to suggest that they went much further, perhaps because they caught sight of Rupert's covering force waiting silently nearby. Hampden's and Grantham's Foot approached Kineton along the main Warwick road and, now joined by Fiennes's composite command, they constituted a significant force as they made their way forward to join Essex on the field of battle. No eye witness reports survive to detail what happened to them, but it is likely that they saw action – perhaps they were charged by Rupert – as seven men from Hampden's and seven from Willoughby's are included in the lists of casualties compiled in Warwick and Coventry shortly after the battle. This may seem an insignificant number until one considers that deaths and non-hospital wounds were not recorded and that Fairfax's Regiment had only seven men listed in the same documents and they had been broken and caught by Horse in pursuit!

To return to the Royalist Foot, having been driven back in a melee and then, withdrawing across the little stream, they found time and space to reorder their ranks and files. Having lost contact with Wentworth's on their left, Gerard's and Belasyse's realigned along a ditch, diagonally across their original position in the Royalist army's start line. By so doing, the army's senior commanders managed to achieve a satisfactory position. They secured their lines of communication with the Banbury road to their rear, their right flank rested on the northern war ground and was further protected by the returning troops of Rupert's command. Their left rear was covered by the fortified village of Radway and the remnants of Wilmot's Brigade, and the whole line now came under the protection of their army's big guns on Bullet Hill, although they may still have been in some disarray.

Placing the ditch accurately can be a problem, but not if we turn, once again, to that early battlefield walker, Rev. Miller, who interprets it as the brook which diagonally crosses the field. The upper reaches of Ramsey's little stream, after running from north to south for a short distance parallel to the great hedge, turns eastwards and runs diagonally away towards Radway. If the Royalist line had been pushed off the slope of Essex's Ridge, pivoted along a forty-five degree axis, and had then been driven back the 400 yards generally conceded, it would have arrived at this brook. Miller states 'barely any traces of the battle have been found on the Radway side of the brook or where the brook turns up towards the hill beyond a straight line drawn in the direction the brook has hitherto run'.[9] It would seem that the little stream Ramsey had placed such faith in and which had proved no stay to Rupert's gallant troopers, now provided shelter for the Royalists.

The soldiers were now joined by the King and his tiny retinue. The presence of his person must have encouraged some and strengthened their resolve by projecting an image of Charles in the role of a warrior king taking his place on the field of battle, unafraid to do whatever was required of him. Under the eyes of their monarch they had turned a disorganized push backwards into an orderly retirement, even Ludlow commented that they had 'retired orderly, and at last made a stand'.[10] This was no rout or hurried retreat. They must have also fallen back deliberately to get closer to their magazines in order to replenish powder and bullet, for they 'continued firing until night put an end to the dispute.'[11] During one attempt to repowder an unthinking Royalist musketeer went to a budge barrel and 'clapt his Hand carelessly into a barrel of Powder, with his Match lighted betwixt his Fingers, whereby much powder was blown up, and many kill'd'.[12] This must have brought some relief for Essex's men for, as well as being exhausted, they too were low on ammunition as recorded in the Official Parliamentary

Account; 'by this time it grew so dark and our Powder and Bullet so spent that it was not held fit we should Advance upon them'.[13]

One cannot but admire the Parliamentarian infantry for, nevertheless, having fought all afternoon and being low on shot, they reformed their bodies and once again marched forward to attack. Some other accounts of Edgehill interpret the battle as an initial Royalist attack followed by a simple, if not prolonged, melee. This was far from being the case as a considerable part of the entire day was taken up by a sequence of attack, melee, fall back, regroup and attack again, alternating musket and pike fighting wherever appropriate. For Ballard's exhausted Brigade this final move forward must have been the third full brigade advance that they had made as a cohesive unit. However, it was not to come into contact. The Royalists had chosen their position well, behind their own gun line, with the protection of the ditch to their front. From somewhere, Horse, including some dragoons, appeared and moved to offer them support. Their guns were turned upon the Parliamentary troops but, although the guns fired occasionally, they seem to have caused little hurt. The dragoons also joined in by providing 'a Volley or two of Shot, which made the rebels instantly retire'.[14] In reality, both lines held fast and stood.

Where had these newly arrived Royalist horsemen come from? In the past historians have been tempted to ascribe their presence to Rupert, basing their assumptions on the rhetorical question 'for where else could he have been?' Tradition has it that Rupert eventually returned and covered the retreat of the Royalist army as it withdrew up Edgehill, but there is no evidence to support this story, nor is there much to suggest the Royalist army fell back up the hill. The more likely scenario is that this group of mounted men were not all Horse but mostly made up of dragoons. There had been three regiments of dragoons on the field earlier in the day and all had successfully driven off their opponents. They then vanish from most accounts of the battle. Having covered the advance of the army, recovered and replenished, it is quite plausible that they now did the same for its withdrawal. If two regiments had been placed upon the wings and fired the volleys that so deterred the Parliamentarian advance, there would still be a dragoon regiment of no less than three troops remaining mounted as a reserve. This provides a far more more likely answer to the puzzle than trying to find such a thoughtful deployment from Rupert's direction.

However, both Rupert and Wilmot did manage to gather some sort of command together during the early evening. Neither were substantial and Clarendon even commented that they:

> could not be persuaded or drawn to charge either the enemy's reserve of horse…or the body of their foot… the officers pretending that their soldiers were so dispersed that there were not ten of any troop together, and the soldiers, that their horses were so tired that they could not charge.[15]

Much of what took place towards the end of the day is speculative. The smoke and the dim light of late evening probably cloaked many incidents from the wider view and recollections of these events are infrequent and less vivid than those referring to earlier parts of the day with general overall tiredness a prominent contributory factor. However, it is necessary to provide a further examination of what happened to Rupert's and Wilmot's horse after they had finished plundering. Many of them must have returned, admittedly not those more widely dispersed, but certainly those who had stayed in small groups and had not ventured far beyond Kineton. Some travelled by circuitous routes, others rode more directly back. We know from Bulstrode that the arrival of Essex's reinforcements hastened the rally and we are also told by Ludlow that those who did return to their lines did not have an easy time of it.

Ludlow reports that, late in the day, some of Rupert's Horse were caught by the Lord General's Horse who, having nothing more to do in the centre with the final attack having come to nothing, and probably loathe to remain exposed to cannon fire, had moved towards their left of the field.[16] There they 'discovered a body of horse marching from our rear on the left of us under the hedges'. Stapleton resolved to attack them and, having unsuccessfully sought the aid of additional troops who declined his request, he moved off. Ludlow describes what happened next. 'We had no way to come at them but through a gap in the hedge, we advanced towards them, and falling upon their rear, killed divers of them, and brought off some arms'. The term 'arms' was used in this context to refer to both weapons and armour and, if one dismisses the hoary old chestnut that men cannot mount easily in full armour, it would appear that Ludlow, along with many of his colleagues, dismounted and stripped cuirassier armour from the wounded and the occasional corpse. These fallen Royalists may, therefore, have been members of an important troop.[17] This was not unusual for, as noted earlier in this chapter, Kightley was doing the same thing in another part of the field. As a result of his accumulated pickings, Ludlow could only remount with difficulty when the Lord General's Horse retired to reunite with Balfour's and Bedford's in the rear of the exhausted Parliamentarian infantry.

The end of the fight came almost by mutual consent. Both sides had expended all of their energy and their corporate will to fight just as the day ran out of light. Essex's men had advanced but had failed to reach as far as Radway. The King's men held their original deployment ground and, bloodied and bowed, both sides prepared for night. The Official Royalist Account suggests there was still fight left in the King's army but continues 'It was grown so dark, that our Chief Commanders durst not Charge for Fear of mistaking Friends for Foes'.[18] Under the cover of this early nightfall Essex's army bedded down on the ground that they had so magnificently won. Many of the Royalists also remained in the field sleeping behind their ditch, while others regained the high ground of Edgehill. 'Both Armies retreated, ours in such Order, that we not only brought off our own cannon, but 4 of the Rebels, we retiring to the top of the hill from whence we came'.[19]

The King ordered his small guns to be drawn back onto the lower slopes of the escarpment and also called for his carriage to be brought down from Knoll End. Descending the bottom road, now disused and overgrown, it drew up in the rear of the Royalist's final fighting line, near a Radway farm building that later became known as Kings Leys barn, situated about half way between the great ridge and Parliament's line. Here Charles spent the night, either in his carriage or in the barn itself, local tradition favours the latter, and, again according to local tradition, he walked into Radway the next morning to breakfast in a cottage that, subsequently, was demolished in 1882.[20] There are several points associated with this tale that need to be drawn out. It is said that the table off which Charles dined was preserved until the demolition but has since disappeared. A J Sharkey describes this cottage as an ale-house and thinks that Miller was probably being sensitive about claiming that the King would have eaten in such a

The site of Kings Leys barn. The tumulus is in fact a pile of rubble east of Langdon Road. It is all that is left of some modern buildings which were demolished and piled on top of the barn's foundations.

lowly establishment rather than visit 'the Grange – the only property of substance in the village'.[21] Sharkey goes on to state that the building stood adjacent to Radway Grange and that the empty plot can still be seen, along with the doorstep of the former building. However, two other accounts, those of Sir Robert Walsh and Sir Philip Warwick, both stated that the King lay 'that night upon the top of Edge-Hill'.[22] As for the Earl of Essex, in the early hours of the next day he returned to Kineton where his Lifeguard had endured another bitterly cold bivouac in the same nearby fields where they had slept the night before the battle.

Chapter Thirteen
Aftermath

...many poor sick and wounded soldiers ventured their lives and lost their limbs in the public service of the King and Parliament. Journal of the House of Commons

The night of 23 October was bitterly cold. The wind, of which both sides had fought to gain the advantage, dropped, and frost began to form on the bodies of the dead, dying and wounded alike. Many of the King's infantry were ordered back up the eastern slope of Edgehill escorted by Rupert's exhausted cavalry. Others slept where they last stood. Both sides bivouacked as best they could. Essex's army stood guard that night on ground they had gained from the Royalists, thus technically being able to claim Edgehill fight as a Parliamentary victory. Sir Philip Warwick of the King's Lifeguard of Horse styles the battle 'our first and great military misadventure' and places the blame for the defeat upon Byron and Digby, 'for both reserves pursuing the chase, contrary to all discipline of war, left the King and his Foot so alone, that it gave Essex a title unto the victory that day'.[1] Even the desperately loyal Sir Richard Bulstrode says 'I think we had no Reason to brag of a Victory'.[2]

Conditions in the Parliamentary lines were unpleasant in the extreme. No fires were lit, the ground upon which they stood was littered with the dead, and many troops had not eaten in two days. Ludlow describes how, having lost his cloak and 'having nothing to keep me warm but a suit of iron, I was obliged to walk around all night, which proved very cold by reason of a sharp frost'.[3]

In the early hours, John Hampden's weary men came into the lines having spent part of the night in Kineton, but dawn revealed that the Royalists were in no position to renew the action that morning. To the relief of his men, Essex pulled them back into Kineton for a few hours rest before again arraying them in the field from mid-morning to early afternoon. With the Earl's main force off the field for a short time, opportunistic detachments of Royalist Horse descended the hill and carried off a number of abandoned field guns, both their own and the enemy's, but the return of the Parliamentarians further reinforced by the newly arrived Lord Rochford's Regiment put a stop to that. The rest of the day was given over to burying the dead, trumpeters under flags of truce seeking information on missing personnel, and the retrieval of those wounded still left on the field. A Royalist report claimed that the King dined in the field upon a drumhead and stayed within four miles till the dead were buried. The King's infantry took the day to rest and regroup on their hilltop fastness with the bloodstained Banner Royal set up once again, tradition has it, on the site of the present Castle Inn Tower. This lack of activity convinced Essex that the engagement was definitely over, so he again pulled back his forces to Kineton to prepare for a withdrawal to Warwick. The little village was packed with sick and wounded that night, but at least the local country people were bringing in some provisions. Essex himself rode that evening to Warwick while every wagon that still had a team was readied for an early morning start. Despite convincing themselves that the battle had been a victory, Essex's senior officers finished their official dispatch to Parliament late that night with the ominous passage 'its very requisite letters from the Committee should be writ into the Countries which are Southern, to stir them up or assist us at least against them'.[4]

The preparations for Essex's withdrawal had not gone unnoticed by the Royalists and Prince Rupert determined to attack their rear by marching down from the hill at Sun Rising with two regiments of Horse and two of dragoons. By the time Rupert reached Kineton, most of the rebel army were already on the road, concealed by a great mist that prevented Rupert's pursuit. The Royalists had to content themselves with the capture of a number of arms and ammunition wagons and Essex's own transport containing his plate and a cabinet of private letters. This small skirmish marked the end of the Battle of Edgehill, the first and longest of the great field actions of the English Civil War.

We must now turn to the fate of those who were wounded during the fight. Despite the lessons that had been learned during the Thirty Years War by several commanders in both armies, the establishment of a regimental surgeon and two surgeon's mates to each regiment appears to have been the only provision made for casualty care at this early stage of the war, with little or no consideration given to the long term after-care of the wounded or sick.[5] Powick Bridge served to highlight this deficiency and, four weeks later, Edgehill forced the lesson home. For months afterwards, the rebounding effects of this, the first major battle of the war, were reflected in changes of perceptions, attitudes and plans of the belligerents. Parliament in particular awoke to the realization that it faced a national rather than local conflict, and embarked upon the first steps towards constructing a definitive health and welfare service for those injured in its service.

As with so many other battles, contemporary casualty estimates for Edgehill have ranged across widely disparate figures that have, more often than not, been grossly over- or understated according to the persuasion of the author. A combined total of up to 5,000 dead was widely reported by several contemporary writers:

Table 13.1   Alleged casualty figures for the Battle of Edgehill.

Source	Allegiance	The King's Army	Army of Parliament
Lord Wharton	Parliamentarian	3,000	300
Clarendon	Royalist	1,600	3,400
Vicars	Parliamentarian	2,000 to 3,000	200 to 400
Lord Brooke	Parliamentarian	2,000	100
TK	Parliamentarian	3,000	300

Source: BodL, Vet. A3 d. 404, Wharton, *Eight Speeches* ...; Clarendon, *The History of the Rebellion and Civil Wars in England* (Oxford, 1843), p. 310; J Vicars, *Jehovah Jireh, God in the Mount* (1644), p. 198; BL, *TT* E 124 (18): 'TK'.

In addition, the Royalist, Lord Bernard Stuart, claimed that the King had lost 2,500 men, Belasyse quoted 3,000 and Sydenham 8,000.[6] By way of comparison, in his memoires, James II thought that the combined total was 'not above 1,500' and Sir

William Dugdale, a prominent antiquarian and Royal Herald who was present during the battle, claimed to have questioned the local villagers who had buried corpses on the battlefield and he believed their count, less than 1,000, to have been accurate.[7] So, can a reliable estimate of the actual number of casualties suffered during the battle be arrived at from a distance of over 350 years? To do so requires an in-depth study of contemporary casualty care.

The use of local communities to care for sick and wounded soldiers was dependent to a great extent on local sympathies. On 29 October 1642, the Eydon parish register recorded that 'a soldier of the King's Army and wounded in the battle of Edge-Hill was buried with us' but the predominantly Parliamentarian sympathizers of the surrounding villages were generally hostile to the Royalist cause and gave scant care to casualties left behind by the King's army.[8] Although a few were cared for locally, most survivors were transported to Oxford in wagons and deposited in various churches, almshouses, hostelries and private houses. As a result, the city's parish officers found themselves obliged to provide the survivors with succour and sustenance and to bury the dead. At St Aldate's the churchwarden's accounts record payments totalling £4 8s 2d relating to thirty-one shrouds for the burial of wounded soldiers who died in the parish and £2 8s 4d for food 'for the soldiers of the Almshouses when they came from Edgehill fight'.[9] The King's army and its entourage soon filled every available nook and cranny that the city could offer as, apart from the troops, the court, members of the government, as well as servants, dependants, families and a variety of refugees from surrounding areas all descended upon the city where overcrowding and grossly insanitary conditions were made worse by a huge increase in the number of horses and other animals. Both human and animal waste was carelessly disposed of in cesspits, dunghills or open drains running through the middle of the streets. The latter rapidly filled with excreta and rubbish of all kinds that lay festering for days and weeks on end providing an ideal breeding ground for all types of communicable diseases. Inevitably, the army was soon to suffer the ill-effects of overcrowding and poor hygiene during a widespread outbreak of typhus fever.[10]

On 16 November 1642 a tax, payable by the city parishioners of Oxford according to the table set out below, intended to raise the sum of £71 15s 0d, was introduced for the support of sick and wounded soldiers:

Table 13.2 Oxford taxation in aid of sick and maimed soldiers.

Parish	Levy	Parish	Levy
All Saints	£10 10s	St Martins	£10
Binsey	£4	St Mary	£10
Holywell	£6	St Mary Magdalen	Nil
St Aldate	£10 10s	St Michael	£8
St Ebbe	£3	St Peter in the East	£8 15s
St Giles	Nil	St Peter le Bailey	Nil
St John	£1	St Thomas	Nil

Source: M G Hobson and Rev H E Salter, *Oxford Council Acts, 1626–65* (Oxford, 1933), pp 369–71.

Meanwhile continuing expenditure on military items and the strengthening of the city's defences as well as casualty care, resulted in the imposition of a permanent weekly levy of £12. A second levy was introduced on 30 December, this time totalling £150 and, on 18 April 1643, yet a third demand for £2,398 3s 9d, this time to cover both the Mayor's continuing expenditure on the sick and wounded as well as a forced 'loan' of £2,000 to be paid to the King.[11] Eventually, a military hospital was established in the surviving portion of the former St Mary's college that stood in New Inn Hall Street but, unfortunately, documentation bearing testimony to the nature, quantity and quality of the nursing care provided in this hospital has not survived. Even its location has been the source of some debate.[12]

Elsewhere, the experience of the Parliamentary wounded after the battle was somewhat different. While many lay scattered across the countryside, some lying where they fell, others were carried by, or struggled to follow, the retiring army towards Warwick. Up to 200 wounded men lay in the village of Kineton where, according to Ludlow, 'the enemy having notice, sent out a party of horse under Prince Rupert, who on Tuesday night fell into the town of Kineton, where our sick and wounded soldiers lay, and after they had cruelly murdered many of them, returned to their army'.[13] Fortunately, the local population was well disposed to the Parliament's cause as almost all of the local villagers were approached by wounded including the residents of Halford, Pillerton, the Tachbrooks and Offchurch.

The reality of the battle's impact on the local population is evident in the claims submitted by just one Warwickshire village, Ryton on Dunsmore, where fifteen villagers, including three widows, submitted claims for reimbursement of their losses sustained in accommodating well over 2,000 soldiers, men under the command of Colonel Hampden, Lord Manchester and Colonel Devereux, many of them sick or wounded, during their march either to or from the battle of Edgehill.[14] Elsewhere, Hester Whyte a lady who was left destitute by the death of her husband during the siege of Banbury in 1644, petitioned Parliament for relief in 1646 claiming that, after Edgehill, she cared for two wounded Parliamentary soldiers who remained in her house:

> in great misery (by reason of their wounds) for the space of three months
> at the least, she being constrained many times to be up night & day with
> them w[hi]ch was not only a great trouble to her but [also] . . . a great
> charge, she laying out her own moneys to supply their present necessities.[15]

In answer to her plea she received £1. Equally, Katherine Hobson, a lady employed by Lord Brooke to attend, dress and provide 'necessaries' for 140 wounded soldiers 'that came from Kington [Kineton] battle', later submitted a claim for the significant sum of £76 relating to her associated expenses of which, in repayment some five years later, she received only £25.[16]

Elsewhere, a paymaster sent in a claim for £21 that he had paid to villagers who had received billeted wounded soldiers as a temporary measure until long-term arrangements could be made. Yet more wounded attempted to struggle to their own homes, some at a considerable distance, while the most severe cases were carried to Warwick and Coventry in recently captured enemy carts requisitioned for 'the relief of maimed soldiers which were to the number of three or four hundred sent to Warwick to be cared for and cured of their wounds'.[17] One Warwick resident, Joan Harrison, later claimed reimbursement of 11s for her time spent in searching for wounded during the 'hard and frosty weather' during the night after the battle. Contemporary sources attribute the survival of many casualties to the intense cold which, it is claimed, helped to arrest

The Savoy Hospital (private collection).

bleeding.[18] The severity of the weather was reflected in the quantity of coal requisitioned in Warwick. Some forty-five bags costing £2 8s 0d were supplied for the wounded lodged around the town while, additionally, charcoal costing £2 6s 0d was delivered for wounded prisoners being cared for by four men at Lady Hales's house, a large stone edifice at the end of Jury Street. Despite Lacell having funded the fitting of a new door lock, Dugdale recorded that, in 1644, some sixty prisoners broke out of their prison at Lady Hales's house and successfully regained Royalist lines at Worcester, Dudley Castle and Banbury.[19]

Essex returned to London on 7 November taking the walking wounded with him. Many, together with the casualties that arose from Prince Rupert's subsequent attack on Brentford on 12 November, found lodgings wherever they could in houses and villages scattered throughout the western suburbs of London as well as in the City itself. On 25 October, only forty-eight hours after the battle, Parliament had accepted, for the first time in the country's history, that it owed a duty of care to those killed or wounded in its service and formed the 'Committee for Sick and Maimed Soldiers'. This body subsequently assumed responsibility for administering to the needs not only of those wounded in Parliament's cause but also widows and orphans. It remained in being, in one form or another, until the Restoration in 1660.

On 13 November, the Committee for Sick and Maimed Soldiers issued instructions for soldiers requiring medical care to report to the Savoy Hospital for treatment and, on 3 December, ordered the establishment of a daily 'sick parade' at the Savoy, where wounded soldiers carrying a certificate from their officer 'shall with their said certificates, repose to the Savoy Hospital where there shall be a physician and surgeon appointed ready every morning between 8 and 9 o'clock to view their wounds and maims and to dress the same'. The physician's and surgeon's fees were paid by Parliament while additional administrative officials were instructed to pay each soldier who was

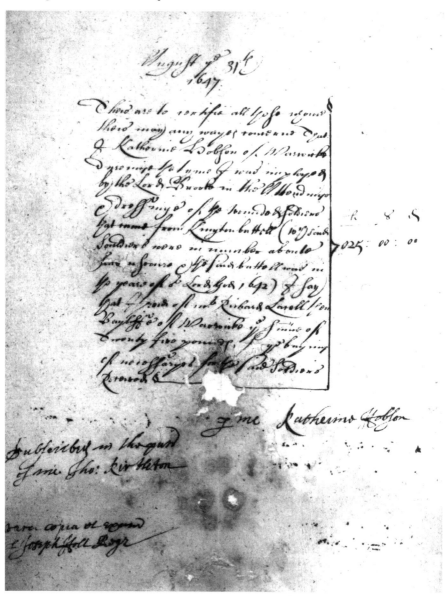

Katherine Hobson's Receipt. Source: National Archives, SP 28/136, f. 16.

sufficiently fit to remain in lodgings the sum of 8*d* a day until his wounds were healed.[20]

Some indication of the work carried out in the Savoy, Brentford and elsewhere, including payments to women widowed as a result of the fighting, can be obtained from the bills subsequently paid by the Treasurers of the Committee for Sick and Maimed Soldiers during the six months following the battle of Edgehill:

Table 13.3 Payments for care of the sick and wounded, 1 November 1642 to 31 May 1643.

Paid to:	The Physician for his pains and charges in visiting the wounded and sick soldiers at the Savoy by the space of seven months, at five pounds a month: £35
	The Apothecaries for physick oils and playsters by them administered to the lame and sick souldiers and delivered to the surgeons, as may appear by their bills and receipts for the same: £75 18s 3d
	The Chirurgeons for their care and pains at the Savoy Hospital: £58 14s
	Widow Paynter, of Richmond in Surrey, for the pains and charges of her husband (since deceased) in letting bloods and administering physick to poor sick souldiers at Richmond who were sent from the General's army to be billeted there: £4
	Sixty-six widows of slain soldiers at 4s 10d: £69
	Three widows of slain souldiers for their present relief whose husbands are supposed to be slain: £3
	Fifteen widows whose husbands were slain: £7 10s

Source: NA, SP 28/141B, Part 3.

Meanwhile, Parliament's attention was also directed towards the care of those casualties who had remained near the battlefield. On 26 November the Committee was ordered to prepare a list of those who had been left behind after Essex had returned from Warwick to London and, in their turn, the Committee delegated the task to Captain Richard Lacell, Bailiff of the Borough and Keeper of Warwick Gaol. Lacell had already documented some 217 wounded soldiers, each of whom was provided with care and subsistence, while, at the same time, another 163 were recorded in Coventry. There, the Governor, Colonel Barker, assumed similar responsibilities for the care of the injured who remained in his town. Elsewhere a significant number also found refuge in Stratford-upon-Avon. In all, somewhere in excess of 400 casualties were treated in Warwick, Coventry and Stratford.

Lacell had in fact already begun to record and locate the casualties some three weeks earlier, on 2 November, having set about his task with vigour. On receiving his further instructions from the Committee, he immediately instituted a collection, raising funds by demanding a contribution of £1 from each of the wealthier townspeople towards the cost of caring for the wounded. His accounts, which show a total expenditure of £101 1s 6d, were divided into five sections. The first, covering the period from 2 to 10 November 1642, listed expenditure on meat, bread, oatmeal and salt for feeding the wounded. The second element, undated, included lists of payments, some to assist soldiers to return to their regiments, and others for food, care and travel for a mixture of wounded soldiers and stragglers. The third sub-division of the accounts, also undated, contained a nominal roll of soldiers discovered during a search of town houses annotated with the names of their sub-unit and regimental commanders. A fourth section contained a further record of payments made to enable soldiers to return to the army while the fifth listed payments related to the nursing care of the wounded and for other services such as burials. In Coventry, where Laurence Lowe, surgeon to the Train of Artillery and personal surgeon to the Earl of Essex, was assisted in caring for the wounded by two additional surgeons, Mr Cotton, and Mr J Sharwood, Colonel Barker's accounts show a similar picture.

Using Lacell's and Barker's figures it is possible to demonstrate, regiment by regiment, the regimental affiliation of some 369 injured Parliamentary soldiers out of the nearly (including those who were just given money to return to their regiments) 800 that were originally listed:

Table 13.4   Parliamentary casualty distribution after Edgehill.

Regiment	Warwick	Coventry	Total
Right wing			
Colonel Browne	1	22	23
Lord Fielding	3	0	3
Colonel Nathaniel Ffiennes	1	0	1
Total right wing	**5**	**22**	**27**
Centre			
Right flank			
Sir John Meldrum	8	1	9
Lord Robartes	0	2	2
Sir William Constable	25	2	27
Sir William Fairfax	6	1	7
Sir Philip Stapleton	1	0	1
Total centre right flank	**40**	**6**	**46**
Left flank			
Colonel Charles Essex	22	6	28
Lord Wharton	13	7	20
Lord Mandeville	16	9	25
Sir Henry Cholmley	17	19	36
The Lord General	50	24	64
Lord Brooke	11	2	13
Colonel Denzil Holles	4	16	20
Colonel Ballard	1	2	3
Lord Grey	1	0	1
Sir William Balfour	3	1	4
Total centre left flank	**139**	**86**	**215**
Left Wing			
Sir James Ramsay[21]	1	0	1
Sir William Waller	1	8	9
Lord Hastings[22]	2	0	2
Colonel Edwin Sandys[23]	1	2	3
Lord St John	2	0	2
Total, Left wing	**7**	**10**	**17**
Late Arrivals			
Colonel John Hampden	7	0	7
Lord Willoughby	3	4	7
Lord Rochford[24]	0	1	1
Total, Late arrivals	**10**	**5**	**15**
Additional			
The Train of Artillery	8	5	13
Not known	5	32	37
Total additional casualties	13	37	50
GRAND TOTAL	**213**	**166**	**369**
Royalist prisoners	4	2	9

Source: NA, SP 28/139, f 11 and SP 28/136, f 19.

Both the Warwick and Coventry accounts were obviously written down verbatim from direct questioning of individual soldiers and, as a result, form an important collection of previously neglected primary source material relating not only to the actual care provided to casualties but also to the distribution of wounded among the regiments of the Parliamentary army with ramifications for students of the battle in determining the course of action. For example, Colonel John Hampden's Regiment of Foot and Lord Willoughby's Regiment of Horse, who had been detailed to provide the guard for the train of artillery and the baggage train during the advance to contact with the Royalist forces, have been described as arriving late on the battlefield, too late to have taken an active part in the fighting. Surprisingly, therefore, we note that these regiments each left seven wounded soldiers in Warwick after the battle, a figure that equals or exceeds that of other regiments known to have been heavily engaged. While it has been variously reported that most of Essex's casualties were suffered during the rout and pursuit of his left wing by Prince Rupert's initial cavalry charge, it is noticeable that Sir William Constable's Regiment, which stood to the right of the Parliamentary centre, suffered more casualties than any other regiment except the Lord General's (a much bigger regiment than many of the others). Despite the devastating Royalist cavalry charge against Parliament's left wing, casualties among the Parliamentary cavalry were evenly distributed among the regiments deployed on both the right and left flank. Equally, the greatest number of infantry casualties were suffered by regiments in the centre of the line. It is, perhaps, reasonable to conclude that on the day of battle the reality for the common dragoon, pikeman or musketeer, whether he stood his ground or ran away, was that his chances of being wounded were much the same wherever he was placed. Even Ludlow commented that 'it was observed that the greatest slaughter on our side was of such that ran away, and on the enemy's side of those that stood'.[25]

Although the Warwick and Coventry documents are primarily concerned with recording the more seriously injured casualties that were too incapacitated to remain with the army, they also list payments made to the 'walking wounded' and stragglers who were issued with travelling money to assist them in returning to their units. The pro-Parliamentarian sympathies of the local population are evident in the reimbursement payments made to them in return for both feeding soldiers and retaining the wounded in their houses, sometimes for several weeks, months or even years afterwards.

The experiences of Warwick householders John Walford and Alexander Dougard were typical. Following promises of reimbursement from John Bryan, the garrison chaplain and treasurer, Walford provided accommodation, food and care for sixteen weeks to a soldier wounded at Edgehill. In April 1647 he eventually submitted a retrospective claim for £12 but, unfortunately, it is not known whether his claim was met. Several mortally wounded soldiers were brought to Dougard's house and lay there for three of four days before expiring. Dougard's retrospective claim for reimbursement included charges incurred for their care, embalming and burials.[26] Meanwhile, in Stratford upon Avon, the Chamberlain's accounts also survive and record payments made there to the local inhabitants who were also involved with providing on-going care to casualties:

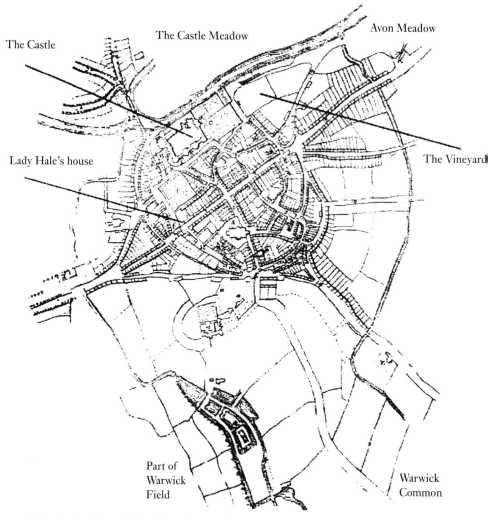

A plan of Warwick, marked to show where significant groups of casualties were treated including Lady Hale's House which was used to accommodate and care for Royalist prisoners.

Table 13.5   Monies disbursed to wounded Parliamentary soldiers at Stratford upon Avon after the battle of Edgehill.

Paid to:		
George Blancher and Morgan Jones, two soldiers who were wounded serving under Sir William Waller:	5s 6d
George Popham who was wounded serving under Captain Cromwell:	2s 6d
John Bennett wounded serving under Captain Robert Hash:	2s 0d
For a metal cooking sheet for eggs, and for a pan to burn coals in for the wounded soldiers:	2s 9d
Nine soldiers who served under Captain Butler and had been left at Worcester (presumably after the skirmish at Powick Bridge):	2s 6d
For three shrouds for three soldiers:	6s 6d
Edward Palmer for carrying a soldier to Evesham:	1s 0d
John Mason for dressing two soldiers:	1s 6d

Table 13.5 continued

A soldier who was wounded:	1*s* 0*d*
For four shrouds for four soldiers:	8*s* 10*d*
Samson Harris and John Cotton who served under Captain Essex:	2*s* 6*d*
Widow Saunders on behalf of John Barker who served under Captain Miles and Lord Roberts [Robartes]:	3*s* 4*d*
Simon Master who served under Quartermaster Dalbeare:	2*s* 6*d*
Francis Ayscue, John Barton and Edward Palmer for carrying wounded soldiers [from Stratford upon Avon] to Warwick:	12*s* 0*d*
Sillye *[sic]* for carrying and care of three men that were hurt:	1*s* 6*d*
Henry Freeman who served under Captain Butler:	1*s* 6d
Total payments:	£2 17*s* 5*d*

Source: Shakespeare Birthplace Trust, Borough of Stratford upon Avon Chamberlain's Accounts, 1622–1647, f 175.

Many more casualties must have straggled into Warwick during the following days or weeks as, although over 400 soldiers were identified in the three towns in November 1642, by September 1643 over 700 wounded remained in Warwick alone.[27] The situation was further confused as a result of the movement of casualties between one town and another. Some were transferred from Warwick to Coventry while others were moved from Stratford to Warwick. In both garrisons, the accounts were recorded in a hurried, random manner but, nevertheless, they clearly illustrate Parliament's growing concern with soldiers' welfare as well as its extensive auditing system that was considerably more sophisticated than that of the Royalists.

As the war progressed, Parliament debated the continuing plight of the Edgehill wounded and, on 13 July 1643, noted that:

> Whereas many poor sick and wounded soldiers ventured their lives and lost their limbs in the public service of the King and Parliament who are in great want and necessity of linen and woollen clothes for relieving them in their distress, which want makes their misery to become more uncomfortable and keeps back the cure of their wounds and sickness.[28]

Awareness of the situation was reinforced when, on 31 July, the Commons received a direct appeal for more funds from Bailiff Lacell in Warwick. However, during the ensuing debate it transpired that, prior to his departure from the town in October 1642, the Earl of Essex had arranged to leave a month's pay with every wounded soldier who remained there when his army departed for London. As a result, the Treasurer at War was ordered to recoup the amount paid to the wounded by deducting a month's pay from the respective regimental colonels' accounts for each wounded soldier involved.[29] An additional, more practical response, required the Treasurers of the Committee for Sick and Maimed Soldiers to appoint three or four suitable individuals to visit every London parish, as well as those in adjacent counties, to encourage those sympathetic to Parliament's cause to contribute clothes, especially linen and woollen items, for distribution to the wounded. Church wardens were to take charge of parish collections with specific instructions to include linen surplices.

Lacell later claimed that 700 Edgehill casualties remained under care in Warwick of whom several remained there for up to three years. As late as 1646, Edward Biddle, a resident in Smithford Street Ward, Coventry, submitted a £10 bill in respect of 'keeping of a wounded soldier two years that had dangerous hurts at Kineton Field'. The garrison chaplain and treasurer, John Bryan, who supported Lacell's petition, was responsible, in addition to his pastoral duties, for supervising expenditure on the care of the sick and wounded within the castle. The accounts of Thomas Hind, the garrison accountant and Bryan's assistant, confirm a continuing expenditure on surgical intervention during this period.[30] Between May and September 1643 surgeon John Tillam received payments totalling £6 for twelve weeks' work and the following year James Cook, another surgeon, was paid over £20 between February and July while the bills of the garrison apothecary, Mr Pargetter, amounted to £16 8s 2d.[31] In February 1643 John Wasse, a Coventry surgeon employed by Sir William Waller's Regiment, successfully petitioned Parliament for payment of arrears of £107 19s 3d relating to food and drink, lodgings, medicines and surgical care that he had given to Edgehill wounded both in Coventry and Warwick over several weeks following the battle.[32]

Bryan's garrison accounts, from which relevant extracts are tabulated below, include expenditure on nursing care for the Edgehill casualties including the laundering of sheets and clothes, the making of beds and the provision of medicines and medical care. They also demonstrate the inequality between payments made to male and female carers. On 29 December 1643, Jane Williams received £1 11s after nursing wounded soldiers at Vineyard House in Castle Street for seventeen weeks. Two men who attended soldiers in Sergeant Ward's house received £2 14s between them while two women shared £1 for a similar task.

Table 13.6   Extracts from Warwick Castle Treasurer's accounts.

Medicines for the Castle	£6 0s 0d	Jane Williams, the nurse	3s 0d
Ditto	£3 15s 0d	Jane Williams, the nurse	6s 0d
Washing beds, bolsters		Jane Williams, the nurse	6s 0d
and soiled clothes	7s 6d	Jane Williams, the nurse	6s 0d
Mr Saunders the surgeon's bill	£33 0s 0d	Jane Williams, the nurse	10s 0d
Making beds and bolsters	4s 0d	Mr Lacell, for wounded soldiers	£33 0s 0d
Making blankets and beds	1s 8d	The keeper of wounded soldiers	6s 0d
Making coverlets and blankets	5s 0d	Mr Wheatley, for cloth	
Washing beds and bolsters	6s 8d	for surgeon's mates	£3 2s 6d

Source: NA, SP 28/136, f. 10.

Many of the wounded were assisted financially to return to their homes, either to recover or to die. This was deemed particularly appropriate where recovery was likely to be prolonged and even appears to have been the widely preferred option during the war's early stages. As the war progressed the increasing realization dawned that the struggle had become both highly expensive and protracted. Recruitment of fresh soldiers was increasingly difficult and, in order to conserve manpower, officers grew more reluctant to release soldiers to return home. Retention of sick and wounded soldiers within the body of the army demanded the provision of more sophisticated facilities and a rising demand for local nursing care with the result that, as military budgets felt the impact of the associated costs, casualties attracted increased attention from senior officers and greater prominence in military thought and planning. By October 1644, Lord Manchester was periodically sending officers into the counties to round up men from the army of the Eastern Association who had previously been sent home and had subsequently recovered, in order to conduct them back to their regiments.[33]

Remarkably little information has been published concerning casualty care during the Civil Wars and much of what has seen the light of day has been poorly researched and misinformed. Contemporary observers paid scant attention to recording details of individual nurses, doctors or their work and subsequent studies of the period have failed to address the subject in any depth. Among the documentation that has survived, particularly within the Exchequer records, Parliamentarian material relating to nursing and welfare far exceeds that available from Royalist sources. It is evident that, in contrast to the apparently lukewarm commitment shown by the King's army towards its casualties, Parliament, influenced by an increasing concern for the 'Commonweal', adopted a very positive approach towards its sick and wounded. By 1645 it controlled an efficient, centrally co-ordinated organization based on permanent efficient military base hospitals in London that contrasted sharply with its enemy's continued reliance on hurriedly arranged and unco-ordinated local facilities.

A huge influx of injured soldiers was, by no means, the only effect of the battle of Edgehill on the local civilian population. One of the more troublesome aspects associated with the passage of an army was its enormous requirement for firewood so that log piles, gates, old furniture, dilapidated barns as well as woodlands and even orchards were often arbitrarily seized and consumed. Soldiers of most armies caused disturbances wherever they went, especially during war, when living off the land, including requisition and quartering, was a common necessity. The Edgehill armies were no exception, and although one does not expect to see acts listed which today we would term atrocities, both sides afforded a degree of license to their men, who frequently overstepped the boundaries of the law. Whereas we have no record of any sympathetic ear in the Royalist camp, Parliament did offer to pay for the expenses or damages incurred by the local populace during their army's occupation of the Kineton area. There is no way of telling if the claims submitted were all attributable to Essex's men, or if they were accurate, exaggerated or even true, but these statistics do provide us with a reasonably comprehensive picture of the implications of having an army passing through a community and fighting a major engagement!

Table 13.7 A statement by the village of Kineton of the villagers' expense due to the army presence between 1642 and March 1645.

Charges paid by the inhabitants in the service of Parliament and other expenses, including free quarter, as a result of the army's presence.

a) Two troops of horse under the command of Colonel Ffynes quartered here one night in August 1642

b) The Lord Saye's Regiment of Foot quartered here one night in August 1642

c) The Earl of Essex with his whole Army at the Battle October 1642 lay here

d) Colonel Fairfax Regiment of Horse under the command of Sir William Waller quartered here three nights from 26 June 1644

e) Colonel Fiennes and his company when they went to besiege Banbury quartered here one night July 1644

f) Colonel Aynhoe's troops quartered here five days and nights in October 1644

g) There was a guard kept in the town when Major General Browne lay at Southam by several troops of Lieutenant General Cromwell's and Colonel Ffynes Regiments for 5 nights from 20 May 1645

h) Colonel Kirke, his regiment in part under the command of Sir Thomas Fairfax quartered here three nights from 20 June 1645

Table 13.7   continued

i) Colonel General Poyntz his army marched through the town in August 1645

Of the General Expenses incurred by the town:

    a) A Horse, saddle and bridle sent to Lord Brookes for a dragoon 27 September 1642 at a cost of £4 8s 0d

    b) Paid for providing three horses for Captain Cotton for the Constabulary by warrant of the Earl of Denbigh dated 15 April 1643 – £18 0s 0d

Additional payments levied on the town by the army in the form of contributions:

    a) A warrant dated 1 November 1643 required £5 0s 0d per week to be paid for a term of six months. Following a petition this was reduced to four months at a total cost of £80 0s 0d

    b) The above warrant was abated after four months to 20s 0d per week for two months at a total cost of £32 0s 0d

    c) A further warrant dated 26 April 1644 required a payment of £5 0s 0d per week which continued for twenty-two months at a total cost of £440 0s 0d

The total overall taxation bill paid by the town was £703 1s 4d

Source: NA, SP 28/182, unfolioed.

Individual expenses were also listed by the inhabitants of Kineton for the same period and are reproduced in the following table in which the second column relates to losses suffered as a result of the presence of Essex's army in October 1642. The 'total' column refers to losses suffered over the entire period from 1642 to 1645.

Table 13.8   Individual financial losses incurred by Kineton villagers between 1642 and 1645.

Name	Essex's Army	Total Claimed
Mr Dalbie of Brookhampton	NIL	£18 7s 3d
Samuel Highworth	£27 0s 0d	£37 8s 0d
Ed. Winter	£20 0s 0d	£25 0s 0d
John Butler	NIL	£1 9s 11d
John Butler	£4 15s 0d	£7 10s 0d
John Freeman	£2 1s 0d	£3 11s 9d
Will. Norton	£6 0s 0d	£7 0s 6d
Will. Taylor	£3 10s 0d	£4 15s 0d
Margaret Westbury	£6 0s 0d	£6 13s 9d
Henry Jones	£1 18s 4d	£2 1s 8d
Ralph Ellis	£5. 0s 0d	£9 10s 0d
Humphrey Norton	£2 10s 0d	£16 1s 6d
Ralph Wisdon	£10 0s 0d	£11 17s 4d
John Heron	£0 8s 0d	£2 10s 4d
Leonard Court	£9 5s 4d	£9 7s 4d
Robert Coates	£7 6s 8d	£17 10s 0d
Thomas Warren	£16 6s 0d	£20 16s 0d
Nathaniel Cooper	£6 10s 0d	£8 18s. 0d
Henry Spires	£10 0s 0d	£13 12s 0d
John Worrall	£6 10s 0d	£8 6s 0d
Ed. Eaborne	£1 4s 0d	£2 3s 0d
Thomas Taylor	£4 6s 8d	£5 3s 0d
Thomas Towned	£18 0s 0d	£18 15s 0d
Will. Coup	NIL	£1 7s 7d
Richard Gibbs	£5 0s 0d	£5 0s 0d
Widdow Dixon	11s 4d	£0 19s 10d

Table 13.8 continued

Name	Essex's Army	Total Claimed
James Wake	£0 12s 0d	£5 5s 0d
Thomas Nicholls	£2 8s 0d	£2 8. 0d
Will. Burrell	£3 7s 0d	£5 5s 6d.
Joan Basley	£9 2s 0d	£9 2s 3d
Edmund Savige	NIL	£1 6s 0d
Ann Savige	£10 7s 0d	£10 7s 0d
Thos. Norton	£0 10s 0d	£1 14s 0d
Will. Harkin	£7 0s 0d	£7 9s 2d
Phillip Stanford	£0 15s 0d	£5 16s 1d
Richard Jackson	£19 3s 0d	£22 6s 6d
Richard Norton	£5 0s 0d	£5 10s 0d
Tobias Norton	£11 15s 0d	£13 10s 10d
Thos. Hakener	£3 10s 0d	£5 7s 3d
Hugh Lumbard	£28 18s 0d	£30 12s 0d
Ann King	£0 6s 0d	£0 16s 0d
Ann Savige	£1 2s 0d	£2 10s 9d
Richard Baron	£12 0s 0d	£17 16s 8d
Humphrey Hurt	£1 0s 0d	£2 2s 8d
Kathryn Potipher (widow)	£2 0s 0d	£3 2s 2d
Thomas Savige	£50 0s 0d	£52 11s 0d
Thomas Crosbie	£7 17s 4d	£11 19s 1d
Thos. Dunn	£7 0s 0d	£7 0s 0d
Widdow Norton	£1 10s 0d	£1 10s 0d
Thomas Chandler	£5 10s 0d	£6 2s 0d
TOTAL	£272. 14s 8d	£497 5s 9d

Source: NA, SP 28/182, unfolioed.

An example of an individual claim from Margaret Westbury is as follows:

Table 13.9 Margaret Westbury's claim.

a) Spent by the Earl of Essex's Army in hay, corn, wood, provisions for men and horses	£4 0s 0d
b) Lost by them three hides of beef	£1 0s 0d
c) Lost by them in clothes and linen	£1 0s 0d
d) For provisions for two men and horses of Sir William Waller	£0 6s 3d
e) For four men of Colonel Askew's	£0 4s 0d
f) For one man and horse of Sir Thomas Fairfax	£0 3s 0d
g) For provender for Colonel Poyntz	£0 0s 6d.
TOTAL	£6.13s. 9d.

Source: NA, SP 28/182, unfolioed.

Chapter Fourteen
Subsequent Events

For what reason I know not, we marched to Warwick. Ludlow

On the Tuesday night after the battle, the King made his quarters at Aynho House, south of Banbury, with his army spread throughout the surrounding villages. While preparations were being made for the delayed reduction of puritan Banbury, the King created the old, gout-stricken but experienced Patrick Ruthven, Lord Forth, his new general in place of Lindsey who had died of his wounds the previous day. The strength of Banbury lay with its ancient medieval castle, but its defenders had no stomach for a fight, and very soon entered into surrender discussions. After a short negotiation, they capitulated and marched out to be stripped of their arms and most of their clothing. A Royalist regiment took their place in the castle. The erstwhile garrison had consisted of about 800 men of the Earl of Peterborough's Regiment and a small detachment of Lord Saye and Sele's men. Ludlow commented that 'pretending it not to be sufficiently provided for a siege, they surrendered it'.[1] What happened to the prisoners is not made clear, some of them changed sides, after all the inaptly named Lieutenant Colonel Sir Faithful Fortescue had done so a few days before. Most of the other officers however, appear again within a matter of weeks in a reformed Lord Peterborough's Regiment. Another detachment of Lord Saye's men made a slightly better showing four miles down the road at the old moated Broughton Castle, the home of their Colonel, but after bombardment, they too were forced to surrender and the castle subjected to plunder 'defacing, tearing and burning'.[2]

With these two successes under their belt, the Royalists began to bolster their depleted ranks. With Essex temporarily out of the way, Prince Rupert was anxious to push on to London, suggesting that he took most of the Horse and dragoons directly to Windsor with 3,000 Foot following him as quickly they could march. However, the majority of the King's Council rejected this plan, preferring a more cautious advance on the capital in easy stages fearing Prince Rupert might 'in heat of blood to fire the town'.[3] The King spent the next night at the old royal palace at Woodstock and the following day, 29 October, entered Oxford unopposed. Here he set up his court while Rupert made his headquarters with the cavalry at Abingdon. On the very same day, having received a number of conflicting accounts of the results of Edgehill, the House of Lords heard a proposal to restart peace negotiations and two days later the Commons agreed to lend their support.

In the meantime, Parliament's Lord General had marched his bruised army from

Contemporary map of Brentford in 1642.

the safety of Warwick castle to Northampton and then south to Olney, Woburn and down the old Roman road via St Albans, reaching London on 7 November. Here he received a hero's welcome and a vote of thanks from Parliament, having beaten the King in the race to the city. Charles had left Oxford on 3 November and the following day was at Reading, the Parliamentary garrison having been evacuated by the governor, Colonel Henry Martin, a Member of Parliament, without firing a shot. At Reading, Charles received Parliament's peace Commissioners but stalled them for two days before declaring one of them, Sir John Evelyn, a traitor and further delaying negotiations. Prince Rupert had by now been taken off the leash and with a flying column struck at Windsor castle whose governor, Colonel John Venn, had arrived with a garrison only a few days before. Rupert set up a battery of five guns in the grounds of Eton College and opened fire across the Thames. The bombardment lasted for about seven hours, leaving

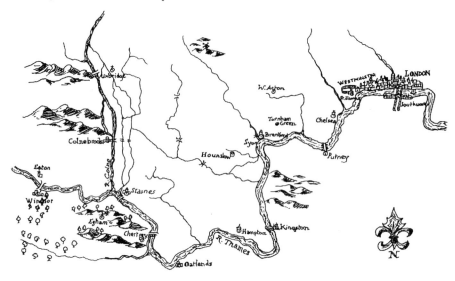

The London area, based on Speed's map.

the town of Windsor 'mightily battered and ruined, and the inhabitants very much damnified'.[4] However, in the castle, Venn remained defiant, eventually causing Rupert to call off his attack and withdraw two hours before daylight to Egham. The King with the main army arrived at Colnbrook on 11 November and Rupert marched over and joined him there. Again Parliamentary commissioners approached the King with proposals for a conference which Charles, tongue in cheek, suggested should be held in Windsor castle, although he would consider other venues. As Charles had failed to mention any cessation of arms to the Commissioners, Parliament sent Sir Peter Killigrew, the King's emissary, back to clear up this all-important point while ordering Essex to refrain from any further hostilities. Killigrew failed to reach the King for, under the cover of mist, early on the morning of 13 November, Rupert launched an all-out assault upon the Parliamentary outpost of Brentford.

The town of New and Old Brentford was a single street settlement about one mile in length with the river Brent looping around its western end. The Brent was joined by a number of tributaries before joining the Thames, which in turn ran roughly parallel to the street. An arched bridge carried the street over the Brent to join the road to Isleworth at Brentford End. Here the straggle of houses was surrounded by enclosures and orchards and backed by the park of Syon House, the home of the Earl of Northumberland. The defenders of Brentford consisted of the battle-scarred regiments of Holles and Brooke, which together numbered about 1,300 men plus a single troop of Horse. They had arrived on the morning of 11 November short of the muskets, pikes and powder that they had been promised. Lieutenant Colonel James Quarles of Holles's deployed the majority of his men among the orchards at the bridge head with an out-post a short distance along the Isleworth road at Sir Richard Wynnes's house, while Brooke's men occupied Brentford itself and emplaced a number of light pieces of artillery. Rupert's initial attack with cavalry and dragoons at Wynne's house took the Parliamentary troops completely by surprise for they were expecting a cessation of hostilities, but the London redcoats put up a stiff resistance until Royalist infantry and

The remains of Essex's 'bridge of boats' at Putney. Copied from an early nineteenth-century drawing.

artillery support arrived and pushed them back over the Brent. Here Lord Brooke's men, according to Clarendon, 'barricadoed the narrow avenues to the town, and cast up some little breastworks at the most convenient places'.[5] Eventually Holles's and Brooke's soldiers were forced from these defences by superior numbers. A Royalist, Captain John Gwyn, stated that they 'beat them from one Brainford to the other, and thence to the open field' where an 'abundance of them were killed and taken prisoner besides those drowned in their attempt to escape by leaping into the river'.[6]

Only with the arrival of Colonel John Hampden from Uxbridge at the head of his own green coats was the Royalist's further advance halted, and the survivors of Holles's and Brooke's evacuated. With the little town now in Royalist hands, it was thoroughly sacked; Prince Rupert having ordered it 'as a punishment for having attached itself to the side of the rebels'.[7] Besides the loot from the town, the Royalists took hundreds of prisoners, between six and eight colours and two guns.

Essex had heard the sound of the guns as he sat in the House of Lords that morning and, as soon as he had received confirmation of what was happening, he left to join the bulk of his army which, by chance, he had ordered to a muster that day on Chelsea Fields. He also summoned the Common Council of the City of London to call out their Trained Band regiments to come to his assistance. By early evening, when news of the sack of Brentford reached London, the citizens (including those of Royalist leaning) were horrified and they resolved never to let the Royalist army into the city, accusing the King 'of Treachery, Perfidy and Blood; and that he had given the Spoil and Wealth of the City as Pillage to his Army which advanced with no other purpose'.[8] The citizen soldiers of the London Trained Bands answered the call with determination and

A Thames barge of the period.

marched out of the city in the early morning of Sunday, 13 November. They rendez-voused with Essex's troops on Turnham Green, a heath one mile east of ransacked Brentford, from which the Royalists had pulled back overnight.

Over 20,000 men had appeared in the field when Essex arrived at the head of a party of MPs and Lords, and as he rode around the individual regiments, he was greeted with loud cheers of 'Hey for Old Robin'. The Trained Bands had been led out by their redoubtable Sergeant Major General Philip Skippon whom Bulstrode Whitelock remembers saying to them 'Come my Boyes my Brave Boyes, let us pray heartily and fight heartily'.[9] Essex intermingled his Foot regiments with battle-tested units standing next to those with no experience, in one long defensive line making use of hedges and ditches and with his cavalry on the wings.[10] The train of artillery was brought to Hammersmith from its park at Knightsbridge to await deployment. Further reinforce-ments were raised by abandoning Kingston, where Sir James Ramsey was quartered with a force of 3,000 men. Ramsey was ordered to cover London south of Thames. The abandonment of Kingston meant that Essex had lost control of the lowest bridged crossing point of the Thames before London, so to counter this he ordered the building of a bridge of boats at Putney using barges and lighters brought down from the city. The watermen and workmen were paid £150 for its construction.[11]

While Essex arrayed his army, the King was on the march down the Western Road from his overnight campsite at Hounslow. Charles's army had been awoken early that morning by the sound of guns from the Thames. A number of large sailing barges were making their way down river from Kingston carrying some of Ramsey's troops and artillery to London and as they drew level with Syon House they came under sustained fire from musketeers and guns sited in the park by Colonel Thomas Blagge. The barges returned fire but were outgunned and one, under the command of Captain George Phillips, was blown up after he ran out of shot. None of the other vessels got through.

Two hours after the river fight, the King's advance was halted by the sight of the rebel army 'in their brightest Equipage upon the Heath' an army 'fit to have decided the Title of a Crown'.[12] The Royalist army, its troops 'harassed, weather-beaten and half-starved' deployed in battle order.[13] The hours passed without any movement on either side until at about 3:00 p.m. Essex's guns opened up on the Royalists causing, according to Clarendon, only the loss of only four or five horses.[14] This bombardment was probably carried out to cover a proposed flank attack on the Royalist left, spearheaded by Hampden's Regiment of Foot that was ordered to take some high ground near Acton. Before this could be fully developed, Hampden and his men were recalled to the main body because of disagreements in the Parliamentary high command.

By now it was apparent that Essex was not going to risk anything but a defensive action and the King in his turn was vastly outnumbered and, having obviously lost any support in the City, would not commit his army to an attack. As darkness was falling, the King ordered a retreat. Prince Rupert had advised that the withdrawal be covered by 500 musketeers positioned at Brentford Bridge, but when the Prince arrived, he found Sir Jacob Astley with just a handful of men covering this all important crossing, and so 'in ye water set his horse till ye others marched over ye Bridge'.[15] The retreat continued as far as Kingston where the army billeted that night in peace, Essex having decided not to harass their withdrawal. The King himself slept that night in his palace of Hampton Court. Meanwhile, Essex's army re-occupied Brentford and did what they could for the shocked inhabitants. Nearly 100 wagons of food had been donated by the citizens of London for the troops in the field, and some of this was distributed for the relief of the people of Brentford.

Charles rested all day at Hampton then removed to Oatlands Palace while his army continued in Kingston. The King thought that more peace overtures would now be made by Parliament, but on the contrary, he began to realize that the storming and sack of Brentford had hardened their resolve and that they would 'keep off all Propositions for Peace whilst the Army lay so near London'.[16] He therefore directed his army to retire to Reading and ordered the release of prisoners taken at Brentford. With no prospects of an early peace, the King made his capital and court at Oxford while, on 9 December, his field army took up their winter quarters in outlying garrisons at Wallingford, Reading, Abingdon and Brill. In the meantime, the Earl of Essex made Windsor castle his Headquarters and ordered his troops into billets for the winter. So ended the Edgehill campaign. The war was not going to be over by Christmas.

Chapter Fifteen
Concluding Implications

The first dry rattle of new drawn steel changes the world today. Rudyard Kipling

After terrible events we become accustomed to hearing such dramatic statements as 'The world will never be the same again', so we ought to consider what changes, if any, were wrought by the terrible events of October 1642. It is hard to divorce the implications of the battle from those of the war, but we should try to focus upon the question, what did Edgehill alter?

The authors maintain that the battle brought about a fundamental change in the mindset of the nation. Up until the first shots were fired it had been a something of a 'phoney war', with most people believing that no-one would actually physically challenge the authority of the monarchy. We have discovered a lot of unsubstantiated stories about Parliament's opening cannon fire being directed at the King's person but believe this to be an expression of the magnitude of the challenge; a symbol of an attitude rather than a direct record of a specific event. Previous armed rebellions in England's bloody history had been personal, either in the form of a usurper or pretender wishing to replace or make a prisoner of the King, as occurred frequently during the so-called Wars of the Roses, or an attempt to coerce him into some sort of specified reform, as in the Peasants Revolt. Essex had no pretensions of becoming a usurper, and it is doubtful that he had an agenda beyond the defence of Parliament's rights and liberties. Edgehill marked something different. It was the physical manifestation of a growing individualism that was pervading all aspects of society; a movement that rejected Divine Right and most of the things for which it stood. At Edgehill the nature of the struggle between King and Parliament changed. This battle was a direct physical threat not only to the reigning monarch but to the Crown itself.

Surprisingly, it was the undecided nature of the outcome that set the greatest changes in motion. Parliament gained the field and the King kept the London Road, both could claim a tactical victory. Had either side won outright, Edgehill would have marked the beginning and the end of the war. Instead, indecision led to nine years of misery for the people of this country and others in Scotland and Ireland. Had the King lost he would never have been executed. Despite the threat to the Crown there was no desire to remove it, only control it, and that only in a limited way such as ousting Charles's 'evil counselors', among whom were numbered the infamous Digby. A decisive victory for either side would probably have found the King back on his throne in London within weeks. The drawn result merely served to fan radical arguments and gave time for them to grow. This did not take long. There was also time for attitudes and circumstances to change, and change they did. Less than a year later, by the time of the next major action of the war, the first battle of Newbury, in which the leading Royalist moderate, Lord Falkland, was killed, Parliament's equivalent, Hampden, was dead and their chief negotiator, Pym, was dying of cancer. The indecisive outcome of the battle of Edgehill ensured that the opposing forces recognized that the time for talking was over and that, for the forseeable future, they could only expect more bloody conflict.

Militarily, Edgehill proved that the war could not be won with well-intentioned amateurs. Cromwell's famous remarks about 'plain, russet-coated captains' and the quality of Parliament's soldiers described the need for a trained professional army succinctly. Edgehill placed in motion a train of thought that would culminate in the creation and maintenance of a standing army in England. It also saw the return of the charging cavalryman to the battlefield. Discounting Richard III's desperate thrust at the Duke of Richmond at Bosworth, the mounted charge had not been seen in England since the early Middle Ages, while on the Continent its death throes had been at Nancy in the face of massed pike, and at Pavia against firepower. The Horse had lost their traditional role as shock troops that charged into melee and swept Foot before them. Gustavus Adolphus had shown the way in which they could regain the initiative when fighting enemy Horse, but it was Rupert at Edgehill who proved that they could overcome the mobile platform tactic by a determined charge. His practice of relying on cold steel and only using pistols in the teeth of the enemy in melee was also proven. Wilmot copied it at Roundway Down with dramatic effect and, as a fighting style, it was adopted and perfected sixty years later by Marlborough's English and Allied Horse.

Edgehill also taught the worth of Horse and Foot operating together as a unified force, capable of inflicting serious damage on even the best infantry that the enemy could muster if the latter was unsupported. Push of pike struggles could be prolonged and, although one side might get the upper hand and drive the other back, it would seem that neither could break the other by virtue of its weaponry alone. When Foot pinned the front and Horse crashed into the flank and/or rear it was another matter. We can see just how far the practice of combined arms had become entrenched in more recent military thinking when we examine the prominent nineteenth-century historian Gardiner's summary of the outcome of Edgehill where he states that 'the claim of victory advanced by either party is little to be heeded... Only amongst the Parliamentary troops had there been that co-operation between infantry and cavalry which distinguishes an army from a fighting crowd'.[1] It would seem that Gardiner was judging the battle using a criterion which it had helped establish!

Edgehill also established the necessity for controlling the Horse. Rupert was criticized for his lack of battlefield control and no matter how hard his apologists work in print, his inability to exert influence over his second line was a battle-losing factor, whereas Cromwell's appreciation of the Edgehill lesson, which resulted in him training his men to reform after an initial success, was to prove a battle-winning innovation. One can only speculate on the battlefield success Wellington could have enjoyed had his cavalry commanders learnt and practised the cavalry lessons of Edgehill.

We also see the importance of training in the Foot, as well as the need for supplying correct and modern equipment. Both sides' infantry fought virtually all afternoon and although Rupert's interference with the Royalist's deployment had a detrimental effect,

Parliament's Foot won by a combination of longer training and better equipment. The use of body armour may have been on decline as plate-piercing ball increased in range and accuracy, but it certainly proved itself a valuable commodity at Edgehill, especially in the pike melees. Edgehill also improved the Treasury's attitude towards arming soldiers with quality muskets and supplying them with adequate ammunition. It gave birth to an awarenes of the need to standardize materials of war.

While, for the King's Army, 23 October 1642 wrought little change in its traditional, paternalistic approach to casualties, for Parliament it brought home the final realization that an all-out shooting war had begun. When the news of the battle reached London it acted as a powerful catalyst for change in providing for sick and wounded soldiers. In the days that followed, Parliament quickly acknowledged the need to establish a centralized organization responsible for the provision and supervision of casualty care.

Although both sides established hospitals for the sick and wounded of their armies, it is unfortunate that considerably less Royalist medical documentation has survived than Parliamentarian. Nevertheless sufficient evidence does survive to demonstrate that there was little difference between the attitudes and practice of the doctors and nurses who gave hands-on care to either side. Parliament's superior achievements were gained through better administration, legislation, and clerical support. Its members' altruistic motivation, to improve the lot of the 'Commonweal', contrasted markedly with the King's reliance upon the beneficence of individual unit commanders. Unquestionably, Parliament's unlimited access to the City of London's financial resources was a determining factor in its establishment of an efficient military medical and welfare support system that served its Army well throughout the ensuing years of warfare. Sadly, by way of contrast, the later years of relative peace during the Protectorate, characterized by an unstable national economy, shrinking financial power and increased public debt, witnessed an inevitable decline in these services.

So, is it possible to arrive at a judgment regarding the quality of care provided? Regretfully the answer must remain equivocal and yet, while it would be invidious to attempt an accurate overall 'quality assessment' of the standard required in a modern hospital, it is possible to draw significant conclusions from the available evidence.[2] Sufficient material survives to enable us to infer that the nursing and medical staff of the Savoy hospital, and the later Ely House hospital opened in 1648, provided a significantly greater contribution to the work of caring for their soldier patients than has previously been credited to them.

To date the majority of published battle studies of the period have either ignored or failed to mention casualties and, where comments do exist, these are usually limited to vague quotations of total deaths in battle. Occasional references refer to the victims of disease, especially plague, while comments about the wounded are usually restricted to noteworthy personalities such as noblemen who fell at Edgehill or Major General Skippon, wounded at Naseby. In most combat studies there is an almost universal absence of comment on wounded or sick soldiers, what happened to them or who cared for them. Indeed, in a high percentage of battle books casualties and their care do not even merit a mention in the index. References to military hospitals and nurses are even harder to find.

It is truly amazing just how little attention has been paid to the significant quantity of battle casualty returns and other associated documentation that survives from the period. This mass of material has been almost completely neglected and, as a result, many authors have missed the opportunity to capitalize upon the hidden potential for the development of many interesting, alternative perspectives into historical events. Such a deficit is the more remarkable given that the impact of Civil War casualties upon the nation as a whole was greater in terms of percentage of population than both of the two World Wars of the twentieth century combined.[3]

Finally we should consider how Edgehill affected Parliament's Lord General. Robert Devereux, Earl of Essex, who according to Clarendon 'wished only to be kindly looked upon, kindly spoken to, and kindly to enjoy his own fortune', had been chosen as supreme commander of its army by Parliament, not only for his military experience but for his unshakeable fidelity to the cause. His lack of an initial convincing victory over the King at Edgehill robbed Essex of much of his support, particularly in the House of Commons, and his later achievements, such as the taking of Reading and his deft handling of the Relief of Gloucester Expedition were undermined by the drawing upon his army for recruits and equipment to build a southern army for Sir William Waller. Essex, understandably, was outraged by this, a move that caused bitter friction between the Lord General and his subordinate commander and contributed in no small way to the disastrous West Country campaign of 1644. Despite this, and failing health, Essex continued faithfully in the service until his resignation on 2 April 1645, just before the implementation of the Self Denying Ordinance. He died the following year from a chill, alledgedly caught while out hunting. The portly, pipe-smoking Earl has seldom caught the imagination of historians and his courageous and dogged attachment to Parliament was soon forgotten by his more radical successors, yet, had he lived, his influence would certainly have had a profound effect on the events of the late sixteen forties.

Overall, Edgehill, had far-reaching implications. From a military point of view it led directly to a realization of the importance of logistics and training, and the tactical possibilities of the cavalry charge coupled with the necessity for its ability to rally. It pioneered thinking in combined arms action and saw the creation of military hospitals, long before the days of Florence Nightingale. It also gave rise to the formation of a professional standing army, yet undermined the man who might have been able to wield it even more effectively than the great 'Black Tom' Fairfax. However, the political outfall was even more significant as it gave time for opposition to the King to solidify and for attitudes to become embittered for, rather than regaining his throne, the next time Charles Stuart set foot in the capital it was to stand trial for crimes against this nation.

Edgehill or 'Kineton Fight', as it was more commonly known at the time, by its hard-fought and yet indecisive outcome, was to set in motion ideas and events which were to propel this county on its difficult path to democracy.

Chapter Sixteen
Edgehill Today

Rest assured, none of us ever walks a battlefield, least of all one fought over by our own countrymen, without an awareness of that inestimable factor common to all fields of war – that they are hallowed by the courage of self-sacrifice of the soldiers who fought upon them. D Featherstone.

The battlefield of Edgehill lies in the Midlands, in Warwickshire, between Stratford upon Avon and Banbury. Come off the M40 at Junction 12 near Gaydon. Take the minor road, the B4451, southwest through Chadshunt to Kineton. Alternatively use the B4455 Fosse Way, in either direction, and turn off eastwards to Kineton on the B4086 Wellesborne to Banbury road. Otherwise refer to SP 354 492 or Ordinance Survey Explorer 206.

Touring the field helps understanding, so we offer this route and recommend you contact the Commanding Officer, Kineton Depot, Warwickshire whose authorization is needed to visit both the depot, and the farmed land inside the unfenced outer perimeter.

Begin the tour in Kineton. Most of this large village has been rebuilt since the 1640s but the street plan is reputedly much the same. Look at St Peter's Church (no. 1 on the map). It is mainly Victorian but the medieval tower was there in 1642, although the ground level has risen considerably. The Earl of Essex was reputedly here when he heard that his enemy was near!

Leave by the B4086 Banbury Road. The ground is rolling and from the first rise (no. 2) there is a good view of the northern end of the great ridge. It is likely that near here a Parliamentarian patrol, or even the Worthy Divine Bifield himself, watched Rupert's Horse assemble on Knoll End. Continue driving and there will be MoD signs either side of the road. About half way to the ridge you will see a battle monument on the right (no. 3). It is on Parliament's left, but a long way from the infantry fight. Further on the route passes between two sets of military gates, approximately where Essex's line crossed the road. As the road dips and bends to the left there is a pull-in on the right; note it for later. Turn left following signposts to the Depot Headquarters.

At the B4100 turn left for Kineton but take the Depot slip road to the left and stop at the guardroom. (no. 4) Present all entry letters and personal identification. If permitted, visit the Officers' Mess where two musket balls, one carbine and one pistol, all found on the field, are mounted in a small frame and displayed on the foyer wall. There are also several copies of period engravings of the commanders, a sketch map, and a spectacular model of a Civil War regiment composed of 25 mm figures. Afterwards, an escort guides visitors through the Depot to those gates on the B4086. Before crossing the road pull over onto hard-standing at a field entrance and walk down into a dip. Eastwards (no. 5) is the rear of the enclosed land which was held by the commanded

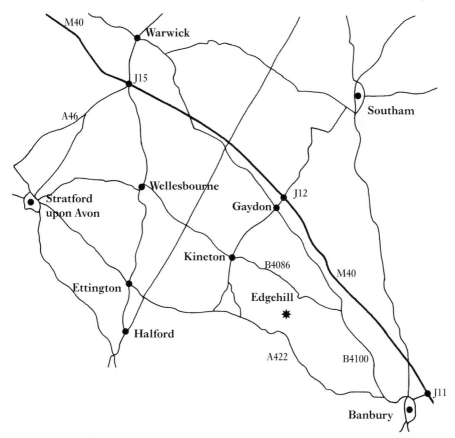

How to find Kineton, Warwickshire.

musketeers on Parliament's left. We cannot tell if these hedges were there at the time, but these are the fields across which the King's Lifeguard chased the fleeing musketeers. Turn around and try to imagine them in those fields, cutting down men as they ran for the safety of their parent regiment or distant Kineton.

Once across the road and beyond the next locked gate, glance at the ridgeline some fifty yards to the left. This was the position of Ramsey's Brigade – twenty-four troops in a two line Dutch formation. Just over the rise is a hedge, probably on the site of 'the Hedge which crost the Field'.[1] Having passed another checkpoint, and inside the inner perimeter, go left at the junction, then round to the right and up a small rise, then first right and, swing right off the road onto an expanse of grass, (no. 6). This is the flatter, northern part of Essex's small hill and the woodland aligning the road marks an approximate position for Parliament's front line about half way through the fighting. In the wood there is ridge and furrow evidence of cultivation – the ploughed land which stopped Royalist cannonballs bouncing. On the southern side of this wood stands another 1949 memorial – the resited grave marker whose pits are said to be nearby.[2] The name of the wood is Grave Ground coppice. Burne maintains finding the grave pits pinpoints the area of the bloodiest fighting. Imagine the units of Foot and intervening guns drawn up along the length of this gentle ridge. Then climb one of the nearby

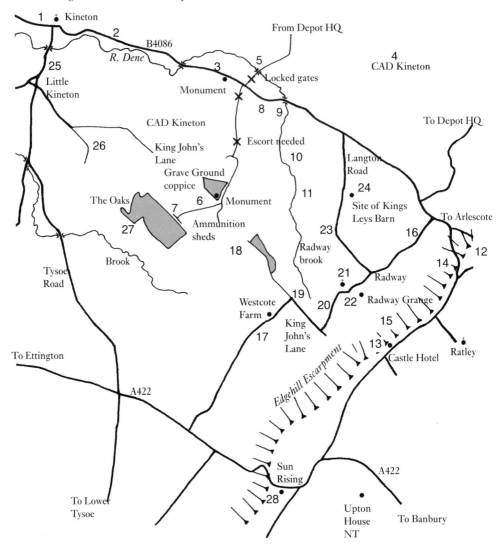

A suggested tour.

bunkers, to look forward across the tops of the sheds and visualize this as a major killing ground. The best bunker to climb is across the railway line which affords not only the desired view but, by turning round, a vista of Essex's line stretching from Oaks Coppice to the left, where Meldrum's right-hand Regiments stood, across to the right to the ridge line where Ramsey's Wing was deployed. One cannot help but lament the development.

A walk down to The Oaks also tasks the imagination, (no. 7) but pacing out distances and matching them to known strengths and formation depths will help gauge frontages. Finally, climb one of the rear bunkers and gaze back towards Kineton. Here is the rolling landscape across which the fleeing Parliamentarian Horse, dragoons and Foot all ran, pursued by Wilmot's and Rupert's exuberant troopers. Before leaving this inner

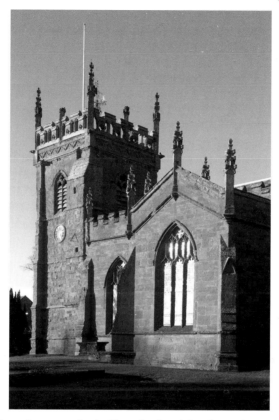

Kineton Church. It was here or nearby that Essex first heard that the royal army was in the vicinity.

part of the Depot, look at the area of the guardhouse. It was here that Ballard's Brigade drove forward to fight their way up to the line, trying to close the gap created by the flight of Charles Essex's Brigade.

After leaving the Depot go back to the B4086 and that pull-in mentioned earlier. Park opposite in a farm gateway and look over the gate at the field beyond. To the right (no. 8) is a thin hedge and a row of pollarded willows which are quite old. Could this be the extreme left, where the famous hedge turned towards the hill and where some of Ballard's commanded musketeers were broken by Usher's dragoons? Cross the road,

Relics of the field, displayed on the wall in the Kineton Depot Officers' Mess. Two musket, one carbine and one pistol ball, found somewhere on the field. Their round shape means it is likely they never hit their target.

The monument to the fallen. The resited monument stands in a little enclave at the side of what was once the farm track which became known as King John's Lane. You can just make out the Castle Inn on the skyline, but the bunkers have ruined this crucial part of the field.

walk down to the 'pull-in' and look over that gate. Is this more remains of that famous hedge? Look left and see the ground over which Rupert's men charged. Look right, to the other side of the hedge. In these fields the Royalist Horse hit Ramsey's. Out to the front, Fortesque's traitors changed sides.

Continue eastwards a short distance. Just before a right bend there is a small bridge with another gateway on the right. Park here and walk along the track, (no. 9). There are woods to the left and an open field on the right that gradually climbs away. This is the slope up to Ramsey's position, the 'uphill' Stuart was 'fain to charge', and Parliament's left almost certainly extended across the road in order to block it. Imagine the sight of the ranks of Horse on the skyline. Follow this track through a few woodland

The rolling plain back to Kineton. A peaceful, rural setting in 2003, but in 1642 this was open heath and full of men running for their lives.

The Old Road. It was down this road that the Royal artillery was laboriously manoeuvred. It was improved by Sanderson Miller to make an attractive country walk but it is still steep in places.

glades running parallel to the stream. Do not go into the pheasantry management centre but keep to the path and over a culvert. Follow the stream and scramble down to water level so as to appreciate the nature of the brook behind which Ramsey deployed his left wing. Near the pheasantry much of the ground was landscaped during the construction of an ammunition railway line, but examine the brook beyond these workings (no. 10),

Rupert's deployment ground Out in those fields, probably on a line with the grey, modern barn Rupert arrayed his Horse. Byron was a little nearer the camera somewhere perhaps along the road line, while the barn is approximately where the first of the infantry brigades, Gerard's, stood.

The Kingsmill memorial in Radway Church. Below, detail of the Kingsmill effigy.

where even today it is still a significant obstacle, even at its kindest. Follow this brook across the central farmland. After a couple of hundred yards it turns east and runs towards the ridge, then meanders off again to the south east, cutting this northern half of the field diagonally, parallel to Langdon Road. Could this be the 'ditch' behind which the beaten Royalist infantry regrouped at dusk (no. 11)? It's in the right place and diligent searching cannot find any other contending feature. We believe Radway Brook provided the literal last ditch defence for the Royalists, and to the left they stood arrayed in their tired ranks.

Return to the vehicle and continue up the Banbury Road ignoring both right turns for Radway. Take the second left towards Avon Dassett and Fenny Compton. After a short distance there is a group of houses and farm buildings. The one on the left is Arlescote House (no. 12). It is mostly late seventeenth century, but the original house provided shelter for Clarendon, Harvey and the two Princes during the battle.

Returning to the Banbury road again, go left, up the hill. This road was not here in 1642. As it breasts the incline it turns sharp left for Banbury, so turn off for Edgehill village where there is a spectacular panorama of the whole battlefield from The Castle Hotel (no. 13). This building is a converted eighteenth-century, medieval-revivalism folly and has a car park opposite. The driveway is interesting, in that this should be the summit of the old highroad to Banbury that was nicknamed King Charles's Road after the battle. The great advantage of this hostelry is the view from its garden terrace.

The Old Church, copied from a drawing in Radway's new church. There is some doubt that the porch actually existed.

Binoculars will enhance appreciation but even without them the various features inside the Depot are discernable. The ammunition sheds are all too easy to spot, but behind them is the flat space bordering the memorial. The Oaks are to the left, Grave Ground Coppice to the right. The trees of Radway Brook can also be made out. In the foreground stands Radway, the centre of the Royalist start line. Although significantly enhanced, Radway Grange has not moved. Radway Church has been relocated since the 1640s but maps suggest that, although the village has spread to the north, its layout remains much as it was.

Return to the B4086, back towards Kineton. Midway down the hill, pull onto the left verge near a style. Cross the style and walk beyond the hedge where the vista opens, (no. 14). These are the fields of the Royalist right. Across the road, out to the right were

Site of the Old Church. The Miller tomb can be seen in middle ground. One of the authors is standing where the small chancel once stood.

Usher's Dragoons, while to the left, where the land flattens off, Rupert's Horse deployed in their two lines. The fields near the barns contained Gerard's Infantry Brigade with Belasye's to their left. Also visible is the 'bump' of the Kings Leys barn site!

To see the field from the Royalist perspective follow the public footpath along the foot of the hill, across Bullet Hill where the Royalist six gun battery thundered, behind Radway and Radway Grange, past the obelisk (no. 15) commemorating the gallant deeds of Lieutenant Colonel Miller at Waterloo. The path eventually links up with King John's Lane as it runs down from the top of the escarpment on its way over to Little Kineton.

Return to the car and set off downhill again. Take the first left for Radway. Pull off the road into the first field gateway on the left. (no. 16). Look up the hill. This is the front of Bullet Hill and this is the view that those on the left of Balfour's little party would have had as they charged the Royalist battery.

Drive through the village past the church, towards Tysoe. King John's Lane joins from the left as you turn a sharp right bend. Follow this 18th century Edgehill to Little Kineton road for a couple of hundred yards then turn a sharp left bend, although the lane carries on. Look for a place to park with a reasonable view of the landscape. There is a pull-in on the right just after the farm (no. 17). These are the fields over which Wilmot's and Digby's cavalry wing attacked. Turn around and go back to the sharp bend. With permission, turn left and follow King John's Lane westward. Go to the far end where the lane ends in a mass of bushes (no. 18). There is room to turn a car between two gateways either side of the track. Park and inspect the fields beyond both gates. Tony Pollard told the author some battle detritus had been found here, although not featured in the BBC television programme *Two Men in a Trench*, and at the time of writing the report is yet be published.[3] However, you are probably standing in the place where the cuirassiers of Bedford's Parliamentarian reserve pursued Fielding's broken Regiments, and behind you, in the south field, Byron's Brigade fled. In these cornfields the King's Lifeguard and Lord General Lindsey's Regiments were cut up and their colours, including the Banner Royal, taken; also in that southern field Meldrum's and Wentworth's Brigades were locked in deadly combat as tiredness and circumstances forced the Royalists to fall back.

Drive back down the lane; on your left, the gap in the battle line would be gradually opening as Ballard's began to pivot about their left forcing Gerard's and Belasyse's Brigades back until they were able to draw up behind their protective ditch. Stop where the track rejoins the road. Around this crossroads (no. 19) it is believed Wentworth's finally dug in. There cannot be a precise location until somebody detects, excavates and plots the finds that possibly lie beneath the soil here.

Back towards Radway and pass a mound on the left (no. 20). It has trees growing on it and is called King's Clump because tradition says that Charles used it as a vantage point during the later stages of the fight. A little further on is Radway Church (no. 21). Although constructed several centuries after the battle, it does contain items taken from the old building, including a monument to Henry Kingsmill Esquire, of Sydmonton Court, Hampshire, killed by a cannon ball while serving as a Royalist Captain of Foot. Now head for the village centre but turn first right. Radway Grange is through the trees to the left. The house existed at the time of the battle and was owned by the Washington family, whose descendant became President of the United States. Park near the pond then find the row of cottages on the southern side of the green. Take the unmarked footpath between Dale Cottage and Ferndale House. It looks like a private drive but it is a public right of way. Behind the houses, on the right, is the site of the old Church (no. 22) which tradition says was used as a Royalist field dressing station.[4] Some sources state that near the churchyard entrance is the gravestone of Elizabeth Heritage; she died in 1645-6 and supposedly helped the wounded of both sides. Unfortunately, there is no proof of this and we could not find the stone.

Return to the main thoroughfare, turn right into the village and then turn left for Kineton, up Langdon Road which runs diagonally across the field. There is a parking bay on the left (no. 23) by what appears to be a failed building project. Over the low wall and through the trees to have a good view of the final Royalist position and the tree line that marks Radway Brook. Crossing the fields to these trees affords another view of the brook. It runs in the right direction, is in the correct location and it has sizeable banks for a considerable part of its length, making it a natural defensive feature. As it stretches towards Radway and its source, it becomes shallower and the banks flatten out, but the surrounding ground becomes marshy.

A little further up Langton Road there is another pull-in on the right by some farm gates. In the field to the right is something resembling a small tumulus (no. 24) but it is a pile of rubble from a WW2 structure that was heaped on top of the remaining foundations of Kings Leys Barn where the King spent the night after the battle.

At the T-junction with the B4086, turn left and head back to Kineton. Imagine the cavalry pursuit over this rolling countryside. Stop again in Kineton and try to envisage this quiet Warwickshire village as a scene of panic and pandemonium, and with Digby's troopers riding in, one of looting, destruction and murder. Just beyond the War Memorial turn left towards the church, then, opposite, left again into Bridge Street. The road dips down to the bridge (no. 25). Park on the left, in the entrance to a field a few yards over the bridge. This is one contender for the infamous Kineton Ford, where many of the fleeing men were cut down. Miller says that skeletons were found when the nineteenth-century bridge was built. The other possible location is near an avenue of trees east of the present bridge, but the archaeological dig featured in *Two Men in a Trench* discovered little evidence of a track or ford. Obviously, further work is needed to clarify the true site.

Head into Little Kineton, turning left for Tysoe and Oxhill; then left again at a crossroads in the village centre. This is the western end of King John's Lane and soon runs out of tarmac. King John's Lane branches off to the left, past a disused brick works to the Depot perimeter fence. It is a pleasant walk to see the reverse slope of Essex's ridge but a lot of it has disappeared or is no longer visible. Continue down the main lane, preferably on foot. The lane rises steadily until it turns sharply to the right (no. 26) through a gate leading to a Farm. This rise is known as Lucas's Knoll, where supposedly Lucas rallied and reformed his small force of Horse. From here they charged the fleeing remnants of Charles Essex's Brigade and, somewhere in the fields to the north, Captain Smith retook the Banner Royal.

With permission from the farmer, continue to walk the lane round the southern end of The Oaks to see the right rear of Essex's position and the nature of the small hill he recognized as a crucial fighting area. Further on is the area where Fielding's Regiment was broken, and further still where Wilmot hooked Essex's line (no. 27). Note the

Kineton Ford. The traditional site of the Ford where Miller says skeletons were discovered.

difficult nature of the land and how the rising ground would have encouraged a drift to the left.

Go back into Little Kineton and take the road again for Tysoe and Oxhill, by following signposts to Tysoe and Compton Wynyates cut across to the A422 and turn left. Follow this road up the ridge through an area known as Sunrising Hill. It was down this hill, two days after the battle, that Rupert returned to Kineton and continued plundering the baggage of Essex's departing army. On the right is a large house. This is the Sun Rising (no. 28) on the old Stratford upon Avon coach road. Reputedly, it was where the mortally wounded Lindsey was taken and it once contained various battlefield memorabilia including arms and armour. Walford makes an intriguing reference to 'a sword supposed on the evidence of emblems in its decoration to have belonged to the

The authors on Edgehill, still enjoying walking the field and discussing various points.

Earl Lindsey' , but these have long since disappeared.[5]

Further afield visit: Chadshunt Church where Rupert's men supposedly dragged some Parliament men out of holy sanctuary; Warmington Church for the headstone of Captain Alexander Gourdin or Gaudin who died 24 October 1642; or Windmill Hill. The view is spectacular but placing Fiennes and Cromwell there does not fit the evidence. Most of Ratley's picturesque houses were not built when the King's army was quartered there, although some Royalists who died of their Edgehill wounds are supposedly buried behind the church. Also visit Tysoe which was occupied by the Parliamentarians prior to the battle and who, locals will tell you, sequestered the village's bread as they marched out. The Manor at Little Wolford supposedly has bloodstains on the stairs from the time of the battle while in Oxhill there is grave of a Royalist soldier who died in 1681. Newbold Pacey's parish register has the following entry, 'A souldier wounded in that great battell between ye king and the parliament oct 23rd was buried ye oct 29th'. We are indebted to Peter Ellis, a fellow Trustee of the Battlefields Trust, for many of these snippets.

For battlefield walkers we also recommend Halford Bridge, the scene of a skirmish in 1643, while those who like visiting stately homes will find Upton House nearby and the fascinating home of Lord Saye and Sele, Broughton Castle, near Banbury. It has a 'plotting room' where the early resistance to the King was orchestrated. For those seeking restaurants or shopping, Banbury and Stratford Upon Avon are short drives away. Yet, to the true enthusiast, one day on Edgehill will not be enough and we hope we have provided such visitors with sufficient information and thoughts to keep them not only absorbed and walking for a full day, but also for them to return time and time again, as we have, to this most exciting, engaging and enigmatic of battlefields.

Appendix A
Battlefield Interpretation

Battlefield interpretation is a skilled art. It is a combined art, where three distinct skills are fused together in creating the one experience. It calls for knowledge of the nature of warfare during the age in which the conflict took place, an understanding of the ground over which it was fought and an appreciation of what evidence has been found and how time has changed things – that is the historical, the landscape and the archaeological perspectives. This too is further complicated by the complexities of each skill.

The Historical Perspective:
- sifting truths from historical accounts, distinguishing the bias or the nature of sources often written in Latin, old French or English secretary script;
- collating who took part and the alliances, allegiances and vested interests that brought them to fight;
- linking the period standards and conditions to contemporary values and beliefs and their influence upon the behaviour of men in certain social groups and in large numbers;
- appreciating the technological advantage games played out between designers and manufacturers of weapons and protection;
- having knowledge of strategy and tactics, military formations, command and control and the practice of offensive and defensive manoeuvres; as well as logistics and supply of the materials of war including animal husbandry.

The Landscape Perspective:
- the geographical importance of a place, how it relates to the goals of a campaign and its proximity to towns, castles, river crossings or any other major or minor objectives;
- the contours of the ground and the various viewpoints offered to general officers for command and control;
- the form and lie of the land which decides the nature of the battle and its influence upon decisions to defend or attack or indeed shelter or move troops in secret;
- the nature of the ground in deciding the minor tactics of how & which type of troops will fight on or in particular types of terrain;
- the feasibility of specified areas to accommodate unit frontages and allow the

execution of manoeuvres as dictated by period drill manuals;
- the state of the ground in various weathers ;
- the contemporary fauna's ability to provide cover or mask moves;
- the ability of the land to sustain an army's consuming needs for firewood, forage, fresh water and food.

The Archaeological Perspective:
- the understanding of historical topography, what the terrain was like at the time of the battle: road systems dictate why and where the armies were - control and use: enclosures impede movement but provide cover - choice of ground in deployment;
- the viewing of the ground as the commander on the day might have seen it, by knowing what was there, not what is there - thus appreciating constraints and opportunities influencing decisions taken regarding the battle;
- the analysis of found artefacts - whole finds or pieces of armour, arms-blanches, projectiles, small arms, or other war impedimenta;
- the gleaning of relevant information provided by the position of found artefacts - patterns of fallen shot indicating areas of engagement and intensity of shooting, backtracking via knowledge of ranges for position of firing units, etc;
- the relating of objects to their original owners - specific shot or calibres of shot determining guns or small arms for Foot or Horse and referring discoveries to stores issues or regimental order books;
- the appreciation of excavation revelations and material - shot-marked or rebuilt walls, burnt soil layers, grave pits, entrenchment, field rubbish pits and kitchens, etc.

Many battlefield visitors may not have the necessary historical, topographical and archaeological expertise to appreciate and interpret what went on across several remote fields in the English countryside. It is the job of those who do have these skills to work for them, to enable them to understand, to fire up and stimulate their imagination and, above all, ensure they take away from any visit an understanding of the battle that took place upon the ground they have chosen to visit. It is this fusion of history, geography and archaeology that provides the key to enjoying a visit to a battlefield.

Appendix B
Battlefield Finds

By the Rev. George Miller[1]
1 On some rising ground near to Lower Westcote.
2 South of the hedges of those fields which served Little Kineton and about half a mile in front of that village:
    a) Light bullets.
    b) Other debris of battle.
3 In front of a great hedge that ran alongside a track between, what was in his day, Battleton and Thistleton Farms (although the hedge most probably did exist, it is very unlikely that these farms existed in 1642):
    a) The largest portion of battle debris.
4 In the area of the Bridge between Kineton and Little Kineton:
    a) Several skeletons.
    b) Pieces of armour.
5 In the fields northeast of Langdon road:
    a) Kings Leys Barn, near to which Charles's coach was stationed for the night after the battle.
6 In Radway village:
    a) A cottage with a table upon which the King breakfasted the following day.
7 On the rising ground in the centre of Essex's position:
    a) A grave pit.
8 One field from the old turnpike gate on the Kineton Road:
    a) Another grave pit.

Reported by Walford[2]
1 The slopes at Lower Westcote near the Sun Rising:
    a) Cannon balls and other remains.

Recorded by Brigadier Peter Young[3]
1 No specified location:
    a) Several musket balls.
2 Grave Ground Coppice:
    a) A musket ball.

3 Reported as coming from the area of Thistleton Farm about 1941:

    a) Two cannon balls, 23½ lb (demi-cannon) and 12 lb (demi-culverin).

    b) Three cannon balls, one 19 lb (culverin) and two ½ lb (robinet).

4 In a ditch a quarter mile NW of the modern Radway church:

    a) A musket ball.

5 In the vicinity of the Graveyard – during the construction of the depot in 1942:

    a) Six or more cannon balls, varying in weight from 6 lb to 22 lb.

6 In a disused brick-kiln, 300 yards east along the Arlescote Road below Knowle End:

    a) Some cannon balls.

7 In a general search of the Great Grounds (outer perimeter?) in 1967:

    a) Metal tyre of a heavy vehicle.

    b) Two spear or pike heads – one at Upland Farm.

8 Broughton Church Yard:

    a) A sword.

9 Unspecified location possibly in Ratley:

    a) A sword.

Leedham tells of Peter Young (1960s) making discoveries himself:[4]

1 Embedded in the wet ground west of the Radway Brook and before the area of the trees which surround the pheasantry:

    a) Several cannon balls of varying weight and calibre.

Captain J G Grant of the Kineton Depot (1978/79) North Warwickshire County Museum Archaeology Department:

1 To the north and east of Grave Ground coppice, adjoining fields.

    a) 24 balls

2 To the north and east of Grave Ground coppice, fields further out.

    a) 19 balls

    b) A 3½-inch diameter cannon ball – saker shot not minion as Grant states

3 On Essex's Ridge

    a) 2 balls

4 On the slope of The Oaks

    a) 2 balls

5 Along the northern bank of Ramsey's Stream

    a) 5 balls.

Although Grant gives a complete breakdown of the numbers of various sizes of balls found, which vary between musket, carbine and pistol balls, and plots exact locations of all finds, he does not say which weight of ball was found where.[5]

Oliver & Pollard have currently written of their findings:[6]

1 In the fields just outside the southern perimeter of the depot, quite close to the site of the battlefield grave at Grave Ground coppice:

    a) Musket balls both round and flattened.

    b) Pieces of grapeshot and caseshot.

    c) Buttons, some silver-plated and etched.

d) Pieces of horse harness.

e) Knife blades.

f) Buckles.

g) Possible musket fittings.

2 On the slopes overlooking the ford on the Dene, about 100 m east of King John's castle, about midway between the two disused sluices:

a) Pistol or carbine balls, clipped and still with sprue.

b) Lumps of solidified lead splashes.

c) Two pewter spoons.

d) Two lead cylinders.

e) Possible lead dice.

3 In the fields northeast of Langdon road:

a)The foundations of the walls of Kings Leys Barn.

4 Shown by local residents without any reference or location published.

a) An unspecified number of musket and cannon balls

There is a widely held belief that another metal detector survey was done by an officer called Scott during the 1960s and that he made significant discoveries, although we can find no record of his work or evidence that he existed.

Appendix C
Frontages

A fascinating exploration is to try to determine which regiments fought each other. In order to do so it is necessary to make a few calculations and, to do that, the first task is to establish the strengths of the various units involved in order to estimate their frontages. These following statistics have suffered from a great deal of manipulation in the past and, in order to instil as high a degree of accuracy as possible into these calculations, the figures presented here are drawn from pay warrants surviving in the National Archives. The numbers given are for private sentinels and do not include officers, inferior officers, non-commissioned officers, drummers or other attached personnel. The figures quoted below in table C1 list the total numbers that the colonels proposed to raise on first muster, the number of men actually counted on reconstructed musters listing pay drawn prior to Edgehill, the numbers of men paid after Edgehill, and the number of files that an eight-deep deployment would have produced in a fighting line.[1] Tincey and Roberts do not provide a detailed overall breakdown, but their estimate for Essex's Army of between 9,000 and 10,000 seems accurate. Young estimated the Parliamentarian regiments to have all numbered around 1,000 each, and gave an overall total of 12,000; this figure seems to be an improbable over-estimation.[2]

Table C.1   Supposed establishments for regiments of Foot in Parliament's army

Regiment	Proposed establishment	October 1642	Nov–Dec 1642	Edgehill files
Meldrum	800	799	400	100
Fairfax	800	750	unknown	94
Constable	800	700	450	88
Robartes	800	500	unknown	62
Total		*2,749*		
Charles Essex	800	600	unknown	75
Mandeville	800	600	139	75
Wharton	800	600	unknown	75
Chomley	1200	1,128	552	141
Total		*2,928*		
Lord General	1500	958	unknown	120
Brooke	800	740	480	92
Ballard	800	776	439	97
Holles	1200	1,130	unknown	141
Total		*3,604*		

Table C1   continued

Regiment	Proposed establishment	October 1642	Nov–Dec 1642	Edgehill files
Hampden*	1200	963	unknown	
Grantham*	800	unknown	unknown	

*excluded from subsequent calculations.

Total of ordinary soldiers estimated at 9,281

To calculate an overall estimate for the Foot, it is necessary to include a company officer, a lieutenant, an ensign, a sergeant and a musician for every company – perhaps five supernumeraries for every sixty men, thereby adding around a further 773. The overall estimate for the numbers of Parliament Foot at the outset of the battle of Edgehill is, therefore, something over 9,000, some 3,000 less than that provided by Young. The figures for the Royalist regiments are even more difficult to gather. Young bases his estimates on returns gathered in Oxford during November 1642, but it should be remembered that these were compiled after the battle of Edgehill and also after part of the army had fought the action at Brentford and had been obliged to retreat from Turnham Green. Table C.2 below repeats Young's figures:

Table C2   Supposed establishments for regiments of Foot of the Royalist army.

Regiment	16 Nov.1642		Regiment	16 Nov.1642
G Gerard	560		Blagge	690
Salusbury	91		Belasyse	505
Molineux	320		Pennyman	685
	Total 971			*Total* 1,880
Lifeguard	670		C Gerard	740
Lord General	840		Dyves	575
Beaumont	320		Dutton	670
	Total 1,830			*Total* 1,985
Fielding	460			
Lunsford	350			
Bolles	560			
Fitton	460			
Stradling	715			
	Total 2,545			

Total of ordinary soldiers estimated at 9,211

These figures appear, therefore, to indicate that the minimum number of Royalists Foot present at the battle of Edgehill was in the region of 9,211 men. It is not known whether these numbers include supernumeraries, but Young goes on to state that the Royalist army had had time to recruit and were sufficiently successful to replace losses. This would thus argue that these November figures are reasonably close to those actually present at Edgehill.

To identify who the opposing regiments were on either side, it is necessary to examine the battle array of both sides, make allowance for their 'figure of battle', and then pair off the fighting files. This can, of necessity, only ever hope to produce a crude calculation but it may possibly throw some light onto several associated combat issues. Because the Royalists were in Swedish formation a substantial number of each regiment's files would not be in the fighting line at the same time. An estimate of the number of files may be readily achieved by dividing regimental numbers by six to arrive at the number of individual files mustered by each regiment, but it is then necessary to deduct an overall 25 per cent for each regiment's contribution to the companies that formed the rear block of the lozenge. Similarly, a further 12½ per cent has to be deducted from the remaining files to compensate for those placed behind the front block of the central divisions. It is not proven, but if it is accepted that, on contact with the enemy, the muskets passed through the pike to fire, and that the pike then advanced through them when the fall on was ordered, it is still necessary to reduce the brigade's allocated frontage because these two blocks were arrayed behind one behind the other rather than side by side. Although this was designed so that the line could be self-protecting from attack by Horse, Rupert and his co-conspirators had convinced the King to adopt a battle order that would effectively negate 37½ per cent of his Foot's strength in an infantry combat.

The authors crave the reader's pardon for not pursuing an examination of the divisions between files of musketeers and files of pikemen. The numbers are simply not available and the whole process would be both speculative and byzantine in its complexity. However, as a rough rule of thumb, at Edgehill, whereas the King's army fielded an approximate ratio of one pikeman to every musketeer, Essex's army was more likely to field two musketeers to every pikeman. It is accepted that opinions do vary on these ratios. Another popular theory has the King employing a two to one, musketeer to pike ratio while Essex was able to produce three to two. Whichever arrangement is believed to be correct, and the authors of this work prefer the former, both accept that Parliament achieved greater proportionate firepower.

Calculating the length of the opposing lines is an interesting exercise. Although appreciating the difficulties and assumptions this involves, we believe it to be useful if only to give a general idea of the distances occupied by the various formations. Our arithmetic is based upon distances recommended by several period drill manuals, the above musket-to-pike ratios and allowing for the pike to be at Order with an allocation of one metre of frontage per man, while the musket are reckoned to be in Open Order at two metres of frontage per man. For the Horse we allow two metres per trooper and mount. We have decided to convert our yards to metres, for two reasons. Firstly, we wish our book to make sense to younger generations for whom yards will mean very little and, secondly, in this way we gain some eight metres per 100 men which can be used to account for minor intervals. We believe these are reasonable presumptions based upon period drill experience. Figures have been rounded to make the arithmetic simpler. With these provisos we estimate the following frontages:

Table C3 Suggested frontages for the battle of Edgehill.

Parliament	Strength	Files	Troops	Metres Frontage
Lord General's	360	60	6	120
Balfour's	360	60	6	120
Fielding's	360	60	6	120
Ramsey's	240	40	4?	80
Waller's	240	40	4?	80
Goodwin's	360	60	6?	120
Sandys'	240	40	4?	80
Bedford's	120	20	2?	40
Urry's	240	40	4?	80
Holles'	400 muskets in 66 files 11 divisions			132

Table C3   continued

Parliament	Strength	Files	Troops		Metres Frontage
			Pike	Musket	
Meldrum's	799	100	35	65	165
Fairfax's	750	94	30	65	160
Constable's	700	88	30	60	150
Robartes'	500	62	20	40	100
Charles Essex's	600	75	25	50	125
Mandeville's	600	75	25	50	125
Wharton's	600	75	25	50	125
Chomley's*	1,128	141	45	95	235 or 115/120
Lord General's*	958	120	40	80	200 or 100/100
Brooke's	740	92	30	65	160
Ballard's	476	59	27	32	86
Detached	300				
Hollis'	730	91	44	47	135
Detached	400				

* Given the size of these two regiments it is likely that they were drawn up in two bodies called 'Grand Divisions'. This would be in line with the period practice of creating battalia of about 550 men.

Royalist	Strength	Files	Troops	Metres Frontage
Wilmot's	355	120	6	120
Grandison's	200	65	4	65
Caernavon's	200	65	4	65
Digby's	150	50	3	50
Aston's	150	50	3	50
Lifeguard	150	50	1	50
Wales'	500	165	8	165
Rupert's	465	155	7	155
Maurice's	180	60	4	60
Lifeguard Servants	150	50	1	50
Byron	250	83	6	85

Because of the Swedish formation the Royalist fighting frontages are more complicated. We can estimate the number of files easily enough but we must then deduct an overall total of 37½ per cent for each regiment's contribution of companies to the rear block at the back of the lozenge, and to those placed behind the front block of the central divisions. It is not proven, but if we accept that on contact with the enemy, the muskets passed through the pike to fire, and the pike then advanced through them when the fall on was ordered, we still have to reduce the brigade's allocated frontage because these two blocks are arrayed in depth not width.

Table C4   Royalist fighting frontages.

Strength	Files	-37½%	Pike	Musket	Metres	
Molineux's	320	53	34	17	17	51
Salusbury's	910	151	95	48	47	142
G.Gerard's	560	93	59	29	30	89
Beaumont's	320	53	34	17	17	51
Lord General's	840	140	88	44	44	132
Lifeguard	670	111	70	35	35	105

Table C4 continued

Strength	Files	-37½%	Pike	Musket	Metres	
Fielding's	460	76	48	24	24	72
Lunsford's	350	58	37	19	18	55
Bolle's	560	93	59	29	30	89
Fitton's	460	76	48	24	24	72
Stradling's	715	119	73	37	36	109
Blagge's	690	115	72	36	36	109
Belasyse's	505	84	53	27	26	79
Pennyman's	685	114	72	36	36	109
Gerard's	740	123	77	39	38	115
Dyve's	575	95	60	30	30	90
Dutton's	670	111	70	35	35	105

In order to envisage brigade frontages it is necessary to allow for intervals between both the constituent divisions of the homogenous weapon blocks, and between those blocks themselves. In addition allowance must be made for intervals between battalia, both foot and horse, although these can be largely negated in the case of certain deployments due to the practice of checker-boarding. Provision is thereby made for a second line battalia to come up to the fighting line into a gap left specifically for that purpose, roughly equal to the front of the unit for whom it was intended. In Ramsey's deployment we have allowed the same notion to stand for, although not checker-boarding, we believe that he left sufficient space at the side of each body in order that it could fall back. Into these intervals he placed his commanded musketeers who should not be calculated as an additional extra.[3] In the case of the Royalist Foot, allowance for their deployment has already been made in the calculation of their individual regimental frontage.

Obviously we cannot produce anything other than approximations for the frontages taken by these bodies but even these rough calculations are better than nothing when we apply them to the scaled map in order to get some idea of how much space each formation occupied on the ground at Edgehill.

Table C5 Rounded approximations for frontages.

Parliament		*Rounded approximations****
Balfour's Brigade	360m	350
Meldrum's Brigade	575m	575
Charles Essex's Brigade	610m	600
Ballard's Brigade	585m	575
Ramsey's Brigade	480m or 612 if giving room to interlard muskets	500 or 600
Royalist		
Wilmot's wing	310m	300
Wentworth's Brigade	282m	275
Byron's Brigade	288m	275
Fielding's Brigade	397m	400
Belasye's Brigade	297m	300
Gerard's Brigade	310m	300
Rupert's wing	565m	550

* Rounded figures are for use in roughly pacing out or estimating distances on the field. One can never get an accurate picture but these approximations, no matter how crude, do help place units on the ground and supply comparisons in size of deployment areas.

Table C6 below is an attempt to identify the opposing regiments. As previously mentioned, the table is based on crude calculations but it does, nevertheless, provide a reasonable answer to the question 'which regiment fought which' that, in the absence of records is, if nothing else, of interest.

Table C6   Opposing units I.

Royalist			Parliamentarian		
Name	*Files*	*Frontage*	*Name*	*Files*	*Frontage*
Molineux	34	51m	Meldrum	100	165m
Salusbury	95	142m			
G.Gerard	59	89m	Constable	88	150m
Brigade total		282m			
Beaumont	34	51m			
Lord General	88	132m	Robartes	62	100m
Lifeguard	70	105m			
Brigade total		288m			
			Additonal:		
			Fairfax	10	15m
			Charles Essex	20	30m
Combined totals	326	570m		280	460m

These figures include approximations of the remnants of Fairfax's Regiment (believed to have been Sir William himself, and about 100 officers and men) and, for those from Charles Essex's entire Brigade who reached to Meldrum's, we allow about 160, although it could have been considerably more. We have no record of where either body made their gallant contribution to the line. Meldrum's remaining three Parliamentarian regiments were engaged all along its length and, having lost most of Fairfax's, they must have been overlapped on both flanks and put under very heavy pressure but, thanks to the Royalists' Swedish formation, the threat appears to have been contained. It seems likely that Meldrum's Brigade was on the far right engaging Wentworth's Brigade, possibly helped by the presence of Balfour's Regiment of Horse, for it was Constable's and Robartes's Regiments who added the Foot's contribution to the attack that finished Byron's.

The following scenario is based upon primary source material and what is known of the deployment and methods of fighting. It also allows for division, company and regimental intervals and includes differences that might accumulate from the pikes and muskets forming 'close' or 'closest' order. Any spaces left for manhandled light guns also have to be borne in mind, not only within the ranks but also among those of the opposing enemy occasioned by involuntary shying away. Regardless of how many factors are included, any answer can only be a best 'guestimate' and is offered merely as an informed personal interpretation rather than a serious hypothesis.

Starting from the basic premise that, in the Royalist army's Swedish system, there is nothing to suggest that a specific regiment was left to maintain the rear position. It is assumed that the rear unit was formed by drawing men from companies belonging to the brigade's constituent regiments, with the result that each of the latter took a place in the fighting line. Young concurred with this argument. With the amalgamation of the regiments into four grand divisions of musket and pike blocks it is, therefore, impossible to determine exactly which regiment fought where, but if we apply what is believed to have been normal contemporary practice, Meldrum's would have been placed on the right and would, therefore, have engaged a combination Molineux's and Salusbury's men. Then Constable's would have faced an amalgam of mostly Gerard's and Beaumont's Regiments and, perhaps also assisted Robartes's to face Lord General Lindsey's Regiment and the Lifeguard. Robartes's must also have received help from Charles Essex's Regiment. Meldrum's line must have been shorter than their opponents' and included some gaps. Finding themselves overlapped was a desperate situation but the depth of the line would have compensated during 'push of pike' as the pike blocks, despite being wrapped around by the enemy, would continue to 'lock-in' on themselves and hold their ground. In practice, the Dutch order proved highly effective against the Swedish system. The centre of the Royalists's pike line could easily have been reinforced by bringing up the brigade rear guard, but this action would have demanded expert and thoughtful handling on the part of inexperienced regimental officers fighting in an unfamiliar formation.

To investigate the picture at the other end of the line we must again use regimental numbers to determine the number of files and, for the Royalist formations, it is first necessary to deduct 25 per cent for each regiment's contribution to the brigade's rear companies and a further 12½ per cent for the second line of its front companies.

Table C7   Opposing units II.

Name	Files	Frontage	Name	Files	Frontage
C Gerard	77	115m	Holles	91	135m
Dyves	60	90m	Brooke	92	1 60m
Dutton	70	105m	Ballard	59	86m
Brigade total		310m	Lord General	120	200m
			Brigade total		446m
Blagge	72	109m			
Belasyse	53	79m	*Additional:*		
Pennyman	72	109m	Charles Essex	20	30m
Brigade total		297m	Holles	12	24m
			Brooke	10	20m
Fielding	48	72m	*Additions*		74m
Lunsford	37	55m			
Bolles	59	89m			
Fitton	48	72m			
Stradling	73	109m			
Brigade total		397m			

The additional figures are for rallied men. If a similar number of men joined Ballard's from Charles Essex's Brigade as Meldrum's received from the same source, some 320 from a total of 2,828 does not appear unreasonable. It is also probable that a significant proportion, perhaps 25 per cent, of the commanded musketeers recently ridden over would have returned to the safety of their parent units rather than risk the hazards of the open countryside infested with enemy cavalry.

Although unproven we offer this speculative series of calculations to possibly deliver greater insight into the fighting.

Appendix D
King Charles I's Speech

The Kings Majestie's Speech to his Whole Armie immediately before the Battell.[1]

The King riding up to the forefront or head of his Armie, made a Royall Speech unto them all, the effect whereof, I have signified unto you in this my letter.

Friends and Soldiers, I look upon you with joy, to behold so great an Armie as ever King of England had in these latter times, standing with high and full resolutions to defend Your King, the Parliament, and all my loyall subjects. I thanke your loves offered to your King with a desire to hazzard your lives and fortunes with me, and in my Cause, freely offered, and that in my urgent necessitie, I see by you, that no father can relinquish and leave his son, no subject his lawful King, but I attribute all this unto God, and the justnesse of my Cause; hee that made Us a King will protect us. Wee have marched so long in hope to meet no Enemies, we knowing none at whose hands we deserve any opposition, nor can our sunne-shining through the clouds of malignant envie, suffer such an obscuritie, but that some influence of my Regal authority, derived from God, whose substitute and supreme Governor under Christ I am, hath begotten in you a confidence in my intentions. But matters are now not to be declared by words, but by swoards, you all thinke our thoughts endeavour to defend our Person, which I reign over your affections as well as your persons. Now therefore know, my resolution is to trie the doubtful chance of warre, which with much griefe I must stand to, and endure the hazard; I deme not the effusion of blood, but since heaven hath so decreed that so much preparation hath been made, We must needs accept of this present occasion and opportunity of gaining an honourable victory, and some addition of glory to Our Crowne, since reputation is that which doth guild over the richest gold and shall be ever the endeavour of Our whole raigne. The present action of this battell makes me speak briefly and yet lovingly and royally unto you, Our loyall Armie. I put not my confidence in your strength or number but confide, that though your King speaks unto you and that with as much love and affection as ever King of England did to his Armie; yet God and the justnesse of Our Cause together with the love I bear to the whole kingdome must give you the best encouragement. In a word, your King bids you all be courageous and heaven make you victorious.

Appendix E
The Earl of Essex's Orders

The Earl of Essex's orders[1]
I shall desire all and every officer to endeavour by love and affable carriage to command his souldiers, since what is done for fear is done unwillingly, and what is unwillingly attempted can never prosper.

Likewise 'tis my request that you be very carefull in the exercising of your men, and bring them to use their armes readily and expertly, and not to busy them in practizing the ceremonious formes of military discipline, onely let them be well instructed in the necessary rudiments of warre, that they may know to fall on with discretion and retreat with care, how to maintaine their order and make good their ground: also I do expect that all those which voluntarily engaged themselves in this service, should answer my expectation in the perfomance of these ensuing articles.

1. That you willingly and chearfully obey such as (by your owne election) you have made commanders over you.
2. That you take speciall care to keape your armes at all times fit for service, that upon all occasions you may be ready when the signal shall be given, by the sound of the drumme or trumpet, to repaire to your colours, and so to march upon any service, where and when occasion shall require.
3. That you beare yourselves like soldiers without doing any spoile to the inhabitants of the country, so doing you shall gain love and friendship, where otherwise you will be hated and complained off, and I that should protect you, shall be forced to punish you according to the severity of law.
4. That you accept and rest satisfied with such quarters as shall fall to your lot, or be appointed you by your quarter-master.
5. That you shall (if appointed for centries or per-dues) faithfully discharge that duty, for upon failure hereof, you are to undergo a very severe censure.
6. That you shall forbeare to profane the Saboth, either by being drunke, or by unlawfull games, for whatsoever shall be found faulty must not expect to passe unpunished.
7. Whosoever shall be knowne to neglect the feeding of his horse, with necessary povender, to the end that his horse be disabled or unfit for service, the party for the said default shall suffer a month's imprisonment, and afterwards be cashiered as unworthy the name of a souldier. These things faithfully performed, and the justice of our cause truly considered, let us advance with a religious corage, and willingly adventure our lives in the defence of our king and parliament.

8. That no trooper or other of our souldiers shall sufer his Paddee[2] to feed his horse in the corne, or to steal mens hay, but shall pay everyman for hay 6d a day and night, and for oats 2s the bushell.

Lastly; that you avoid cruelty, for it is my desire rather to save the life of thousands, than to kill one, so that it may be done without prejudice.

Notes

Introduction
1   See appendix A for further comments regarding battlefield interpretation.
2   C H Firth (1895).

Chapter One: Preceding Events
1   Howard and Paret (1974/1986), pp 75–89.
2   Clarendon (1843), p. 306.
3   *Ibid.*, p. 307.
4   *Ibid.*
5   Warburton (1849), vol. 2, p. 12.
6   BL, *TT*, E 126 (38): Bifield.

Chapter Two: Weapons
1   There is no contemporary evidence for the use of the term 'twelve apostles' which appears to be a 20th-century re-enactment myth.
2   Clarendon (1843), pp 73 and 83.
3   For example, BL, *TT*, E 126 (38): Bifield.
4   For example: BL, *TT*, E 126 (13): Keightly; BL, *TT*, E 126 (38): Bifield; BL, *TT*, 669. f 6 (88): Ramsay.
5   Tests performed by the Royal Armouries under controlled conditions, recorded on film, were conducted during the 1970s and 1980s at various ranges at HM Tower of London and Fort Nelson. Richard Ellis and Chris Scott also undertook live-firing experiments at targets in the summer of 2000 on private property at Minchinhampton, Gloucestershire.
6   Roberts and Tincey (2001), p. 20.
7   Akehurst (1972), p. 16.
8   Honeywell and Spear (1993), p. 38.
9   *Ibid.*
10 NA, SP 28/2, f 668.
11 NA, WO 55/1754 and WO 55/1927.
12 Chris Scott experimented with mounted dragoon live-firing at a re-enactment battle at Powderham Castle in Devon during the late 1970s. Although one of his six-man command was able to perform reasonably well, he and the rest had great difficulty in controlling their mounts after firing. Other attempts performed over the years by various re-enactment groups have had similar results except in cases where owner-riders were able to spend time getting their mounts accustomed to the noise before putting the drill into practice.

13   Polybius (1537); Lipsius (1598); Connolly (1977), pp 29–32.
14   Kellie (1627).
15   A very wide range of drill books was available to officers as the country headed into war. Some were of British authorship others were translated, either in original or amended form, from German, Dutch, Swedish, Latin, Italian, French or Greek texts. There was no reason for any officer to be without a drill manual.
16   Davies (1934), quoting from *The Parliamentary or Constitutional History of England* (24 vols, London, 1751–1761), XI, pp 436–9.
17   These are transcribed in appendix F below.
18   Ward (1638).
19   BodL, 4° X 44 (38), King Charles I, *Military Orders...*; Elton (1649).
20   Smyth (1590).
21   *Ibid.*
22   No evidence has yet been found of pikemen wearing sleeveless buffcoats under their armour, nor of this type of garment being issued to anyone. Several members of the London Trained Bands did wear them, but they were expensive pieces of equipment and evidence suggests they were more a musketeer accoutrement than that of pikemen who had their breastplates. The universal wearing of buffcoats appears to be a re-enactment myth.
23   Captain H Barrett, (London, 1652) cited in Duthie (1985), pp 16–17.
24   Roy (1971), p. 107.
25   *Ibid.*, p. 108.
26   C E H Chadwyk Healey (1902), p. 43.
27   Smyth (1590).
28   Thompson (1927).
29   *Ibid.*
30   Because of the diversity of guns in use it has become fashionable among modern writers to say there was no regularized system. However, King Henry II of France had introduced *Les Six Calibres de France* for his artillery in 1550, which was copied by Maurice of Nassau, except that he styled his light pieces as 'infantry guns'. At the beginning of the English Civil Wars, guns of varying ages and manufacture were gathered in from many sources so that the array of pieces assembled thereby posed problems for the standardization of supply.
31   Roy (1963), I, p. 18; Young (1938), pp. 145–51.
32   Moone (1903).
33   Eldred (1646).
34   Conversation with Robert Leedham, a member of the Inner Council of the Sealed Knot and a good friend of the late Brigadier Peter Young. He is a recognized local Civil War historian who conducts tours of Edgehill for the Army and private individuals.
35   Clarendon, (1843).
36   Lion Television production, *Royal Deaths and Diseases*, 2002, episode 1.
37   Tennant (1992), p. 46.
38   Vicars (1644), p. 166.
39   Nehemiah Wharton's letters provide considerable insight into the military life and experiences of the times. They commence on 16 August 1642 and end at Worcester on 7 October 1642. It is possible that he was killed at Edgehill two weeks later: Peachey (1989), p. 18.
40   Atkin (1995), p.39

Chapter Three: Command

1   These included illness, detached duties, absence or in some cases individuals holding two posts or superseding an inferior's command. However, many of the duties were clearer and more specific. These are taken from the period drill book written by John Cruso,

Militarie Instructions for the Cavalerie (1972 edn), pp 1–16.

2   Roberts and Tincey (2001: pp 16 and 62) style him Lieutenant General yet acknowledged the titling of his regiment of foot as 'the Lord General's'.

3   Cruso, *op. cit.*

4   *Ibid.*

5   *Ibid.*

6   BodL Vet. A3d. 404, P Wharton, *Eight speeches...*

7   Roberts and Tincey (2001) p. 14.

8   Clarendon (1843).

9   *CSPD, 1641–1643*, p. 353.

10 *Ibid.*

11 BL, Harl. MS 3783, f 60: Stuart, *A Brief Relation...*

12 Vicars (1644), p. 201.

Chapter Four: Combatants

1   Young and Holmes (1974), p. 55.

2   *Ibid.*

3   Clarendon (1843), p. 202.

4   Young and Holmes (1974), p. 56.

5   Young (1967), p. 69.

6   Clark (1891), I, p. 64.

7   Ede-Borrett (1983) p. 16.

8   Wiltshire County Record Office, *Extracts of Wiltshire Quarter Session Rolls*, p. 349; Somerset County Record Office, 'Somerset Quarter Session Roll' quoted in Young, (1967), pp. 220-221; Ede-Borrett (1983), p. 30.

9   Lawson Dick (1976), p. 265.

10 *CSPD, 1642*, p. 367.

11 Adair (2001), p. 15.

12 Gregg (2000), p. 99.

113 *Ibid.*, p. 86.

14 Whenever things are written on Edgehill, reference is always made of Barkham's regiment as mentioned by Bifield. Barkham's were not part of Essex's army but probably a local militia regiment based in Coventry. None of their number feature in any of the hospital lists, so it would seem they arrived belatedly, only in time to march back to Warwick.

15 BL, *TT*, E. 108 (23): *The Parliaments Resolution...*

16 Ede-Borrett (1983).

17 Peachey and Turton (1987), p. 4.

18 NA, SP 16/492, f 49.

19 NA,, SP 28/28, f 367.

20 Bod L, Tanner MSS 61, f 149.

Chapter Five: Deployment

1   The term senior in this instance could mean either in rank, experience, social status or years!

2   This order of could change daily on a rotating basis. It was not an ideal situation but it could mollify personal egos.

3   P Young, (1967), plate 9. It is interesting to read the various interpretations of the Royalist deployment written by earlier scholars who did not have the luxury of this source: Ross (1887).

4   Bulstrode in Firth (1895).

5   It would probably have unwise to contradict James II's account, no matter that it was a personal recollection.

6   Moone (1903).
7   BL, *TT*, E 126 (13): Kightly.
8   Official Parliamentary Account.
9   Bulstrode in Firth (1895); Clarendon (1843).
10   The Banbury garrison was probably augmented by two companies from Meldrum's (formerly Saye & Sele's) thought to have been in Broughton & Banbury.
11   P Young, (1967), p. 254; HMC, Portland MSS, I, p. 65.
12   BL, *TT*, E 126 (13): Kightly; BodL Vet. A3d. 404, A Wharton, *Eight speeches....*
13   Fiennes mentions 'half the Lord Generall's Regiment, which his Excellency himself led up.' BL, *TT*, E 126 (39): Fiennes.
14   Ludlow in Firth (1894).
15   Official Parliamentary Account.
16   *Ibid.*
17   BL, *TT*, E 126 (39): Fiennes.
18   Ludlow in Firth (1894).
19   BL, *TT*, E. 126 (38): Bifield.
20   BL *TT*, E. 126 (24): Anon, *A Relation...* It is believed that this document, frequently referred to as the 'Official Royalist Account', was written by William Dugdale. Young suggests that it was submitted to the Royalist Council of War before publication. Young, *op. cit.*, p. 132. (hereafter the 'Official Royalist Account').
21   Bulstrode in Firth (1895).
22   Clarke (1816).
23   BL, Harl. MS 3783, f 60: Stuart, *A Brief Relation...*
24   Moone (1903).
25   Miller (1896, repr. 1967).
26   A significant part of the Earl of Bedford's Regiment was in the West Country at the time of the battle.
27   Sandys' regiment had been badly cut up at near Worcester, many of its troop commanders being either cP (captured) or kP (killed) at Powick Bridge.
28   Although Fiennes states that Sergeant Major Hurrey was part of the Lord General's regiment of Horse, that was his initial appointment. By October 1642 he had his own regiment which had been raised in September, and by cross referencing names of his troop captains from hospital and other accounts we can place him on the left with Ramsey. Fiennes also claims that Cromwell was on the right when alternative evidence shows he was not.
29   Official Royalist Account.
30   The spelling of the family name varies in sources between Fielding and Feilding.
31   Clarendon states that 'it cannot be denied that the earl, with great dexterity, performed whatsoevercould be expected from a wise general': Clarendon (1843), p. 307:
32   Official Parliamentary Account.
33   Bulstrode in Firth (1895).
34   Hexham (1642).
35   Warwickshire County Record Office, CR 319/8.
36   Previous writers have taken references to 'some 24 troops' to mean 'twenty-four exactly'. This does not fit the evidence. We may not have unearthed every troop present but conclude the rounding out to two dozen was an estimate qualified by the word 'some'.
37   See footnote on previous page.
38   NA, SP 28/36, f 482.

Chapter Six: The Field
1   Miller (1889), pp 36–45. Beighton's map of 1725 indicates the King's Tent.

2   *Ibid.*

3   Miller, (1889), pp 36–45.

4   Roberts and Tincy (2001), pp 51–4.

5   Young and Holmes (1974).

6   P Young, (1967), p. 96.

7   Warwickshire Museum Archeology Records Office, *Grant, Letter and Report.*

8   Walford (1904), pp 18–19.

9   Harvey and Thorpe (1959), p. 23.

10   Archer, '*Letters*', Oakley Park, f. 76 quoted in Styles (1978), p. 10.

11   Smith (1821), p. 289.

Chapter Seven: Opening Moves

1   Probably a piece of Victorian romance. See Johnson (1870), p. 11.

2   Clarendon (1843), p. 357; BL, *TT*, 669, f 6, Ramsey, *Vindication.*

3   Bulstrode in Firth (1895).

4   Walford (1904), p. 21

5   Bulstrode in Firth (1895).

6   P Young, (1967), p. 108

7   Ludlow in Firth (1894), p. 42.

8   *Ibid.*

9   BL, *TT*, E 124 (18): Anon., *A True Copy...*

10   BL, *TT*, E 126 (13): Kightly

11   BL, Harl. MS 3783, f 61: Stuart, *A Brief Relation...*

12   *CSPD, 1659–60*, p. 434.

13   BodL Vet. A3d. 404, P Wharton, *Eight speeches...*

14   Bulstrode in Firth (1895).

15   Official Royalist Account.

16   *Ibid.*

17   *Ibid.*

18   Philip (1947) I.

19   Clarendon (1843), p. 308.

20   BL, *TT*, E 126 (13): Kightly

Chapter Eight: The North

1   The Second Troop of His Majesties Lifeguard of Horse comprised the First Troop's servants and was commanded by Sir William Killigrew. If the message regarding Fortesque's impending defection did not reach him, could it be that this troop was actually in the second line? Admittedly there is a status assumption here, but it is doubtful that once granted the honour of 'the right of the line', Lord Bernard Stuart would then assign it to his servants' troop. If they were deployed to Stuart's left, then whatever messenger Rupert sent would have to ride past Killigrew's to reach Stuart's. For Stuart's to have received the message and not Killigrew's, it is more than likely that this troop was deployed along with the other non-recipient of the message, Byron, in the second line: this could explain why there was insufficient time for the message to be delivered. However, it could be that his troop was on Bullet Hill as shown by De Gomme and riding late to the fray, after the charge had begun, missed the message. Whatever their initial position, we think we can assume they were not in the front line.

2   We know that Killigrew's charged with Rupert's Wing but yet De Gomme shows them on Bullet Hill. For some reason they either got permission to join their first troop on the right or moved off without it!

3   Warwick (1702) pp 228–32.

4   Bulstrode in Firth (1895).

5   Prince Rupert's diary quoted in P Young, (1967), p. 111.
6   *Ibid.*
7   *Ibid.*
8   Official Parliamentary Account.
9   Bulstrode in Firth (1895)
10   BL, Harl. MS 3783, f 61: Stuart, *A Brief Relation...*
11   *Ibid.*
12   BL, *TT*, 669, f 6 (88) Ramsey, *Vindication.*
13   BL *TT*, 669. f 6 (85) Marshall, *A Most True...*
14   Bulstrode in Firth (1895)
15   Clarke (1816).
16   *Ibid.*
17   Official Royalist Account
18   BL, *TT*, E 126 (38): Bifield.
19   Bulstrode in Firth (1895)
20   Burne and Young (1998), pp 29–30.
21   Clarendon (1843), III, pp 278–9.
22   Bulstrode in Firth (1895).
23   Official Parliamentary Account.
24   BL, *TT*, 669, f 6 (88) Ramsey, *Vindication.*
25   Conversation between B Leedham and C L Scott. We remain unconvinced, particularly with regard to the presence of women so close to the fighting.
26   Miller (1889), p. 40.
27   Walford (1904).
28   BL, Harl. MS 3783, f 61: Stuart, *A Brief Relation...*
29   Robert Bennet of Exeter, a wagoner pressed into service, petitioned for and was granted the sum of £82 in May 1643 in compensation for his wagon and seven horses that had been stolen in Kineton: *CSPD, 1641–1643*, p. 459.
30   Davies (1921) 25, p.35.
31   BL, *TT*, E 126 (39): Fiennes.
32   BL, *TT*, E. 669f (85): Marshall.
33   NA, SP 28/182.

Chapter Nine: The South

1   Fiennes may not be 100 per cent accurate in his detail but even the fog of war could not have concealed the broader picture: BL, *TT*, E 126 (39): Fiennes.
2   Bulstrode in Firth (1895).
3   Professor Richard Holmes, in conversation with author at the launch of 'The Guild of Battlefield Guides', Uxbridge, November 2003.
4   These can only be estimates as greater detail has yet to come to light about the allocation of troops to regiments. It is possible that even with the detail we have discovered that sources are wrong.
5   Ludlow in Firth (1894).
6   *Ibid.*
7   Miller (1889), p. 79.
8   Ludlow in Firth (1894).
9   Walford (1904) map facing p. 20. This is not possible. There were just not enough men to cover that amount of ground. However, that the focus of the battle was centred upon the highest part of Essex's little ridge, his extreme left, is plausible. Wilmot, at some point would probably have studied his ground from the vantage of the hill before coming down. He had seen the open ground to Essex's right and saw a way in which he could outflank

the position. Added to which he probably became aware that there was little between his troops on his own left flank and the houses of Little Kineton and Kineton.

10   Clarke (1816).
11   BL, *TT*, E 126 (39): Fiennes.
12   BodL, Vet. A3d. 404, Wharton, *Eight Speeches...*
13   Young, (1967), p. 114
14   Miller, (1889), p. 79
15   We were recently made aware of unpublished letters written by Sir Arthur Aston to his wife after the battle. He commanded one of Wilmot's regiments. Regrettably, we have not been permitted to read these documents.
16   Young, (1889), p. 116
17   BL, *TT*, E 126 (38): Bifield.
18   BL, *TT*, E 126 (13): Kightly.
19   BL, *TT*, 669, f 6 (85), Marshall, *A Most True...*
20   On 20 August 1998, the *Wiltshire Gazette & Herald* disclosed The English Courtyard Association's plan to name its housing development in Marlborough after George Digby. Faced with a local outcry accusing Lord Digby, whose men had sacked seventeenth-century Marlborough and committed atrocities under his personal direction, of being a war criminal, the Association renamed their retirement home St Luke's Court. See also BL, TT, E 245 (8), Anon., *Marleborowes Miseries...*
21   Young, (1967), p. 114.

Chapter Ten: The Centre – Attack

1   Warwick (1702), pp 228–32.
2   Clarke (1816).
3   Official Parliamentary Account
4   *Ibid.*
5   Wade even did it at Sedgemoor 42 years later: BL, Harl. MS 6845, Nathaniel Wade, *Narrative* and *Further Information.*
6   Official Parliamentary Account.
7   *Ibid.*
8   Miller (1889), p. 79–80.
9   Official Royalist Account.
10   Clarke (1816).
11   *Ibid.*; Ludlow in Firth (1894), p. 44.
12   Contemporary accounts appear to paint a picture more akin to re-enactment battles than most of their critics and detractors would care to admit!
13   Regrettably, although it must have been done, (twelve charges are just not enough for several hours' fighting) we have no source for this essential activity.
14   G Davies, (1934), p. 35.
15   Official Parliamentary Account.
16   *Ibid.*; Bulstrode in Firth (1895); Moone, 1903.
17   See chapter 8 above.
18   Bulstrode in Firth (1895).
19   This version of events is speculative as the exact order of these regiments cannot be stated with certainty.
20   Official Parliamentary Account.
21   BodL Vet. A3 d. 404, Wharton, *Eight Speeches.*
22   See Chapter 12 below.
23   BodL Vet. A3 d. 404, Wharton, *Eight Speeches.*
24   *Ibid.*

25   Marching on the right-oblique by throwing forward the left shoulder is too complex a drill for this early in the war. We are asking a lot for them to be allowed to wheel in line of divisions!

26   Johnson (1870), p 16.

27   Miller (1889); Ross (1887).

28   Pollard and Oliver (2003), p. 111. The description fits the site but regrettably the full findings and maps have yet to be published

29   Official Parliamentary Account.

30   Clarendon (1843).

31   Details of these figures including numbers ordered and produced both home and abroad are drawn together in Brassey's *History of Uniforms*: Elliot-Wright (1997) p. 77.

32   Questions following a lecture at the Battlefield Archaeology Conference 2003 at the National Army Museum attended by the author .

Chapter Eleven: The Centre – Counterattack

1   Ludlow in Firth (1894), p. 42.

2   *Ibid.*

3   Miller, (1889)

4   Davies, (1934), p. 36.

5   *Ibid.*

6   BL, *TT*, E 126 (39): Fiennes.

7   Official Parliamentary Account.

8   A Phillipson, conversation with the author; Clarendon (1843), VI, p. 73.

9   This was established practice. If they had time, troopers who rode among undefended enemy guns would use shoe-hammers or their pistol butts to hammer their spare horseshoe nails down the touch-hole. The gun was thus rendered incapable of firing until the laborious task of removing the nail could be undertaken.

10   Clarke (1816).

11   *Ibid.*

12   Johnson (1870), p 19. It is a shame Johnson does not quote his sources.

13   BL, *TT*, E 126 (39): Fiennes.

14   Official Parliamentary Account.

15   This could not be Kings Leys Barn as it would be in the wrong direction.

16   Hinton (1679).

17   Ammunition must have been brought up, either in barrels or more likely already broken into charged bottles on reserve bandoliers, but nobody tells us which or indeed of it happening. The Royalists were desperately short of bandoliers. They would have had no spares available and must have relied upon budge barrels.

18   It was common for gentlemen's servants to serve in another troop of the same regiment – see Royalist's Battle Order for the Lifeguard.

19   Ludlow in Firth (1894), p. 42.

20   It is presumed that the majority of shot had flown high and a stray low ball caught this unlucky man's hand.

21   Strangely, Davies asserts that Robartes's regiment was accompanied not by Constable's, which was in the same brigade, but by the Lord General's. It is more likely that one battalia of the Lord General's came to the assistance of both regiments joining the attack on Robartes's side of the melee: Davies (1921), p. 36.

22   Miller, (1889), p. 42.

23   Ludlow in Firth (1894) p. 43.

24   Official Parliamentary Account.

25   BodL Vet. A3d. 404, P Wharton, *Eight speeches...*

26   T Barker, (ed.) *The Military Intellectual and Battle; Raimondo Montecuccoli and the Thirty Years War* (Albany, State University of New York Press, 1975), quoted in Tincey and Roberts (2001), p. 28.

27   Walford (1904) p. 28. Unfortunately Walford, who was a well-read writer who normally added substantiating notes to his text, failed to cite his source in this instance. The tale is also recounted by the 'great romancer', P Johnson, who includes the dramatic intervention of a Royalist 'lion' called 'Adam Hill of Spaldwick'. Although his first edition was written in 1886, Walford republished Johnson's book four years before his own revised edition came out in 1904.

28   *Ibid.*

29   BL, *TT*, E 126 (39): Fiennes.

30   Official Parliamentary Account.

31   BodL Vet. A3d. 404, P Wharton, *Eight speeches...*

32   Clarke (1816).

33   *Ibid.*

34   Verney (1963).

35   Fiennes states that Essex himself brought up half of his own foot regiment. It is possible to deduce how it was that Essex's Regiment appeared capable of being in two places at the same time and also substantiate the fact that this unit was divided into two grand divisions. One attacked Byron's brigade and the other fought further along the line: BL, *TT*, E 126 (39): Fiennes.

36   Official Parliamentary Account.

37   Miller, (1889), p. 42.

38   Moone (1903).

39   Conversation between Bob Leedham and C L Scott: apparently, plotting documents do exist but their whereabouts is unknown. As with most tales by respected authors, we have to take them on trust, even if we remain a little sceptical.

40   Official Parliamentary Account.

41   *Ibid.*

Chapter Twelve: Disengagement

1   BL, *TT*, E 53 (10), Walsingham.

2   *Ibid.*

3   Ludlow in Firth (1894), p. 43.

4   A different version of these events can be found in Ludlow who says that it was retaken by disguise and duplicity.

5   D Featherstone, conversation with author.

6   BL, *TT*, E 126 (13): Kightly.

7   Firth (1895): Bulstrode has mistakenly identified Grantham's for Holles's regiment.

8   *Ibid.*

9   Miller, (1889), p. 42.

10   Ludlow in Firth (1894), p. 42.

11   Clarke (1816).

12   Bulstrode in Firth (1895).

13   Official Parliamentary Account.

14   Official Royalist Account.

15   Clarendon (1843), p. 309.

16   Ludlow in Firth (1894), pp 42–3

17   According to Ian Eaves, former Keeper of Armour at the Royal Armouries, the winching of medieval knights on to their mounts is a fictional invention of Mark Twain's that was later translated into 'popular truth' by Olivier's film *Henry V*: conversation with author.

18   Official Royalist Account.
19   *Ibid.*
20   Miller, (1889), p. 44.
21   Sharkey (2003), p. 10.
22   Walsh (1679).

Chapter Thirteen: Aftermath

1   Warwick (1702).
2   Bulstrode in Firth (1895).
3   Ludlow in Firth (1894), pp 44–5.
4   Official Parliamentary Account.
5   . Wellcome Institute, Howell papers, f 123; Firth (1902), p. 256.
6   Quoted in P Young, (1967).
7   Clarke (1816); Dugdale (1681) pp 109–10.
8   Underdown (1981), pp 69–94; Underdown (1979), pp 25–48; J S Morrill (1976), pp 99–100 *et seq.*
9   Oxon Record Office, Ref. MSS DD Par. Oxford, *St Aldate's Parish Churchwarden's Account*; Crossley and Elrington (1907–96), IV, pp 376–9.
10   Eddershaw (1995), pp 59–60.
11   Hobson and Salter (1933), p. 370.
12   These buildings, now part of Brasenose College, were later renamed 'Frewen Hall'.
13   Howell (1904), p. 301; Ludlow in Firth (1894), I, p. 45.
14   NA, SP 28/182.
15   *CSPD Add, 1623-1649*, p. 693; Hamper (1827); P Young, (1967), pp 131–2; Tennant (1990), pp 66–8.
16   NA, SP 28/136, f 16 and SP28/140, part 2, f 19, np; Ratcliff and Johnson (1935–41), VI, p. 68.
17   NA, SP 28/253B, *CSPD,1625–49*, p. 693; *CSPD Add.*, p.345; *Journal of the House of Commons*, III, p. 187; Firth (1902), p. 260; Kempthorne (1941), pp 192–202.
18   Sir Richard Bulstrode, *Memoirs & Reflections* (1721) quoted in Young (1967), p. 272.
19   Personal correspondence G M D Booth to the author; NA, SP28/136, f 16; Burke (1841), pp 236–7; Ratcliff and Johnson (1935–1941), pp. 75–6; Warwickshire County Records Office: CR 1908/75/4; CR 1886/9230, 9231 and Naworth's transcript of MS notes by Sir William Dugdale; Dugdale (1652–1673); Hamper (1827), p. 75.
20   *Journal of the House of Commons*, II, p. 874.
21   Sir James Ramsey commanded the Parliament Horse deployed on the left wing. He would also have held nominal command of his personal troop but, during the battle, command of his troop was probably delegated to another officer.
22   After the battle, Henry Lord Hastings was imprisoned in London with Ramsey to answer for the failure of the Left Wing. Presumably, he led a troop during the debacle.
23   Sandys was mortally wounded at Powick Bridge. His regiment was subsequently dispersed, but the remnants formed part of the Horse stationed on the left wing of the Parliamentary army.
24   Lord Rochford's Regimentt of Foot were in Coventry during the fight and arrived late on the 24th
25   Ludlow in Firth (1894), p. 45.
26   Return of losses submitted by parishioners of St Margaret's and St Nicholas's parishes: NA, SP 28/140, part 2, pp 15 *et seq.*
27   *Journal of the House of Commons*, III, p. 528.
28   *Ibid.*, p. 528
29   *Ibid.*, pp 560 and 866.

30 NA, E 101/612, Warwick Garrison Accounts, f. 64, p. 27; Farr (1904–69), vol. VIII, p. 473; Submission for restitution of losses by Coventry parishes: NA, SP 28/182, nf.
31 NA, E 101/612, Warwick Garrison Accounts, f 64.
32 *Journal of the House of Commons*, II, p. 980 and III, p. 83.
33 NA, SP 28/243 nf, warrants of 2, 14, 18 & 25 October 1644; Holmes (1974), p.174.

Chapter Fourteen: Subsequent Events

1   Ludlow in Firth (1894), p. 46.
2   Tennant, (1992), p. 76.
3   Clarke (1816), p. 280.
4   'Joyful Tidings from Windsor' quoted in South (1991), p. 33.
5   Clarendon (1843), p. 319.
6   Young and Norman (1967) p. 46.
7   *CSP (Venetian) 1642/43* (London 1925), p. 205.
8   Clarendon (1843).
9   Adair (1976), p. 199.
10 Notice how, even when he has the luxury of numbers, Essex did not create an infantry reserve not did he place one brigade behind another, but adhered to the established practice of one long line.
11 NA, SP 28/3A/96.
12 Clarendon (1843), p. 320.
13 *Ibid.*
14 *Ibid.*, p. 76.
15 Wiltshire County Record Office, 'Prince Rupert's Diary' quoted in P Young, (1967), p. 286.
16 Clarendon (1843), p. 322.

Chapter Fifteen: Concluding Implications

1   Gardiner (1987), I, p. 51.
2   E E Gruber von Arni (2001).
3   *Ibid.*, pp 9–10.

Chapter Sixteen: Edgehill Today

1   Official Royalist Account.
2   It originally stood some fifty yards to the southeast but whether it was erected on or near the original Sanderson Miller stone is unknown.
3   Pollard and Oliver (2003), pp 111–113.
4   As with many local traditions, there appears to be no contemporary evidence for this. Equally, there are no grounds for disbelief as a solid stone-built shelter would make a safe haven and what better place for a God-fearing soldier to endure pain? However, it makes a refreshing change from tales of Cromwell scurrying down church towers or stabling his horses in the naves.
5   Walford (1904), p. 6.

Appendix B: Battlefield Finds

1   Miller (1896, repr. 1967), pp 79–80.
2   Walford (1904), pp 25–6.
3   Young (1967), pp 330–1.
4   Robert Leedham, in conversation with the author, autumn 2003.
5   A couple of Grant's finds are displayed in the Officer's Mess, CAD, Kineton.
6   Pollard and Oliver (2003) pp 110–9. Several of their finds also featured in their television programme broadcast on BBC 4, February 2004.

Appendix C: Frontages

1 This could have been inflated in line with the connived at corrupt officialdom of later Stuart administration, but we believe it to be unlikely in Parliament's ranks at this stage of the war.

2 Roberts and Tincey (2001), pp 28–32; P Young, (1967), pp 57–61.

3 Although we concede they could be so regarded if we allow that, during the morning, Ramsey extended his deployment to the left in order to counter the overlap that he could perceive Rupert developing against him.

Appendix D: The King's Speech

1 BL, *TT*, E 200 (67), *Three Speeches...*

Appendix E: The Earl of Essex's Standing Orders

1 BL, *TT*, 200 (64): *A Worthy Speech...*

2 The meaning of this word is unclear but probably refers to Irish boys, many of whom served as grooms to the troopers.

References

For abbreviations used in the References please see page xv.

Primary Manuscripts

National Archives: State Papers, Commonwealth

SP 12/242	SP 28/139
SP 16/492	SP 28/140
SP 28/2	SP 28/141B
SP 28/3A	SP 28/182
SP 28/28	SP 28/243
SP 28/36	SP 28/253
SP 28/136	

National Archives: Exchequer Papers
E 101/612

National Archives: War Office
WO 55/1927   WO 55/1754

Oxfordshire County Record Office
Ref. MSS DD Par. Oxford

Shakespeare Birthplace Trust
Borough of Stratford upon Avon *Chamberlain's Accounts, 1622–1647*, f 175.

Warwickshire County Records Office
CR 319/8
CR 1908/75/4
CR 1886/9230
CR 1886/9231
G Naworth (ed.), *MS Notes by Sir William Dugdale in his Diary 1644, A New Almanack & Prognostication for the year of our Lord 1644.*

Wiltshire County Records Office
Extracts of Wiltshire Quarter Session Rolls.

Primary Printed Sources

Bariffe, W, *Military Discipline, or the Young Artillery-man, Wherein is Discoursed and Showne the Postures both of Musket and Pike* (London, 1635).

Bodleian Library

Vet. A3 d. 404: Wharton, P, *Eight Speeches Spoken in Guildhall* (London, 1642).

Vet. A3 e. 2108: Wharton, A, *A True relation of a Great and Happy Victory* (London, 1642).

4 ° X 44 (38) King Charles I, *Military Orders and Articles… for the Better Ordering and Government of His Majesties Armie* (Oxford, 1643).

Tanner MSS 61.

British Library

Add MS 34713: *Miscellaneous historical papers, 1642–1817* f 1, Warrant from Charles I to Matthew Brodley, Paymaster-general of the Army, for payments to various regiments.

Harleian MSS

Harl. MS 3783, f 61: Lord Bernard Stuart, *A Brief Relation of the Battle at Red Horse Field under Edgehill* (London, nd) .

Harl. MS 6845: Nathaniel Wade, *Narrative and Further Information*.

Thomason Tracts

E 53 (10): Walsingham, E, *Britannicae Virtutis Imago; or, The Effigies of True Fortitude expressed to the life in the actions of Major General Smith, who is here represented* (Oxford, 1644).

E 85 (41): Anon., *A Great Wonder in Heaven, shewing the late Apparitions seen on Edge-Hill* (London, 1642).

E 86 (23): Anon., *The New Yeares Wonder, being a relation of the disturbed inhabitants of Kenton and other villages neere unto Edge-Hill, in which place is heard and seene fearfull and strange apparitions of spirits* (London, 27 January 1643).

E 108 (23): *The Parliaments Resolution concerning the Volunteers that are to be raised under the Earl of Essex* (1642).

E 124 (18): 'TK' [anon.], *A True Copy of a Letter sent to the Lord Maior of London. Written on Monday morning 24 Oct. after the Battell* (London 1642).

E 124 (21): Anon., *A Letter from a Worthy Divine to the Lord Mayor of London, being a relation of the battaile between His Majesty and the Earl of Essex* (London, 1642).

E 124 (26): Anon., *An Exact and True Relation of the late Battell neere Kineton* (London, 1642).

E 126 (13): Kightley, E., *A Full and True Relation of the Battle between the King's Army and the Earle of Essex, in a letter from Captain Edward Kightley* (London, 1642).

E 126 (24): Anon., *A Relation of the Battel fought between Kineton and Edgehill, by His Majesty's Army and that of the Rebels* (Oxford, 1642).

E. 126 (38): Bifield, Rev. A., *A Letter sent by a Worthy Divine to the Rt. Hon. The Lord Mayor of London, being a true Relation of the battaile* (London, 1642).

E 126 (39): Fiennes, Captain N, *A Most True Relation of the battels fought against the Cavelliers; the one neer Edge-Hill, the other at Worcester* (London, 1642).

E 128 (20): TC, *A More True and Exacter Relation of the battaille of Keynton than any formerly* (London, 1642).

E 200 (64): *A Worthy Speech spoken by his Excellency the E. of Essex in the Head of his Armie before his arrival at Worcester, on Saturday last, being the 24th September, 1642* (London, 1642).

E 200 (67): King Charles I, *Three Speeches made by the King … before the late Battell at*

Keinton neer Banbury (London, 1642).

E 245 (8), Anon, *Marleborowes Miseries; or England turned Ireland by the Lord Digby and Daniel Oneale* (London, 1642).

669 f 6 (85): S. Marshall, *A Most True and Succinct Relation of the late Battell neere Kineton* (London, 1642).

669 f 6 (88): Ramsay, Sir J, *The Vindication of Sir James Ramsey from aspersions concerning his carriage in the fight at Kyneton* (nd).

Clarendon, Edward, Earl of, *The History of the Rebellion and Civil Wars in England* (Oxford, 1843).

Clark, A, (ed) *The Life and Times of Anthony Wood, Antiquary of Oxford, 1632-1695 described by himself* (5 vols, Oxford, Oxford Historical Society, 1891).

Cruso, J, *Militarie Instructions for the Cavalerie* (London, 1632, republished Kineton, Roundwood Press, 1972).

Dugdale, Sir W, *A Short View of the Late Troubles in England* (Oxford, 1681).

Dugdale, Sir W, *Monasticum Anglicanum* (1652–1673).

Ede-Borrett, S L, (ed.) *The Letters of Nehemiah Wharton* (London, Tercio Publications 1983).

Eldred, W, *The Gunner's Glass* (London, 1646).

Elton, R, *Compleat Body of the Art Military* (London, 1649).

Hexham, H, *The Principles of the Art Militarie* (1642)

Hinton, Sir J, *Memoirs of Sir John Hinton, Physitian in Ordinary to His Majesties Person* (London, 1679).

HMC, *Calendar of the Manuscripts of the Duke of Beaufort, KG, and others* (London, 1891).

HMC, *Calendar of the Manuscripts of the Duke of Portland* (London, 1892), vol. I.

Hobson, M G, and Rev. H E Salter, *Oxford Council Acts, 1626–65* (Oxford, 1933).

Kellie, Sir T, *Pallas Armata or Militarie Instructions* (Edinburgh, 1627).

King Charles I, *Military orders and Articles… for the better ordering and government of his majesties armie* (Oxford, 1643).

Firth, C H, (ed.) *The Memoirs of Edmund Ludlow* (2 vols, 1894).

Firth, C H (ed.) *Bulstrode, Sir Richard, Memoirs and Reflections* (originally published London, 1721) in English Historical Review (Oxford, 1895), vol. X.

Lipsius, J, *Iustus Lipsii de Militia Romana Libri Quinque* (Antwerp, 1598).

Moone, J, 'A Brief Relation of the Life and Memoirs of John, Lord Belasyse', HMC, *Calendar of the Manuscripts of the Marquis of Ormonde*, new series, (London, HMSO, 1903), vol. II, pp 376–99.

Philip, I G, *Journal of Sir Samuel Luke* (2 vols, Oxfordshire Record Society, 1947).

Polybius, *De Romanorum Militia et Castrorum Metatione* (Basle, 1537)

Roy, I (ed), *The Papers of Captain Henry Stevens, Waggon-Master-General to King Charles I* (Oxford, Oxfordshire Record Society, 1962).

Roy, I (ed), *The Royalist Ordnance Papers, 1642–6* (2 vols, Oxfordshire Record Society, 1963–4).

Smyth, Sir J, *Certain Discourses Military* (London, 1590).

Vicars, J, *Jehovah Jireh, God in the Mount* (1644),

Walsingham, E, *Brittannicae Virtutis Imago* (Oxford, 1644).

Ward, R, *Directions for Musters* (Cambridge, 1638).

Ward, R, *Animadversions of Warre* (London, 1639).

Walsh (Walch), Sir R, *A True Narrative and Manifest* (London, 1679).

Secondary Manuscript

Wellcome Institute
History of Medicine Library, RAMC 562, The Papers of Colonel H A L Howell.

Secondary Printed

Adair, J, *By the Sword Divided* (second imp., London, 2001).

Adair, J, *The Patriot: A Life of John Hampden* (London, 1976).

Akehurst, R, *The World of Guns* (Hamlyn, 1972).

Andrews, W, *Byegone Warwickshire* (Hull, Hull Press, 1893).

Anon., *Kineton, The Village and its History* (HMSO, Kineton Local History Group, 1999).

Atkin, M, *The Civil War in Worcestershire* (Stroud, 1995).

Bearman, R, *The History of an English Borough, Stratford Upon Avon.* (Stratford upon Avon, Shakespeare's Birthplace Trust & Sutton Publishing, 1994).

Burke, J, *A Genealogical and Heraldic History of the Extinct and Dormant Baronetcies of England, Ireland and Scotland* (1841).

Burne, A and P Young, *The Great Civil War* (London, Eyre & Spottiswood, 1959 republished Kineton, Windrush Press, 1998).

Clarke, T S, (ed.) *The Life of James II* (2 vols, London, 1816).

Connolly, P, *The Greek Armies* (London, MacDonald, 1977)

Chadwyk Healey, C E H, (ed.) *Sir Ralph Hopton's Narrative of his Campaigns in the West, 1642–1644 XVIII* (Somerset Record Society, 1902).

Crossley, A and C R Elrington (eds), *Victoria County History of Oxfordshire* (13 vols, Oxford, 1907–96).

Davies, G, 'The Parliamentary Army under the Earl of Essex' *English Historical Review* (Oxford, 1934), XLIX, pp 35–6 quoting from *The Parliamentary or Constitutional History of England* (24 vols, London, 1751–1761), XI, pp 436–9.

Davies, G, 'The Battle of Edgehill' *English Historical Review* (Oxford, 1921), XXXVI.

Donagan, B, 'Code and Conduct in the English Civil War', *Past and Present*, 118, 1988, pp 65–95.

Duthie, R, 'Pike Points I', *English Civil War Notes and Queries*, no.14, (Leigh on Sea, Partizan Press, 1985).

Eddershaw, D, *The Civil War in Oxfordshire* (Oxford, 1995).

Elliot-Wright, P J C, *Brassey's History of Uniform, English Civil War* (London, Brassey's, 1997).

Farr, M, *Victoria County History of Warwickshire* (8 vols, 1904–69), VIII.

Featherstone, D, *The Battlefield Walker's Handbook* (Airlife, 1998).

Firth, C H, 'Journal of Rupert's Marches' *English Historical Review*, 1898, XIII, pp 729–41.

Firth, C H, *Cromwell's Army* (London, Methuen, 1902).

Gardiner, R S, *The Great Civil War 1642–1649* (4 vols, London, Longman Green, 1893, republished Windrush Press, 1987)

Gregg, P, *Free Born John* (London, 2000).

Gruber von Arni, E E, *Justice to the Maimed Soldier* (Aldershot, Ashgate, 2001).

Hall, A R *Ballistics of the Seventeenth Century* (Cambridge University Press, 1952).

Harvey, N P D and H Thorpe, *The Printed Maps of Warwickshire, 1576–1900* (Warwickshire County Council, 1959).

Hamper, W, *William Dugdale, his life, diary and correspondence* (1827).

Holles, G, *Memorials of the Holles Family* (Royal Historical Society, Camden Third Series, Vol. LV, 1937).

Holmes, C, *The Eastern Association in the English Civil War* (1974).

Honeywell C and G Spear, 'The English Civil War', *Europa Militaria*, no.4. (London, Windrow & Greene, 1993).

Howard, M, and P Paret, (trans.), *C von Clausewitz, Vom Krieg* (Princeton, University Press, 1976/84 from the original German published Berlin, Dumlers Verlag, 1832).

Howell, H A L, 'The Army Surgeon, and the care of the sick & wounded during the Great Civil War', *Journal of the RAMC* (1904), VI.

Johnson, W B, *The Battle of Edge Hill, or, A Guide to the Field* (Banbury, 1870).

Kempthorne, Lt Col G A, DSO, 'Notes on the medical services during the Civil War and the Interregnum 1642–1660' *Journal of the RAMC*, LXXXVII (1941), pp 192–202.

Lawson Dick, O (ed.), *Aubrey's Brief Lives* (London, 1976).

Lion Television, *Royal Deaths and Diseases*, 2002, episode 1.

Marsh, R, G Winton, and P Dix, *A Guidebook to the Battlefield* (Privately published Edgehill, The Castle Inn, nd).

Miller, Rev. G, *Rambles Round the Edge Hills* (Potts, 1896, republished Kineton: Roundwood, 1967).

Miller, Rev. G, 'The Battle of Edgehill', *Journal of the Royal Archaeological Institute*, 46, (1889).

Morrill, J S, *The Revolt of the Provinces* (London, Allen & Unwin, 1976).

Peachey, S, *The Edgehill Campaign & The Letters of Nehemiah Wharton* (Leigh on Sea, 1989).

Peachey, S and A Turton, *Old Robin's Foot* (Leigh on Sea, Partizan Press, 1987).

Potter, R, and G Embleton, *The English Civil War 1642–1651* (London: Almark, 1973).

Peacock, E, *The Army Lists of the Roundheads and Cavaliers* (London, Chatto and Windus, 1874).

Pollard, T, and N Oliver, *Two Men in a Trench II* (London, Penguin, 2003)

Ratcliff, S C, and H C Johnson, *Warwick County Records* (8 vols, 1935–41), VI.

Roberts, K, and J Tincey, *Edgehill, 1642* (Oxford, Osprey, 2001).

Ross, W G, 'The Battle of Edgehill' (in *Notes and Documents*), *English Historical Review* (1887), 2, pp 541–3.

Roy, I (ed.), *The Habsburg-Valois wars and the French wars of religion [by Blaise de Monluc, translated from the French by Charles Cotton]* (London, Longman, 1971).

Sharkey, A J, *Forgotten Heroes, The Millers of Radway and their links with the Battle of Edgehill, Waterloo and a Royal Artillery Crimea VC* (Hampton in Arden, Edgehill Enterprises, 2003).

Smith, F, *Warwickshire Delineated* (F Smith and Longman, second edition, 1821).

South, R, *Royal Castle, Rebel Town* (Buckingham, Barracuda, 1981).

Styles P, *Studies in Seventeenth Century West Midlands History* (Kineton, Roundwood Press, 1978).

Tennant, P E, *Edgehill and Beyond* (Stroud, Alan Sutton, 1992).

Tennant, P E, 'South Warwickshire and the Banbury Area in the Civil War', *Journal of the Banbury History Society*, 11 (1990), no. 6.

Thompson, Sir T, (ed.) *Sir James Melville, Memoirs of his Own Life* (London, 1927)

Timmins, S, *A History of Warwickshire* (London, Elliot Stock, 1889).

Turton, A, *The Chief Strength of the Army, Essex's Horse 1642–1645* (Leigh-on-Sea, Partizan Press, 1992)

Underdown, D, 'The Chalk and The Cheese: Contrast Amongst the English Clubmen', *Past and Present*, LXXXV (London, 1979).

Underdown, D, 'The Problem of Popular Allegiance in the English Civil War', *Transactions of the Royal Historical Society* XXXI (London, 1981).

Verney, P, *The Standard Bearer: the story of Sir Edmund Verney, Knight-Marshal to King Charles I* (London, Hutchinson, 1963).

Walford, E A, *Edgehill: The Battle and Battlefield* (London, second edition, 1904).

Warburton, E, *Memoirs of Prince Rupert and the Cavaliers* (2 vols, London, 1849).

Warwick, Sir P, *Memoires of the Reign of Charles I* (London, 1702)

Wiltshire Gazette and Herald, 20, 27 August and 3 September 1989.

Young, A R, *The English Emblem Tradition, Emblematic Flag Devices of the English Civil Wars, 1642-1660* (3 vols, Toronto University Press 1995).

Young, Brigadier, P, 'The Royalist Artillery at Edgehill, 23 October 1642', *Journal of the Society for Army Historical Research*, 31 (1938).

Young, Brigadier P, *Edgehill, 1642, The Campaign and the Battle* (Kineton, Roundway Press,

1967).

Young, P and R Holmes, *The English Civil War, A Military History of the Three Civil Wars* (London, Eyre Metheun, 1974).

Young, P, and T Norman (eds), *Military Memoirs of Captain John Gwyn* (London 1967).

Internet Web Site

www.hillsdale.edu.dept/History/War/17e/ECW/1642-E

Index